Affirming Middle Grades Education

Related Titles

Middle Grades Social Studies: Teaching and Learning for Active and Responsible Citizenship, Second Edition
Michael G. Allen and Robert L. Stevens
ISBN: 0-205-27118-9

Teaching and Learning in the Middle Grades, Second Edition
K. Denise Muth and Donna E. Alvermann
ISBN: 0-205-27859-0

For more information or to purchase a book, please call 1-800-278-3525.

Affirming Middle Grades Education

Edited by

Carl W. Walley
Ashland University

W. Gregory Gerrick
Ashland University

Allyn and Bacon
Boston • London • Toronto • Sydney • Tokyo • Singapore

Series Editor: Frances Helland
Series Editorial Assistant: Bridget Keane
Manufacturing Buyer: Suzanne Lareau

Copyright © 1999 by Allyn & Bacon
A Viacom Company
Needham Heights, MA 02494

Internet: www.abacon.com

Library of Congress Cataloging-in-Publication Data

Walley, Carl W.
    Affirming middle grades education / Carl W. Walley :
W. Gregory Gerrick.
        p.   cm.
    Includes index.
    ISBN 0-205-17128-1
    1. Middle school education—United States.   2. Middle schools—
United States—Administration.   I. Walley, Carl.   II. Title.
LB1623.5.G47   1999
372.24'2—dc21   98-38246
                                                                    CIP

Printed in the United States of America
10   9   8   7   6   5   4   3   2   03   02   01   00

To the memory of

Donald R. Castle:
colleague, scholar, and friend

Contents

Preface

Affirming Middle Grades Education is not only the title of this book but also a statement of its purpose. It is our intent to explore a thoroughly unique environment for a very specific group of students. The middle school stands alone in K–12 education as both a specific organizational design and an exciting opportunity to begin to make sense of the many changes and frustrations of the early adolescent experience. We attempt to paint a picture of this uniqueness from the perspectives of organizational (interdisciplinary curricula, teaming, flexible scheduling) as well as social, emotional, moral, and community dimensions. In addition, we hope to draw distinct lines of demarcation between the middle school and that other institution known as the junior high school.

The book is divided into three sections: First, a philosophical component considers overarching foundational issues related to the peculiar structure of the middle school; second, an organizational component examines how traditional school structures are a "bad fit" for what professional educators need to accomplish and how a community structure is a more appropriate fit; finally, a practitioner component considers what all of this looks like in the daily life of the classroom. It is our hope that the three sections of this book will reveal how theory, organizational structure, and practice combine to create an effective middle school.

Educators who would benefit from the book include preservice as well as practicing teachers. Educators who are becoming exposed to the many dimensions of the middle school movement as they prepare for the transition from a junior high school to a middle school would especially appreciate the many perspectives in the pages that follow. Finally, persons engaged in administrative training in the area of the middle school principalship would certainly find these chapters helpful.

Readers will find four recurring themes throughout the book:

1. Design influences function: Organizational structures directly influence the type and quality of the program offered to students.

2. Middle school programs must be sensitive to the unique developmental needs of this age group (social, emotional, physical, intellectual).

3. The democratic aims of the middle school are tied to democratic actions: Teachers, administrators, and students must be actively involved in the development and implementation of the school programs; students need to have a say in what they will learn and how they will learn it—viable choices must be available to students.

4. The ideas and practices presented in the book are *dynamic*: Middle school is not a static institution: it will continually evolve and change. The book offers ideas for consideration. Notions discussed here are not necessarily universally applied; they can and will change to adapt and fit unique populations over time.

The approach we have taken in this book is to weave together the best ideas and insights we could find from a variety of contributors. The work of scholars, practitioners, and parents comes together under the themes outlined here. Our idea was to give educators a glimpse of theory for successful organizational design and then elaborate on how theory and ideas work out in actual practice. It is then up to the reader to bring these notions to life in the specific settings in which they find themselves on a day-to-day basis.

Consequently, the book is designed as a springboard for further discussion and investigation. Discussion questions are included with each chapter to encourage the reader to take theory to the next level—to ask the question "How does all of this link up with my own experience?" In addition, in the "Wuz Up?" chapter, we consider the students' view of what *they* say about the middle school experience. It is interesting to note that sometimes the views of students are contradictory to those of the experts and "accepted" practice.

The impetus and initial foundation for the ideas and ideals expressed in this book were provided by Donald R. Castle, Ph.D. We are grateful for Don's friendship and his scholarship. We especially thank Don's brother, Doug Castle, for his help in organizing this project following Don's untimely passing.

We would like to thank Brenda McConnell for reviewing the early drafts of the book, and Frances Helland, editor at Allyn and Bacon, for her encouragement and patience. Our appreciation goes also to the following reviewers for their comments on the manuscript: Jane Haskell, Rolla Middle School, Rolla, MO; Jo Ellen Read, Leawood Middle School, Leawood, KS; C. Kenneth McEwin, Appalachian State University; Anita Perna Bohn, Illinois State University; Nicholas Holodick, King's College; and William Croasdale, University of Rhode Island.

Affirming Middle
Grades Education

The Adolescent and the Middle Grades—Introduction

In the 1920s John Dewey endorsed a period in the school continuum devoted to the needs of early adolescents. Dewey viewed adolescents as unique individuals with educational interests and needs different from those of children in the elementary grades. They are more mature, socially sensitive, and intellectually inquisitive than elementary pupils. They are also less sophisticated, emotionally secure, and socially steady than typical high school students. The organizational structure provided for these students, wedged between high school and the elementary grades, became known as the junior high school. This program taught subject area content through classes that encouraged social interaction, individually chosen projects, and vocationally grounded activities. As the decades passed, this system evolved into a program that focused on academic preparation for high school more than it addressed Dewey's concept of meeting the immediate requirements of early adolescents.

By the later part of the century the junior high school mirrored the typical high school. It is unfortunate that the accepted philosophy evolved from placing the social, emotional, and intellectual needs of the early adolescent at the core of the program to emphasizing curriculum content. As in Dewey's time, many current educators recognize the fallacy of placing curriculum interests ahead of adolescent needs. The renewed desire to teach academic content in the context of adolescent traits has fostered the middle school concept.

Effective middle schools are associated with several hallmark characteristics, such as integrating subject area content through selected themes. Furthermore, the activities within the themes are socially embedded; they necessitate interaction between both students and teachers. Teaming, for example, is a popular approach that requires teachers to work together and students to participate as part of a group. The middle school concept, in addition, restores to the curriculum the progressive ideal of creating a democratic society that enfranchises learners to make personal decisions about their education and to accept the unique qualities of others.

In Part I of this book the authors discuss the unique qualities of the early adolescent. In particular, Rick Breault speaks about morally responsible teaching. To Breault, morally responsible teaching is based on the need to "do the right thing." He asserts that we must use our professional authority on behalf of students. This moral emphasis hinges on learning communities that respect all individuals in the school family. If we are to create a society that embraces all its citizens, we must reject structures that marginalize individuals in the name of efficiency, instructional practices that favor selected student groups, or curriculum content that succumbs to pressure for artificial accountability practices. Instead, the guiding principle must be the quest to design procedures that encourage students and adults to work together and that validate the talents inherent in all people.

In order to be a morally responsible teacher, an educator must understand the characteristics of students. In the introductory chapter, Sue Simpson provides a framework for exploring the emotional, social, and intellectual development of middle school students. The background she provides establishes a foundation for organizing a middle school curriculum that is empathetic to the characteristics of this group. As part of this emphasis on the requirements of adolescents, Doug and Don Castle's chapter on at-risk students presents a system for supporting adolescents at a time when they are most vulnerable.

Patrick Slattery's contribution, "The Excluded Middle: Postmodern Conceptions of the Middle School," helps to define what is and should be special about the middle school experience. His chapter presents considerations that should be explored throughout this book. The reader is encouraged, for example, to ask:

- What are the responsibilities of all members of the middle school community?
- How do these responsibilities interact or conflict with the interests and needs of others?
- How do the practices and procedures being described adhere to the qualities and needs of adolescents?
- In what ways do the ideas encourage the founding of democratic actions that enfranchise all people to become productive members of our society?

This initial section of the book should provide a foundation that aids in the exploration and understanding of these and other questions that may emerge through the readings.

$$C \quad h \quad a \quad p \quad t \quad e \quad r \quad \mathit{1}$$

Early Adolescent Development

SUE SIMPSON

*Sue Simpson has been a teacher at the elementary, high school,
and university levels, but the majority of her teaching experience
is at the middle level. She is currently a curriculum consultant,
a reviewer for the* National Middle School Journal, *and
newsletter editor for the Ohio Alliance for Arts Education.*

Life in "the middle" is much like a Hans Christian Andersen tale of transformation. Like scraggly cygnets, adolescents go through a time of change that for many is speeded up and compacted into a few months and for others occurs over a few agonizing years. This time period falls somewhere between the ages of 10 to 14. How, if at all, do these young people fit the stereotypical labels often connected to this age group? What characteristics do most share—or not share? What are the instructional implications? How and what can be done to better serve the middle level student?

For most 10- to 14-year olds during the last century and a half the early adolescent years have posed basically the same set of problems in the areas of growth and development. However, since the mid-1970s the early adolescent experience has become more complex, and critical life issues have catapulted into the earlier stages. The media-influenced images of fashion, self-fulfillment, and sensual experiences coupled with the frightening warnings about smoking, drinking, sex, and even decibel levels and an evaporating ozone layer permeate their real and imagined view of the world.

Their grandparents, as adolescents, dealt primarily with social concerns: "Should I or shouldn't I" dilemmas surfaced during such activities as spin-the-bottle (a rather public kiss); petting (a "rushin' hands and roamin' fingers" approach to physiological exploration); and parties at which alcohol, usually in the form of beer, and cigarettes (and possibly marijuana) may have been available. The fashion quandary for girls revolved around whether to wear slacks or mini skirts; for boys it was whether to "peg" their jeans or wear "chinos." A majority of early adolescents were part of a traditional family unit, and most had at least one meal a day with everyone in the family present.

Today's adolescents face similar but more complex challenges. The dilemma of a spin-the-bottle kiss or clandestine petting is apt to be in terms of sexual experimentation in the form of "life-and-death" risk-taking. Although they may be presented with information about AIDS and other sexually transmitted diseases, they are no less prone to experimenting. And today's adolescents are less likely to have that "inner voice" that encourages them to do the right thing. "Today nuclear families are less common, and more children than ever before are growing up without positive adult role models, particularly fathers" (*This We Believe*, 1995, p. 9).

The middle years have historically been a confusing and challenging stage in human growth and development. The impact of family, community, and school may clash with what early adolescents feel emotionally and psychologically. Sometimes this collision results in concerned, conscientious commitment to causes, such as the environment or world peace. Sometimes they debate what they *know* to be "right" against what they *feel* to be "cool." This tension results in their taking risks that can threaten their futures. Somewhere between childhood and adulthood, early adolescents are frustrated by who they are and who they are trying to become. They expect and want a certain amount of security and support, while at the same time they battle for independence and freedom. Insulted if adults imply they follow the herd without thinking for themselves, they boast of their right to be "their own person" and plead for authority figures to "get off their case."

The Evolving Early Adolescent

Who are these people we call "early adolescents"? How are they different? Frequently they are made to sound more "different" than they are. The early adolescent experience has prompted labels such as "hormones with legs" and "the range of the strange." Although humorous to others, such labels create negative stereotypes, unfair and detrimental to these young people who are trying so desperately to "fit in." Even the less controversial "tags" illicit frowns or quizzical looks; consider the connotation carried by such labels as the following: "juveniles," "youngsters," or "transescents." To genuinely understand the adolescent, adults must look beyond the surface appearance and into the thoughts and emotions of 10- to 14-year old students.

Alike, Yet Different

Like most age groups, adolescents share a set of common experiences, although they may vary in the specific timetable for moving through these experiences.

Stevenson (1992, pp. 77–78) identifies "Four Caveats" of early adolescence that help to illuminate the issues the adolescent will confront:

1. Early adolescence is a time when all youngsters change in many ways.
2. Changes occur at idiosyncratic times as they move through a common sequence.
3. Home, neighborhood, and racial-ethnic identity influence development.
4. The influences and effects of early adolescence are long-lasting.

George and Lawrence (1982, pp. 12–13) modify materials from Kohen-Raz (1971) and Eichhorn (1966) to draw attention to four aspects of early adolescent development that are mutually experienced and cut across all four facets of development: intellectual, emotional, physical, and social.

1. *Adjustment to maturation.* How well they adjust to the maturation process depends, to a large extent, on the kinds of relationships they can achieve with both adult and peer associates.
2. *Erotic interest.* Erotic alertness and curiosity are typical of transescent girls; curiosity is typical of boys.
3. *Experimentation.* They like to indulge in unique and unconventional activities.
4. *Physical testing.* Many exercises and competitions that appear to be sport activities are ways in which transescents satisfy their curiosity and test the limits of their power and range of body functions.

To a degree, the changes early adolescents experience are automatic; they are predestined according to Mother Nature's schedule. Nothing can stop or defer them. Other aspects, such as relationships, "experiments," and the exposure and information shared with them about their world, represent variables that provide an opportunity to mold the adolescent's character. These are the pivotal determiners of who they become and how they feel about themselves as individuals. Beane and Lipka (1986) assert that how adolescents see themselves (self-concept) and their degree of self satisfaction (self-esteem) are redefined during adolescence.

Aspects of Development and Change

Middle level philosophy and practice ideally spring from the recognition of the changes that manifest themselves in early adolescence. A true middle school recognizes this unique stage of development and moves adolescents through this transitional period with the least amount of frustration and the greatest amount of success. Lounsbury (1991) observes that "what the middle school concept advocates is rooted in the realities of human growth and development" (p. 12). These physical, emotional, social, and intellectual characteristics are unique to the adolescent.

Physical

Between the ages of 9 and 14, boys and girls experience growth spurts, possible skin blemishes or acne, and puberty. Most experience problems with coordination, and many begin to become concerned about gaining or losing weight. The onset of these physical changes generally occurs in girls earlier than in boys, approximately 2 years ahead (Stevenson, 1992). By eighth grade the rate of physiological development in girls begins to slow down (Stevenson, 1992).

Physiological changes affect more than appearance; they have their greatest impact on self-image and confidence. Diet, hygiene, and puberty, for instance, may cause skin blemishes or acne. The blemishes alone may cause some frustration and concern, but the reactions of others to the blemishes cause the greatest level of anxiety.

Although somewhat gradual, the onset of puberty reigns as the most life-altering physiological change experienced by the early adolescent. The body reproportions itself, creating self-consciousness, possible incidents of embarrassment, and curiosity about their personal sexuality. For most adolescents, sexual curiosity becomes a major focus of attention, but boys experience it differently than girls. Girls tend to perceive sexuality in romantic and idealistic ways; boys possess a curiosity expressed through jokes and anecdotes shared with male peers. As Stevenson (1992) observes, there is probably "no group more interested in adolescent development and sexuality than young adolescents themselves" (p. 89).

Social

Interest in the opposite sex emerges and dominates adolescents' thoughts and social actions. This intense interest usually emerges between the ages of 10 and 12. Some early adolescents may find it impossible to concentrate on anything other than sexual issues. Any idea or piece of information is translated into an erotic or sexual reference.

Some of this sexual fascination is part of belonging, being accepted by peers. Similarly, distancing themselves from parents or adults in their lives is also, to a certain extent, a behavior that is to be expected, and one that should be interpreted as part of the group acceptance effect, rather than an actual rejection of home and family (George & Lawrence, 1982; Kindred et al., 1976).

As important as the peer group may seem, "friendships are not typically so strong. . . [they are] seldom based on intimate sharing of personal values until later adolescence" (George & Lawrence, 1982, p. 77). The "acceptance" issue is tied more closely to the pursuit of identity and "being their own person" than to close, personal peer relationships (Gutheinz-Pierce & Whoolery, 1995; O'Brien & Bierman, 1988). The transescent seeks to mirror adult behaviors and personality traits (Garner & Yancey, 1994). For as much as they seem to try to be like everyone else, early adolescents want most to find their own identities.

Emotional

The "adult personality" that adolescents may emulate can come from a positive or a negative role model. George and Lawrence (1982) describe this as how the adolescent perceives the role of "the promise" in "successful" lives. The promise is "the belief that success in school is a ticket to successful adulthood" (pp. 78–79). If school seems to be the basic ingredient of the adult's success, the adolescent will pursue the promise of education. However, if the adolescent sees an adult's success as possible without "the promise," he or she may become anti-school-oriented.

For today's early adolescent the promise of the future is also jeopardized by a greater likelihood of encountering incidents of divorce, violence, and poverty than in previous generations. The prevalence of single-parent families, latchkey conditions, and lack of physical and financial security continues to increase, and these conditions influence the adolescents' perceptions of what life holds for them. For many, life can seem hopeless. Herring (as cited in Garner &Yancey, 1994) shares some startling information:

> . . . *first, approximately 10% of child suicide attempts will ultimately succeed; second, in a National Adolescent Student/Health Survey of eighth to twelfth graders, 34% of the eighth graders reported they had seriously thought about suicide and 15% had actually attempted it; third, nearly 200 suicides by children younger than fourteen years of age are committed annually in the United States with an increase from 33% in 1968 to 41% in 1982 and a continued increase in the late 1980s. (p. 8)*

Harter (1990) attributes the adolescents' contemplation of suicide to the new-found experience of self-reflection, observing that some will "agonize to the point of despair" (p. 234).

Intellectual

Equally powerful as emotional development, and far more imperceptible, is the intellectual development experienced by early adolescents. Cognitive development for transescents may begin in concrete, ego-centered thought and evolve to formal operational, reflective contemplations (Inhelder & Piaget, 1958; Schave & Schave, 1989). Most early adolescents reason without processing information; they absorb it like a sponge just as it is given. In Piagetian terms it is assimilation. Stefanich (1990) calls this quality the Mental Experience Storage System (MESS); others might describe it as building schema or a core of basic information from which we later determine a reference point for understanding new concepts. This type of thinking is most prevalent in the first 7 years of life (Stefanich, 1990).

As individuals enter early adolescence (at approximately 10 years of age), most employ concrete operational thought (Piaget, 1966). Stefanich (1990) labels the early adolescents' thought process as Memory Organization Points (MOP).

> *The ability to draw from a number of schema in employing logical reasoning patterns begins to emerge with the advent of concrete operations, generally considered common in the reasoning of individuals after the age of seven. The depth and complexity of reasoning continues to mature and become more complex as*

long as a person continues to actively seek new knowledge and new insights.
(p. 47)

These "new insights" are localized by the data or schema that seems to fit, based on the person's storehouse of past experiences. Transference of concrete operational thought from one situation to another is infrequently demonstrated, if at all.

Later, in the formal operational stage, concepts from one set of data are integrated or meshed with other sets of information to create new levels of understanding. Verging on the abstract, adult stage of cognitive development, the individual no longer needs to actively experience (assimilate) information, but is able to carry out an activity based on information (accommodate) and build or understand the concept as a result (Maier, 1969).

George and Lawrence (1982, pp. 43–44) identify six dimensions of intellectual development that demonstrate the range of early adolescent experiences. They are as follows:

1. From concrete into abstract thinking
2. From an egocentric into a sociocentric perspective
3. From a limited into a broad perspective of time and space
4. From a simplistic into a complex view of human motivation
5. From reliance on slogans toward the construction of a personal ideology
6. Development of a capacity for forming concepts that stretches from lower-order into complex, higher-order conceptualizing

These descriptors represent the possibilities; however, not all are realized by all adolescents. As in the other three areas of development, progressing through the states of cognitive development varies within the early adolescent population. The majority of early adolescents fail to reach formal operational thought (Stefanich, 1990). Lounsbury (1991) reports, "For a rare one or two in the sixth grade, for some in the seventh grade, and for many in the eighth grade, the capacity to think analytically *begins* to emerge" (p. 36). Van Hoose and Strahan (1988) assert that about one-third of the eighth grade population "consistently demonstrates formal reasoning" (p. 4).

Instructional Implications

The true middle school provides for and respects the early adolescent's development socially, emotionally, physically, and cognitively. Traditional "schooling" focuses on ideas, the goals of which are admirable, but its methods or means are flawed. The typical school program insufficiently meets the total needs of the adolescent. Preoccupation with teacher behavior, content, skills, and test performance typically distracts from the real issues "going on in students' minds and lives" (Stevenson, 1992, p. 75). Stevenson (p. 76) prescribes the following equation for "response education."

$$\frac{\text{what to teach and how to teach it}}{\text{developmental assessment}} \quad = \quad \text{Responsive Education}$$

He asserts that by following this formula, the middle school should develop a series of realistic learning expectations and experiences.

The Carnegie Report (*Turning Points*, 1990) observes that "many middle grade schools today fall far short of meeting the critical educational, health, and social needs of millions of young adolescents" (p. 10). Many of the report's recommendations relate directly to early adolescent development and growth:

- Create smaller learning environments.
- Form teams of teachers and students.
- Assign an adult advisor for every student.
- Ensure success for all students.
- Improve academic performance through fostering the health and fitness of young adolescents.

These recommendations clearly suggest emotional and social development but impact intellectual and physical development as well. All of the characteristics of adolescent growth and change discussed earlier and the efforts made to address them in the educational program are crucial to the early adolescent's survival. They directly influence the student's chance of developing into a productive, self-assured young adult.

Dorman (as cited in Martin, 1993, p. S-24) suggests that the school should respond by offering an educational program that provides the following:

1. Diversity
2. Self-exploration and self-identification
3. Meaningful participation in school and community
4. Positive social interaction with both peers and adults
5. Physical activity
6. Competence and achievement
7. Structure and clear limits

These are healthy suggestions that are pedagogically and developmentally appropriate conditions for middle level learners. These seven areas encompass all aspects of a middle level environment and its educational program.

Diversity

This discussion of the wide range of development within the early adolescent population is but the tip of the iceberg. Work done by such individuals as Eisner (1982), Gardner (1983), Dunn and Dunn (1985, 1985), and Cross (1990) has shown that within each of the four basic components (social, physical, emotional, and intellectual) exists yet another set of variables, whether it be the workings of the brain, or levels of needs, or individual styles of learning. The middle level population possesses a range of abilities and interests. They are also at different stages along the developmental time line within each of these areas.

The educational program needs to accommodate this broad range of diversity and attend to the variances within the range. Instruction should offer opportunities for learning through activities using rhythms and words, learning by seeing and creating models and re-enactments, as well as learning by traditional means like listening and reading. Middle schoolers need to learn in diverse ways: in large groups and individually, but also with a partner and in small groups. Affective programs need to be as available as highly academic programs. Teachers need to employ a variety of teaching strategies, including more student-centered approaches that empower students to make choices about how and what they will learn.

Model middle school programs also broaden the definition of "classroom." For example, learning experiences may take place by a stream or in a woods or through a community service project that places a few class members in a different location each day (Obert, 1995; Sherman & Banks, 1995). Ideally, learning goes beyond the confines of school and into the community. It also moves along the "informational highway," using technology to communicate across the country and around the world. The possibilities available through technology are literally limitless.

Self-Exploration and Self-Definition

Transescents should learn in diverse ways as a means of developing character and a sense of self. Being flexible, making choices, and becoming aware of a multitude of resources help students learn the process/problem-solving skills they need in their adult lives. Their choices may be unsuccessful or nonproductive; however, through each experience the student learns and makes progressively more intelligent choices. If choices are never made available, the ability to make choices is never developed. "Learned dependency of helplessness" is frequently the lesson learned instead, creating a rather self-centered and vacuous individual.

Lounsbury (1991) suggests that before academic progress can be realized, we need to "provide for social and psychological development" (p. 25), specifically by providing experiences that help students develop their own value system, behavior code, and self-esteem. The early adolescent is a fragile being; "support and pastoral care needs are greater at this time than at any other" (Renihan & Renihan, 1990, p. 40).

The affective/attitudinal aspects of the early adolescent's education are as important as the cognitive/conceptual aspects. Lounsbury (1991) sees "wayside teaching," for example, the casual exchanges in the hallways, in the cafeteria, or at the local mall, as having a great impact on behavior. The out-of-class interactions with students can be of greater significance than those that occur in the instructional setting.

Meaningful Participation in School and Community

As part of seeing how they "fit in," early adolescents need to be encouraged to contribute to their school and community. Many educational programs involve students directly in service projects. The end result of participating is usually self-satisfaction and pride in a job well done.

The group project experience also meets early adolescents' social needs. In addition, using their proclivity for socialization has an instructional advantage. As Lounsbury observes (1991), "Middle level teachers would do well . . . to plan many learning activities that are built around team learning" (p. 16).

Positive Social Interaction with Peers and Adults

Giving of themselves in school and community projects helps early adolescents evolve from clumsy social neophytes to more self-assured, socially aware young adults. Similarly, "opportunities to learn together aid in establishing meaningful social relationships with various age mates of both sexes" (Lounsbury, 1991, p. 16). They benefit in a variety of ways:

- Learn to consider and value related matters
- Acquire an appreciation of the contribution of others
- Gain self-esteem
- Have opportunities to experiment with leadership skills
- Gain an understanding of how groups operate
- Develop more positive attitudes toward school

Schools that address the social needs of students also provide places, people, and programs that allow for socialization skills to be learned and socializing to be practiced. The adults in these programs are very important. "Students' self-esteem and feelings of well being are correlated closely with the level of interaction with teachers . . . " (Lounsbury, 1991, p. 21). Large multipurpose rooms or one end of a cafeteria may be used to allow students to congregate to talk before school or after lunch, and advisory programs provide a place for discussing concerns and building networks of support (George & Lawrence, 1982; Hootstein, 1994; Lounsbury, 1991). Such environmental accommodations are necessary to enable adolescents to develop positive social interaction skills.

Physical Activity

As early adolescents move from the elementary to the middle school setting, opportunities for physical movement typically lessen. This is problematic because transescents want and need physical exercise and mobility. This may seem to be the responsibility of physical education and intramural programs, but the implications go beyond these areas. Students need freedom to move in the regular classroom setting. Beane and Lipka (1986) cite a study in which students who succeeded academically attributed their success to the fact that they were allowed freedom to move about in the classroom. Mobility does not infer lack of control or an inability to teach. It does require planning, guiding, and a willingness to trust students.

The early adolescent needs to be assured that his or her physical awkwardness is normal, that he or she is "okay." To provide this assurance, the instructional program needs to offer opportunities for learning about and talking about how change occurs; this can be done with an objective approach using science and health information, with a sense of discovery using measurement and data gathering, and, more subjectively, using historical and personal perspectives in the humanities.

Competence and Achievement

Feeling comfortable about who they are and what they can achieve is integral to early adolescents in any program. Opportunities to experience success within and outside the academic program should exist in middle schools sensitive to early adolescents' needs. Such schools offer a variety of ways to recognize students' unique attributes and achievements.

"Academic excellence . . . is more nearly the result of attitude than it is of separate, specialized instruction in the basic subjects" (Lounsbury, 1991, p. 22). Nonthreatening classroom environments in which teachers work with students side by side produce happier, more productive students. Specific contributing factors include keeping students and teachers together for more than one period a day or over more than one year, increasing conversations with students in and out of the classroom, and reducing seatwork (Lounsbury, 1991). There is a growing awareness that the measure of intelligence is not so much in the retention of facts but in the ability to solve problems and work with others in creating those solutions.

Structure and Clear Limits

Probably one of the biggest quandaries the middle level staff must grapple with is establishing limits on adolescent behavior. The early adolescent seeks independence and needs opportunities for developing his or her own identity; yet there is an equal need for consistency in the setting of standards and consequences of inappropriate behavior (Ridley, McCombs, & Taylor, 1994). The early adolescent questions authority and turns to peers more than to adults. The dilemma for adults is how to allow the early adolescent room to grow while channeling that growth in a positive direction.

For the early adolescent, Farris (1990) identifies four basic needs: the need to belong, the need for freedom, the need for power, and the need for fun. Strangely enough, in meeting these needs, the educational program is most apt to provide structure and clear limits. Middle level students are motivated most when they are key participants in identifying what is acceptable and what is not, what the basic expectations are, and what the consequences or repercussions of their actions will be (George et al., 1992). Given the opportunity, early adolescents will set appropriate limits for freedom, power, and fun. In so doing, they will feel valued, as if they belong. Lounsbury (1991) states: "A school is not significant because it has a guidance program, and an exploratory program, and an academic program; it is significant because of what it is in its totality" (p. 91). It is by adhering to the needs and characteristics of the adolescent that a middle school program will be developed that enriches the lives of its students.

Discussion Questions

1. How do the four areas of adolescent development work together to help the student confront issues common to this age group? How, for instance, does physical development relate to the social and emotional growth of the adolescent?

2. If you were a teacher in a middle school classroom, how would you use the information in this chapter to help adapt your instruction to meet the developmental needs of your students?

3. Think of the experiences of your parents when they were 10 to 14. What were their social, intellectual, and emotional pressures and concerns? How do their issues compare to what you experienced? Compare your life and that of your parents to the life of the typical student today. How are the three generations similar and different?

References

Beane, J. A. (1990, 1993). *A middle school curriculum: From rhetoric to reality* (2d ed.). Columbus, OH: National Middle School Association.

Beane, J. A., & Lipka, R. P. (1987). *When the kids come first: Enhancing self-esteem.* Columbus, OH: National Middle School Association.

Cross, C. T. (1990). *Issues in education. Who is the American eighth grader?* NELS: 88. National Education Longitudinal Study of 1988. Washington, DC: Office of Educational Research and Improvement. U.S. Department of Education, U.S. Government Printing Office.

Dorman, G. (1987). *Improving middle grades schools: A framework for action.* Carrboro, NC: Center for Early Adolescence.

Dunn, R., & Dunn, K. (1985). *Learning styles model.* Lawrence, KS: Price Systems.

Eichorn, D. H. (1966). *The middle school.* New York: Center for Research in Education.

Eisner, E. (1982). *Cognition and curriculum: A basis for deciding what to teach.* New York: Longman.

Farris, R. A. (1990). Meeting their needs: Motivating middle level learners. *Middle School Journal, 22*(2). 22–26.

Gardner, H. (1983). *Frames of mind.* New York: Basic Books.

Garner, A., & Yancey, E. E. (1994). If I could only see tomorrow: The transescent years. *Becoming, 4*(2), 4–9.

George, P., & Lawrence, G. (1982). *Handbook for middle school teaching.* Glenview, IL: Scott, Foresman.

George, P., Stevenson, C., Thomason, J., & Beane, J. (1992). *The middle school—and beyond.* Alexandria, VA: Association for Supervision and Curriculum Development.

Gutheinz-Pierce, D., & Whoolery, K. (1995). The reality of early adolescence: Using what we know to guide our classroom practices. *Middle School Journal, 26*(2), 61–64.

Harter, S. (1990). Processes underlying adolescent self-concept formation. In R. Montemayor, G. Adams, & T. Gullotta (Eds.), *From childhood to adolescence: A transition period* (pp. 205–239). Newbury Park, CA: Sage.

Herring, R. (1990). Suicide in the middle school: Who said kids will not? *Elementary School Guidance Counseling, 25*(2), 129–137.

Hootstein, E. W. (1994). Motivating middle school students to learn. *Middle School Journal, 25*(5), 31–34.

Inhelder, G., & Piaget, J. (1958). *The growth of logical thinking from childhood to adolescence.* New York: Basic Books.

Kindred, L. W., Wolotkiewicz, R. J., Mickelson, J. M., Coplein, L. E., & Dyson, E. (1976). *The middle school curriculum: A practitioner's handbook.* Boston: Allyn and Bacon.

Kohen-Raz, R. (1971). *The child from nine to thirteen.* Chicago: Aldine-Atherton.

Lounsbury, J. H. (1991). *As I see it.* Columbus, OH: National Middle School Association.

Maier, H. W. (1969). *Three theories of child development.* New York: Harper and Row.

Martin, T. (1993). "Turning Points" revisited: How effective middle grades schools address developmental needs of young adolescent students. *Journal of Health Education, 24*(6), S-24–S-27.

McEwin, C. K., & Thomason, J. T. (1989). *Who they are—how we teach: Early adolescents and their teachers.* Columbus, OH: National Middle School Association.

National Middle School Association (1995). *This we believe: Developmentally responsive middle level schools.* Columbus, OH: Author.

Obert, D. L. (1995). "Give and you shall receive": School-based service learning. *Middle School Journal, 26*(4), 30–33.

O'Brien, S. G., & Bierman, K. L. (1988). Conceptions and perceived influence of peer groups: Interviews with preadolescents and adolescents. *Child Development, 59*(5), 1360–1365.

Piaget, J. (1966). *Psychology of intelligence.* Totowa, NJ: Littlefield, Adams.

Renihan, P. J., & Renihan, F. I. (1990). Across the wide water: A middle years metaphor. *Middle School Journal, 22*(1), 39–42.

Ridley, D. S., McCombs, B., & Taylor, K. (1994). Walking the talk: Fostering self-regulated learning in the classroom. *Middle School Journal, 26*(2), 52–57.

Rogers, V., & Stevenson, C. (1988). How do we know what kids are learning in school? *Educational Leadership, 45*(5), 68–75.

Schave, D., & Schave, B. (1989). *Early adolescence and the search for self.* New York: Praeger.

Sherman, P., & Banks, D. (1995). Connecting kids to community with survey research. *Middle School Journal, 26*(2), 26–29.

Stefanich, G. P. (1990). Cycles of cognition. *Middle School Journal, 22*(2), 47–52.

Stevenson, C. (1992). *Teaching ten to fourteen year olds.* White Plains, NY: Longman.

Turning points: Preparing American youth for the 21st century (abridged), a report prepared by the Carnegie Council on Adolescent Development's Task Force on Education of Young Adolescents, 1990, Washington, DC.

Van Hoose, J., & Strahan, D. (1988). *Young adolescent development and school practices: Promotion harmony.* Columbus, OH: National Middle School Association.

Chapter 2

A Middle Grades Teacher Advisory System for At-Risk Students

DONALD R. CASTLE
W. DOUGLAS CASTLE

Donald R. Castle (1943–1994) was an Associate Professor of Education at Ashland University, authored numerous publications on middle grades education and the deindustrialization of communities, and designed Ashland University's middle grades licensure program in conjunction with the Ohio Department of Education.

W. Douglas Castle has spent 30 of his 32 years in education in middle school and junior high programs. He currently is a middle school principal at John Simpson Middle School, Mansfield, Ohio, and has served as a speaker and presenter at many middle school conferences and functions.

The organization and design of an effective teacher advisory system that focuses on at-risk students must consider the unpredictable nature of the middle grades child that is often exacerbated by the at-risk factors. The intrusion of "at-riskness" into the lives of middle grades children tends to stagnate and retard development. In many cases some regression or misdirection may occur. On a projection basis, middle grades children are in the pre-early adolescent stages of concrete operations. Typically they move into more formal operations that are marked by the move to higher-order, multiplicity functions. The move from the concrete to formal operations normally equips children to be more intuitive and reflective. Children at this point seem more aware of a wider range of nonegocentric concerns as they begin to consider the nature of the world and societal questions, part of a higher level of logic.

At-risk early adolescent children tend to remain in the egocentric concrete operational stage. They need immediacy and tangibility. Advising middle grades children at risk requires advisors who understand these characteristics. In addition, middle grades at-risk students are often unable to link the long-term value of education to their adult lives. Many view their lives as having limited expectations and potential. To a great extent an "Armageddon" mentality dominates their thinking. Separating the ideal from the real while being extremely subject to manipulation from external focuses is clearly an issue for at-risk students at this level. Such factors lead advisors to work with students in developing self-concept and positive identities and gaining control over their lives.

Much of the efforts of middle grades children in general tend to be social. Children in this early adolescent stage are constantly crying for social acceptance at their peer level. The lack of a social skills repertoire, common among middle graders, leads these youngsters to direct an unusual amount of energy toward social, nonacademic needs. However, these efforts for most children result in fairly predictable outcomes in that social skills are acquired and interpersonal relationships develop by the time the formal operations stage arrives.

Interferences caused by risk elements often rob middle grades students of a positive view of their world. In essence, students at risk are able to deal with people only on a negative level. Problems, for example, can only be solved by violence and confrontation. Perception of self is likely to be negative, while an inappropriate amount of time is spent on emotionally arousing and destructive events. Such titillation arouses in the at-risk children a perspective on life that advisors must attempt to redefine. A good, well-organized teacher advisory system can bridge the gap between the academic learning needs and social process needs. The philosophy and design of the middle grades concept meet the criteria necessary for redirecting the energies of at-risk students toward more long-term expectations. It appears that when students acquire the capacity to control impulsive behavior and disruptive chaotic relationships, at-risk students at the middle grades level are likely to become better school citizens with good cognitive learning skills. Nurturing toward this capacity is essential to the advisory program.

TA System

The teacher advisory (TA) system for middle grades at-risk students must be linked with all facets of middle grades education. Advising students occurs in many forums and addresses an infinite number of issues and topics. Much of what has traditionally been called good advising has to do with directing and inspiring students to overcome their frustrations and futilities in order to become good test takers and proper performers. Although these activities are necessary parts of the educational environment, they are only particular aspects of the process, not the "end all" of the higher-order goal of producing good students who are also good people.

The framework of the advisory system consists of those areas of advising that are at least somewhat predictable as to the needs of at-risk middle grades students. The first area of need for at-risk students is the family. Working with students in regard to interpersonal family problems brings attention to the issues of growth and development. Much of what takes place in the classroom begins and grows at home. In essence, children at risk often come to school ill equipped to deal with the kinds of expected behaviors pertinent to schools. To approach such advising roles by deciding to change the child's home life is ludicrous. At-risk students come from at-risk parents who are preoccupied with problems perceived as much greater than those of their children and who have limited capacity to change the conditions creating risks. As dutiful as parents of at-risk children profess themselves to be, showing them what their children need to be successful in school rarely inspires significant positive change. However, at-risk students can come to understand how to function as students and as children from families with many difficulties. Often when the students begin to experience a positive school role, parents do begin to involve themselves at some level. With this in mind, it is essential that strategies for involving parents be emphasized. It is also important that these strategies communicate to parents that schools are not hostile to them. Few successful programs exist that involve parents, so the potential for innovation in this area is a challenging opportunity.

For the at-risk parents the relationship gap with schools exists partly as a result of socioeconomic differences. At-risk parents have indicated their uneasiness and discomfort when they are involved with their children's schools. As research indicates, at-risk children tend to be more involved in disciplinary action and experience academic failure. The association at-risk parents have had with schools has most often been negative. Yet, in discussion of what at-risk parents want from schools, it has been found that they want communication, involvement, acceptance, and opportunity to help solve problems. In addition, parents want dignity, empowerment, and ownership. Many have indicated that school personnel patronize them by telling them what is best for them. A message from these conversations made it clear that the traditional professional educator-to-parent relationship was not acceptable. Instead, a community teacher advisory program based on collaboration was derived. Partnerships make it possible for parents to collaborate with schools in a variety of ways.

Sample Community Collaboration Program for Teacher Advisory System

The community collaboration program involves parents of student team members. The primary teacher advisor recruits as many parents of the group as possible to meet on a regular basis to organize and develop a team advisory system that operates on a small-group dynamics basis. The entire range of advising needs can be addressed with this approach. Procedural activities and operational roles must come about as a result of collaboration among all facets of the team. It is essential that all individuals involved have definitive primary roles in the process. It is likely that some time will be required for role developing, role identity, and collaborative procedures. Parents may have roles in the advisory system as members of external support groups or mentorship programs, as liaisons between school and community resources and institutions, and as planners for advising activities.

At-risk students often are unable to function at the most basic level as students. The incompatibility between school and home provides a poor model for student school behavior. For example, at-risk students often do not have the tools for school, such as pencils, paper, and books. Homework and general preparations for school are not part of the at-risk students' priorities. This advisory system proposes to teach students and parents how to be students. Such activities represent the limitless number of possibilities for advising at-risk students.

The Ashland University/John Simpson Middle School Partnership for College Enrichment for At-Risk Students

When counseling middle grade students on careers, connecting students with the idea of success in the adult world is an arduous task. Perhaps because of the span of time before leaving school, students at this level usually give little consideration to possible careers. The impact of at-riskness on students exaggerates this condition to the point that a general malaise takes over students' thinking and often leads to total rejection of the concept of school. Overcoming the student condition requires a system that connects what is going on in school with economic career structures. Clearly such an approach carries with it enormous student motivation possibilities. Because this is an advisory system, assisting students in making connections is the critical role of the teaching advisor. Participating with business and industry, internships, volunteer programs, field trips to business and industry, and career-oriented speakers and summer and afterschool workshops are practical strategies for assisting students in making connection.

One strategy currently in place for a middle school in Ohio is a school partnership with a university. The employer in this program provides enrichment experiences for at-risk students by giving them an opportunity to not only visit the university but to actually live there as college students for 3 to 5 days. Such experiences often counter the negative perspective the at-risk have of their world. Although the experiences are sensory and provide immediate satisfaction, there seems to be long-term motivation. Based on interviews with the students who have experienced college life, goals are set and ambition is aroused. Apparently such experiences are compatible with the nature of the early adolescent child. Developing identity, direction, and self-esteem is part of the process of growth and learning for the middle grades child. For the at-risk middle grades child, such needs are even more prevalent. College is a distant dream, something out there for these youngsters. Much of what happens during the college enrichment experience familiarizes these students with college life and allows them to view college as a possibility well within their control.

Components of TA Systems

Conflict Resolution and Peer Mediation

It is suggested that students work with the same teacher advisor throughout the middle school years. The advisor can fill a much needed role in assisting students in coping with the violence that surrounds them. One only needs to look at a newspaper or television to realize that we live in a violent world, and middle grade students (from this writer's perspective) are among the most violent of the age groups. Middle grade students are compulsive and tend to react without thinking about consequences. It is imperative that we teach middle grade students the fourth *R*—resolution. The teacher advisor has an excellent opportunity to do this by meeting daily with advisees and providing information and strategies on dealing with conflict.

The advisory program offers daily opportunities to teach students coping skills through the use of a variety of game-like activities and discussions. These activities should be part of a well-developed conflict resolution program. All students need to know how to diffuse a potential conflict peacefully.

A second piece of the conflict resolution program is peer mediation. Students identified with peacemaking skills need to be steered into the peer mediation program. Advisors are very important to this process because of their knowledge of their advisees. Advisors should encourage and assist students in learning peer mediation skills. These skills obviously can be used to help others resolve conflict peacefully. Advisors will need training in conflict resolution and peer mediation to accomplish this huge task. The alternative is the continued escalation of violence in our schools and ultimately in our homes and streets. Students need to see that there are alternatives and that they have choices.

Overcoming Hopelessness

At-risk students spend so much of their daily lives simply trying to get through the day safely that they are unable to focus on life in 10 years, 5 years, 1 year, or in some cases even tomorrow. They spend so much time in survival mode that they are unable to focus on the daily task of education and they fall further and further behind. Eventually they are so beaten down that they give up (the Armageddon theory mentioned earlier). Many students feel helpless and simply drop out of society, becoming totally dependent or turning to a life of crime. Schools must provide early exposure that will allow students to experience hope as they face overwhelming daily problems. There are students as young as 10 who have already decided there is no world for them.

All students, particularly at-risk students, need to know that there are opportunities out there for them. John Simpson Middle School, in Mansfield, Ohio, has attempted in a variety of ways to demonstrate this to the students. The program that has been perhaps the most effective has involved Ashland University, as mentioned earlier. The program was initiated in the late 1980s and has grown tremendously since then. The program consists of an overnight visit by twelve severely at-risk students to Ashland University. Students are teamed with a mentor. They attend college classes and eat in the dining hall. They attend seminars consisting of presentations on college life, finances, and testimonials from students of similar backgrounds on how they got to Ashland University. The students stay overnight in a dormitory under the supervision of Simpson School personnel.

This visit is conducted twice yearly with two different groups. The result has been that some students came alive and put their past behind them and focused on the future. In fact, on one occasion a young man exited the bus and entered the counselor's office to change his registration for his freshman year to a college preparatory program because he said he had found something that he wanted to do—go to college.

This program has expanded into a project called Grow Your Own, which involves several school systems in the Ashland University area. This author's personal experiences with this program have been most satisfying.

Students who see no hope in their daily lives must be given opportunities to experience this type of reality if we are to change the Armageddon outlook. Teacher advisors are in position to help students explore these types of experiences.

Academic Advising

Academic advising is another responsibility of the TA program. Much of this activity is procedural, such as scheduling. However, there is an intervention component that involves the students' academic performance. Traditionally the focus here is a failure. But our program takes a somewhat different approach. Students are taught that much of what happens to individuals, despite their being at risk, is a result of choice. The advisor asks students to get to know themselves and take control. Such an approach requires students to know the nature of their intellectuality, understand application, accept responsibility for learning, and set goals. Problems such as poor memory and poor organizational skills must be recognized and improved. Students are advised to discover the strength of their learning abilities and to understand how to maximize these strengths. The integration of the advisor's association with the student and the student's academic life makes this approach unique. The advisor works closely with other staff members and the guidance counselor in the effort to assist advisees.

Crisis Management

Teacher advisors have a role of crisis management in that students in general, and especially those at risk, tend to be subject to many chaotic and confusing issues. The stress of searching for identity, family chaos, and confused social standing among peers certainly imposes a responsibility for quality counseling and advising that can address the issue of at-riskness. Antisocial and recalcitrant behavior includes many different kinds of acts. Antiauthoritarian acts, fighting, lying, stealing, cheating, truancy, and property destruction are all common and tend to be part of everyone's behavior to some extent. Such behavior, however, diminishes in time for most individuals. Clearly a reasonably thinking person has little problem controlling such behavior. For children whose growth and development are interrupted, such negative overt acts tend not to diminish. For many students—and especially those at risk—crises are common and not perceived as abnormal conduct.

Strategies employed by the advisor most provide intervention for children before they are classified as having conduct disorders or severe behavior disorders. The intervention also must deal with academic deficiencies often created by conduct disorders. Advisors often can connect with the symptoms of negative behavior. For example, although initially less serious, such behaviors as deformation (profanity), boisterousness, lackadaisical attitude, problems with parents, isolation, and irresponsibility are indicators of deeper problems and more severe interpersonal and social conflict.

The role of the advisor is to provide such students with a forum in which critical student issues may be discussed. In many cases the advisor may be a confidant, a listener, or a friend. Good advisors know that their students often feel powerless and frustrated. These advisors also know that because there are middle grades students whose growth has been interrupted, egocentric thoughts control behavior.

The goals of the advisor are several. To control crisis if necessary is the ultimate demand on an advisor. This program teaches prevention and maintenance. Whether the potential crisis is violent physical conflict or a lack of interest in school, most corrective interaction by advisors encourages students to consider the world beyond themselves. They encourage students to set goals and expectations that deal with all facets of their lives. Much of what advisors must understand is that their advisees worry about friends, family, and academic and social problems. Advisors must be willing to involve others, including parents, in the advising of students. The common denominator for a successful advisory program is compatibility and accessibility. Students and advisors must form a trusting and caring relationship and have both scheduled and unscheduled opportunities for interaction. Much of this can be accomplished with implementation of flexible scheduling.

Transitional Advising for Middle Grades Students at Risk

The move to a middle grades environment from an elementary school environment represents a stressful moment in the lives of students. Such disruption removes students from a situation in which familiarity and comfort provide students with a sense of security that is often lost in the transition to middle grades. The transition process must be designed to diminish the stress while connecting students to a new way of school life. In the elementary school, students are associated with one teacher in a very supportive environment. Students spend most of their time in one room with a group of youngsters they have known for a long time. A product of elementary associations and experiences is that students have ample time to learn to function within their environment. They form strong relationships and alliances and learn how to avoid threatening and hostile situations. Growth concepts such as early pubescent, moral definition, cognitive ability, pure groups, acceptance, self-identity, and growth (physical and mental) differentiation are major considerations for transition advising.

This component of the advising program requires the initiation of the advisory program the spring before entry into the middle school. The advisor visits parents and students in their homes to review the procedure for moving into the middle school. This meeting serves to reduce the anxiety of parents and students. Making themselves known to their advisees and imparting knowledge of how the system functions are also important purposes for the meeting. Advisors do follow-up sessions if there appears to be a problem.

A series of visits to the middle school by parents with their children and later the children on their own is also part of the program. One of these visits will include a small-group team discussion session with teaching team members and advisors.

When school begins in the fall, all first-year middle grades students will meet with their advisor several times a week on a scheduled basis. These sessions are designed to keep students on track by supporting their needs, providing a friendly familiar face, and by providing a liaison between the advisee and other members of the school setting.

As the middle grades experience nears completion, students face a similar transition to the high school. Although students are at the midpoint of early adolescence and are obviously more mature, the move from the supportive middle grades environment to the isolated, more independent environment of the high school can be traumatic and stressful. Oddly, the same kinds of disassociation and separation problems are likely to occur. The implementation of appropriate transitional programs as part of the advisory system is essential. As most high schools do not have advisory programs, the major responsibility for this transition belongs to the middle school.

Conclusion

The middle grades advisory program for at-risk students requires teachers to become advisors as a part of their professional responsibility. In essence, middle grade teachers must perceive guidance and advising as equally important to their role as teachers of specific content areas. Middle grades students are vulnerable to many of the elements of growth and development and socioeconomic factors.

The rationale for this concept is that the best equipped people to help students are those who are with them—teachers. Obviously the teacher advisor must have a professional knowledge of growth and development, group dynamics, learning structures, socioeconomic situations, and human behavior.

In that the middle school concept is a relatively recent notion, a cleansing of the traditional educational system addresses the changes in the structure of American society. With deindustrialization, the demise of the factory model as a basis for education has resulted in a new definition of American education. Students in a middle grades program no longer will be processed through an educational system that ignores the needs of children while labeling and categorizing them to be relegated to careers that go nowhere. Clearly the advisory system seeks to help children grow into successful students and good people. This system supports the development of positive self-concept, self-esteem, and different learning strategies, among the many aspects of a student-centered approach.

A final note: Teacher advisors must be involved in flexible scheduling that accommodates teacher–student advising opportunities on a formal as well as informal basis, as is discussed in detail in Chapter 6.

Discussion Questions

1. How does the role of the teacher advisor differ from the role of the school counselor?
2. In your opinion, what is the most important aspect of your role as a teacher advisor?
3. What are the major roadblocks in implementing a TA program?
4. What are the principal advantages of having a TA program in a school?

Chapter 3

The Excluded Middle: Postmodern Conceptions of the Middle School

PATRICK SLATTERY

Patrick Slattery is an Associate Professor of Education at Texas A&M University where he teaches curriculum theory, foundations of education, and various education courses. He is the author of Curriculum Development in the Postmodern Era *(Garland, 1995),* Understanding Curriculum *(Lang, 1995), and* Contextualizing Teaching *(Longman, 1998). He has published numerous scholarly papers in* Harvard Educational Review, Journal of Curriculum Theorizing (JCT), Childhood Education, *and* Curriculum Inquiry.

The emergence of the popular concept of the middle school is a recent phenomenon that has its roots in the perceived need to create developmentally appropriate, psychologically relevant, and educationally stimulating learning environments for students between the elementary school and the high school. Assuming that early childhood educators and secondary educators have already developed constructs and models appropriate for students in the earliest and later levels of schooling, educators who work with students in the middle grades have sought to create appropriate schooling models for these children. In short, it has been assumed that middle school children have been excluded in an educational system that ignores the special needs of those caught between the elementary school and high school. This is not a unique complaint. The majority of "average" students are usually considered to be overlooked by an educational system that invests its resources at the top in gifted and talented programs, extracurricular activities, honors classes, and advanced placement programs and at the bottom in remedial classes, tutoring, Head Start, and special education. The middle is often considered to be excluded. Adolescent children are marginalized and overlooked.

Journals, conferences, classroom materials, and textbooks—like this one—for middle school students and teachers have proliferated in an effort to overcome the exclusion of middle grades children. On the one hand, this is a positive development. A renewed interest in the needs of the middle school provides incentives and opportunities for growth. On the other hand, the modernist structure of bureaucracy, hierarchy, and positivism that continues to influence these resources does not allow for the emergence of significantly different models of education in the middle school. The philosophy of the middle school that has evolved often replicates the modernist paradigm of traditional elementary and secondary education. Imitating a flawed philosophy fails to produce a curriculum model or instructional program for middle schools that is appropriate for children in the postmodern era. In this chapter I will present a critique of modern education and propose a postmodern philosophy that is more appropriate for the middle school. Particularly, I will explore what it means to say that middle level education is excluded.

There are several contemporary philosophical analyses that reveal the contradictions that currently exist in the philosophical construct of middle level education. Obviously the first issue is the definition of "middle school" itself. While most middle schools include students in grades six through eight between the ages of 11 and 14, variations in the configuration of middle level education range from third grade to ninth grade and ages 8 to 16. Some junior high schools have simply changed their names to middle schools without any significant alteration in the philosophy, curriculum, or instructional programs. Is there anything significantly different in practice between a junior high school and a middle school? Should middle schools even be defined by traditional grade level configurations, levels of experience, and ages of the students? What is the middle school actually between? Or is the middle an imaginary classification? Thus, if we say that the middle school is excluded, must it first exist before it can be excluded?

If, for the sake of discussion, we assume the existence of middle schools, then in what sense is middle level education excluded? Are the voices of students and teachers silenced or erased? If so, is this a self-imposed silence, or is the clamoring voice of the middle unheard by those with the power to silence and ignore? Is there a resistance to being in the middle, or is there only silence in the middle? Is the middle the statistical average, or is it a process of becoming? If the middle is excluded, is it possible that middle schooling could be protected from the contamination of modern bureaucratic and positivistic models of education that permeate other levels of schooling? In this sense, middle level education may be so misunderstood by traditional bureaucratic educators that, in being overlooked, the middle may be free to create itself in a new context. Middle schooling may provide a unique opportunity for reconceptualized and progressive visions of teaching and learning to emerge that are not permitted or included in mainstream educational programs. I propose such an alternative in this chapter; I use the term *postmodern* to describe this philosophical position.

Modern Education

The common schools were founded in the early nineteenth century for the purpose of enculturating all citizens—particularly immigrants—into American society. Common schools were created to establish a common culture in the emerging American democracy. The white, Anglo-Saxon, Protestant majority created a school system that would enculturate, indoctrinate, civilize, and democratize the people of this new country and prepare them for the labor force. Of course, native Americans, enslaved Africans, women, and other minorities were excluded from this process (Spring, 1986). Catholics revolted, fearing for their religious independence. They formed their own school system with the encouragement of their bishops at the Councils of Baltimore (Pinar et al., 1995). The common schools—now called public schools—prepared students for civil society and the work force by teaching them to be compliant, obedient, respectful, and Protestant Christians.

Modern society was linearly organized: military rank and file, farming rows, factory assembly lines, church pews, patriarchal family hierarchies, and the like. Thus, rows of desks, silence, raising hands for permission, repetition of tasks, submission to authority, and standing in lines were of paramount importance in schools (Kincheloe, 1993). Schools were designed to create a common and compliant work force and culture (Spring, 1986). The rhetoric of the American dream, the rugged individual, and manifest destiny all contributed to an attitude that helped convince laborers, immigrants, the poor, and eventually women and minorities that education is the engine of society that levels the economic playing field for all people and builds a democratic society. This attitude has become so ingrained in the American psyche that every politician today aspires to be the "education governor" or "education president."

Some of the features of modern schooling that continue to dominate in the 1990s include the following: segmentation of tasks, linear organization of curriculum on scope and sequence charts, predetermining goals and objectives outside of the context of the school or classroom, universalizing outcomes, emphasizing time on task, mastering proficiency in discrete skills, unquestioning compliance to adult authority, memorizing officially sanctioned information, and promotion of students (and in some states, teachers) based solely on the results of state-mandated criterion-referenced tests. Frederick Taylor designed time and motion studies in the 1930s that would help schools develop models similar to industry to ensure efficiency in this process. The modern school is characterized by efficiency, memorization, predetermined outcomes, segmentation and separation by age and ability, tracking, repetition, rewards for competitive victors, bureaucratic regulation, accountability, written tests with rubrics that simplify complex issues, sorting, and ranking (Oakes, 1985).

Those with a commitment to the status quo modern educational system assume that schooling serves an important credentialing, sorting, and enculturation function in our society. Their commitment to modern schooling is rooted in self-preservation in the economic, political, religious, or social realm. Any deviation in the current social arrangements would threaten those with power. Thus, schooling is seen as the best means of encouraging compliance with the status quo.

Postmodern scholars recognize that the ecological, psychological, economic, political, religious, and social problems of contemporary society require a fundamental shift away from the status quo power arrangements. The survival of the planet is at stake. Education must no longer serve social structures and unjust power arrangements. A postmodern vision is essential. As John Dewey, George Counts, and other educators insisted in the early twentieth century, society must be the function of education. In other words, improving society and creating a just, caring, and ecologically sustainable community must be the primary focus of education. Middle schools must adopt this vision or they will continue to reproduce modern hierarchical and unjust power structures that will never have the effect of empowering students and teachers.

Despite protestations from those who would like to preserve the modern bureaucratic and hegemonic schooling structures, we have now entered a postmodern era. This makes powerful people nervous and angry. They would like to go back to the "good old days" (which were not very good for people who are "different" in race, religion, ethnicity, gender, language, physical challenges, and learning modes—in other words, everyone except white, male, heterosexual, Anglo-Saxon, Protestant land owners). The traditionalists who insist that schools must teach the "basics" must be challenged to understand that the basics have been variously defined over the centuries by different special interest groups: astronomy, rhetoric, geometry, music, and physical education for the Greeks; Latin, Greek, classics, speech, and mathematics in the nineteenth century; reading, writing, arithmetic, and the Protestant Christian Bible in early American common schools; physical conditioning, cranial measurement, and political theory in socialist Germany. What are the real "basics," and who controls the course content and textbooks? Curriculum is a contested terrain (McLaren, 1994) on which various conceptions of knowledge and truth compete for dominance. The issues of power and control must first be addressed before an appropriate middle school curriculum and philosophy can be understood.

The Postmodern Era

John Fiske (1993) in his book *Power Plays, Power Works* contends that the notion of power must be addressed directly in our contentious global society. Before the fifteenth century, premodern societies relied on physical coercion, torture, force, and confrontation to impose order and values on people. With growing populations, particularly in cities, the modern age of the last five hundred years has had to rely on surveillance and monitoring in order to gain compliance of the population

(Foucault, 1979). We are beginning to recognize that there are not enough police and prisons to control the entire population. While churches seek to control the conscience and behavior of people, governments use mechanisms of surveillance, patriotism, economics, and fear to force citizens to comply with rules and regulations. The goal is to develop consensus in the population.

In the postmodern era such consensus has eroded. There are multiple perspectives; competing values; a variety of religious experiences, communities, ideologies, and, for our purposes, curriculums, that are competing for recognition and acceptance. This frightens those who are committed to singular views of society and education. Thus, it is not surprising that powerful communities and constituencies attempt to impose their values on all citizens. National curriculums, state proficiency tests, and standardized accountability models are an outgrowth of this philosophy. Narrow definitions of family values and religious morality are another example. As various minority groups fight for recognition, acceptance, and democratic rights, dominant power groups redouble their efforts to control citizens—particularly minority populations like adolescent children, immigrants, gays, laborers, persons of color, and religious minorities. A return to premodern physical coercion can be seen in the proliferation of prisons, police brutality, hate groups, and militant militias. It is not surprising that schools are often built like prisons and patrolled vigilantly. It is assumed that exerting more control over students will lead to obedience and learning. However, this type of coercion only leads to more turmoil (Slattery & Daigle, 1994).

There is another way to deal with the problems of modern society according to many postmodern writers. John Fisk (1993), for example, writes:

> *The change in the social order, to put it succinctly, will be one from a society organized around a general consensus to one organized around varied points of consent. The United States' social order of the twentieth century was one organized around a broadly shared consensus of values and priorities that stretched across the domains of politics, economics, religion, and culture. It has been legitimated by a long and powerful history in which Greco-Roman and Judeo-Christian influences combined to produce first Europe and the US as major world powers. The consensus was therefore sure of its values, it knew that they were the only ones which could produce a powerful and fair modern society. Any problems that might result, then, tended to be ones of accommodation, not of the values themselves. (p. 44)*

What we are experiencing in the late twentieth century is an explosion of global communities with diffuse influence in politics, economics, religion, and culture. The separation between cultures has been eradicated by mass communication, transportation, computer technology, job migration, and immigration. Despite isolationist rhetoric, it is impossible to return to the independent power centers of the modern era. We live in an interdependent global community where our survival depends on cooperation rather than competition and dominance. Our schools must reflect postmodern values and practices; otherwise education contributes to the divisiveness in our society rather than solutions that are just, caring, and ecologically sustainable.

Postmodern education is a complex process. However, it promotes diversity, understanding, and a new social imagination with "multiple points of consent" (Fiske, 1993, p. 46). Multiculturalism; eclecticism; cooperative practices; interdisciplinary experiences; community-based projects; racial and gender inclusiveness; ecological and spiritual sensibilities; shared power arrangements; and just economic structures that support health, nutrition, and psychological well-being of all citizens will be the hallmark of postmodern learning environments. Education must be prophetic in its condemnation of modern power structures that have resulted in holocausts, genocide, starvation, ecological destruction, massive poverty, slavery, patriarchal domination, colonialization, environmental degradation, and other horrors of the twentieth century. If education does not focus on these issues, then it is complicit in the continuing modern holocausts.

Caught in the Middle as the Postmodern Emerges

The preceding discussion of the emerging postmodern era is unsettling to some. Schooling will now require a realignment of relationships and a reconceptualization of power arrangements by those in control. Middle schools must allow for the emergence of multiple perspectives and multiple forms of representation. The cultures of Africa, Asia, the Middle East, Latin America, and other areas will share stature with European culture. Buddhism, Hinduism, Gnosticism, atheism, pantheism, and Islam—among others—will be respected in society and in schools along with Judaism and various Christianities. Women will share equal opportunities with men. Gender differences, sexual orientations, physical conditions, learning differences, and the like will no longer be the object of ridicule, harassment, and exclusion. Those who continue to resist multiculturalism and multiple communities contribute to the hatred and divisiveness of modern society. Teachers and other school leaders have the opportunity to contribute positively to the emerging postmodern era. However, the middle school movement is literally "caught in the middle" between those who would exert their power and influence to prevent multiplicity from emerging by preserving the status quo social and economic arrangements and those who recognize the needs of middle school children to be actively involved in creating relationships and community practices to improve society.

On the one hand, middle schools have the opportunity to structure the teaching and learning environment based on the postmodern values described here. On the other hand, there is tremendous pressure to create middle schools in the traditional modernist paradigm. I believe that the traditional modern philosophy still dominates middle schools. In the attempt to create middle schools with a focus on discovery learning, spaces for movement, creative projects, interdisciplinary lessons, cooperative relational practices, multicultural celebrations, and constructivist learning, many middle schools find that they remain caught in the modern bureaucratic power arrangements that demand accountability, order, control, measurable data, and compliance. As a result, the emerging middle school has become just another structure at the service of modern technocratic and bureaucratic schooling practices. If the only significant difference between a middle school and other forms of schooling is a new name; a different grade level configuration; a new set of learning materials; rearranged learning spaces; flexible time structures; new goals, objectives, and outcomes, then the middle school perpetuates the disasters of modern society and delays the emergence of the postmodern community. What is needed in the middle school is a total re-thinking of the premises of modern education. Middle schools are the best place for this transformation and new "social imagination" (Fiske, 1993) to occur because, like the modern society in transition to the postmodern, they have an opportunity to reconceptualize their place in the process as a new and emerging educational endeavor.

A Social Imagination for Middle Schools

Giles Deleuze and Felix Guattari (1987) in *A Thousand Plateaus: Capitalism and Schizophrenia* challenge the concept of the middle as a place between two points or a statistical average:

> *A line of becoming is not defined by points that it connects, or by points that compose it; on the contrary, it passes between points, it comes up through the middle, it runs perpendicular to the points first perceived, transversally to the localizable relation to distant or contiguous points. A point is always a point of origin. But a line of becoming has neither beginning nor end, departure nor arrival, origin nor destination; to speak of the absence of an origin, to make the absence of an origin the origin, is a bad play on words. A line of becoming has only a middle. The middle is not an average; it is fast motion, it is the absolute speed of movement. A becoming is always in the middle; one can only get it by the middle. A becoming is neither one nor two, nor the relation of the two; it is the in-between, the border of line or flight of descent running perpendicular to both. (p. 293)*

Thus, as students and teachers are always in the process of becoming, we are always in the middle, yet the middle does not exist as a place between two points. Deleuze and Guattari challenge the whole notion of middle level education by demonstrating that becoming is always the middle. Middle school educators understand this concept. They experience the emotional swings, shifting interests, self-exploration, and emerging literacy of middle school children. Those who live and work with middle school children understand that the middle is a place of becoming and not a rigid point of arrival.

In a postmodern sense, is it possible that there is no middle because of the constant shifting and redefining of self, schooling, and culture in this process of becoming? Autobiographies and narratives from the boundaries of the schooling experience may provide the best understanding of schooling in the middle. Is a phenomenological approach to middle level education ultimately necessary to discover the presence of what is absent or excluded? Through the use of stories and dialogue a postmodern understanding of middle level education may emerge that will address these perplexing questions.

There has been a virtual explosion of the use of the word *postmodern* in recent years: deconstructive postmodernism, constructive postmodernism, eliminative postmodernism, cultural postmodernism, postmodern art, postmodern society, postmodern theology, postmodern architecture, and on and on. Postmodernism can be understood from at least eleven different perspectives: an emerging historical period that transcends the modern industrial and technological age; a contemporary aesthetic style in art and architecture that is eclectic, kaleidoscopic, ironic, and allegorical; a social criticism of unified systems of economic and political organization such as liberalism and communism; a philosophical movement that seeks to expose the internal contradictions of metanarratives by deconstructing modern notions of truth, language, knowledge, and power; a cultural analysis that critiques the negative impact of modern technology on the human psyche and the environment while promoting the construction of a holistic and ecologically sustainable global community; a radical eclecticism (*not* compromise or consensus) and double-voiced discourse that accepts and criticizes at the same time because the past and the future are both honored and subverted, embraced and limited, constructed and deconstructed; a movement that attempts to go beyond the materialist philosophy of modernity; an acknowledgment and celebration of otherness, particularly from racial and gender perspectives; a momentous historical period marked by a revolutionary paradigm change that transcends the basic assumptions, patterns of operation, and cosmology of the previous modern age; an ecological and ecumenical worldview beyond the modern obsession with dominance and control; or finally, a post-structural movement toward decentering in which there is an absence of anything at the center or any overriding embedded truth at the core, thus necessitating a concentration on the margins and a shift in emphasis to the borders.

Middle level education can be understood to reflect many of these postmodern values: It is eclectic, encompassing many genres, styles, moods, and multiple personalities; it is decentered, requiring constant shifting to tangents and narratives; it is critical, challenging traditional convention and authoritarian structures; it is historical, occurring after infancy and before adulthood but not easily defined with precision. Postmodern middle level education includes these things and much more. This postmodern social imagination offers a philosophical basis to support those who would lead middle schools beyond the modern technical and bureaucratic structure to a new vision. What might a middle school program look like in the postmodern era?

Middle School Students as Curators and Tour Guides

An example of postmodern applications in middle level schooling is the Ambassador Jefferson Caffery Project at Cathedral-Carmel School in Lafayette, Louisiana, which began in 1992. In working with many groups of students and parents in the local community, I observed that very few people were familiar with Ambassador Jefferson Caffery, the longest-serving Chief of Foreign Mission in U.S. history, who served as ambassador to Japan, Iran, Cuba, Argentina, Brazil, and France, among other countries. He signed several treaties at the end of World War II and was personally associated with four popes, served under seven presidents, and was received by innumerable queens, kings, and prime ministers. Ambassador Caffery is buried in the cemetery on the grounds of the Cathedral of St. John, the property that also houses Cathedral-Carmel School. Founded in 1821, the church property was donated by Jean Mouton, founder of the Acadian village known as Vermilionville, now Lafayette, and was the settlement of the French Acadians who were expelled from Nova Scotia in the eighteenth century. Cathedral-Carmel, founded in 1846, was the first school, public or private, in Vermilionville. The property is on the National Trust of Historic Places and is visited daily by tourists from France, Canada, Japan, other foreign countries, and all parts of the United States.

In such an atmosphere it was unfortunate that so little attention to local history existed in the school classrooms. As part of the 1992 curriculum, I launched a special interdisciplinary project that brought several middle school students out of the traditional classroom. The students first took tours of the school cemetery, archives, and church. Historians from the local university (University of Southwestern Louisiana) were invited to meet with the students for walking tours of the property and dialogue with the students. During this initial phase of the project the French teacher worked with the students to develop their communication related to the local history using the French language. The speech teacher trained the students in techniques of public speaking on historical tours and began training students to serve as volunteer docents. Visits to local museums, the old family home of the ambassador, and discussions with family members of Ambassador Caffery all took place. Artifacts were collected from various sources.

At the end of this initial phase the students worked with a museum board member to help establish a museum on the campus. The students served as tour guides for visitors, speaking both in English and French. A video tape about local history was made for viewing in the museum and for sale in the new gift shop. The students were involved in every step of the process of establishing the museum: researching local history, collecting and cataloguing artifacts, filming the video, planning and directing tours for both visitors and fellow students, and scheduling upcoming events. In effect, the middle school students took a leadership role in creating a museum, gift shop, video, and tour in the local community.

This project required the students to integrate social studies, language, science, mathematics, religion, the French language, management, speech, language arts, and personal development all in one project. Artificial barriers between subjects dissolved. The leadership and creativity of the students were allowed to flourish. Autobiographical applications of subject matter were allowed to surface. Responsibility for learning was shifted from the teachers to the students. The natural interests of the students were celebrated and supported.

Of course, there continue to be difficulties in the implementation of this special project. There were mistakes made, deadlines missed, frustration with the complexity of the project at times. However, the process was followed through, and the students actually began serving as historical tour guides on their schools campus. There is a functioning museum on the property that the students helped to establish. A video produced with the assistance of the students is shown several times daily to large groups of tourists. The Ambassador Caffery project could serve as an example of postmodern eclecticism, integration, and cultural and aesthetic awareness. While certainly not a perfect model, it is, none the less, a beginning.

It is important to note that simply creating an interdisciplinary curriculum is not sufficient for creating an appropriate middle level education. Integrated units can be implemented using bureaucratic and authoritarian structures or they can be implemented in cooperative, multicultural, inclusive, and holistic environments. The essential element of postmodern middle schooling is a social imagination that examines every aspect of the teaching and learning environment from the perspective of a just, caring, and ecologically sustainable global culture. Middle school educators can contribute to the creation of such a global community or they could perpetuate the technical and bureaucratic power arrangements of the modern world. Having the opportunity to be involved in such a process can be exciting, rewarding, and often dangerous. For the sake of those "caught in the middle," I would encourage educators to move beyond the linear philosophies that have trapped modern schooling in segmentation, hierarchy, bureaucracy, testing, outcomes, and control and accept the challenge to build a just, caring, and ecologically sustainable global culture that is multicultural with multiple perspectives for the middle school children we love so dearly.

Discussion Questions

1. Consider postmodernism and investigate conceptions of the middle school experience in light of this philosophy.
2. What might a postmodern middle school look like?
3. Why have issues of middle school education often been excluded from mainstream schooling practices?
4. How would you design a middle school program to meet the needs of the diverse population of our society?
5. What accounts for the discrepancy between middle school theory and practice?

References

Bowers, C. A. (1987). *Element of a post-liberal theory of education*. New York: Teachers College Press.

Bowers, C. A. (1993). *Education, cultural myths, and the ecological crisis*. Albany: State University of New York Press.

Bowers, C. A., & Flinders, D. J. (1990). *Responsive teaching: An ecological approach to classroom patterns of language, culture, and thought*. New York: Teachers College Press.

Center for a Postmodern World (1990). Position paper on postmodernism. Claremont, CA: Claremont Graduate School of Theology.

Deleuze, G., & Guattari, F. (1987). *A thousand plateaus: Capitalism and schizophrenia*. (trans. by Brian Massumi). Minneapolis and London: University of Minnesota Press.

Derrida, J. (1981 [1972]). *Positions*. Chicago: University of Chicago Press.

Doll, W. E., Jr. (1993). *A post-modern perspective on curriculum*. New York: Teachers College Press.

Fiske, J. (1993). *Power plays, power works*. London: Vicon.

Foucault, M. (1972). *The archaeology of knowledge and the discourse on language*. (trans. by A. M. Sheridan Smith). New York: Pantheon Books.

Foucault, M. (1979). *Discipline and punish: The birth of the prison*. New York: Pantheon.

Foucault, M. (1980). *Power/knowledge: Selected interviews and other writings, 1972–1977* (ed. by Colin Gordon, trans. by Colin Gordon et al.) New York: Pantheon.

Foucault, M. (1982). *This is not a pipe*. Berkeley: University of California Press.

Giroux, H. A. (Ed.) (1991). *Postmodernism, feminism, and cultural politics: Redrawing educational boundaries*. Albany: State University of New York Press.

Giroux, H. A. (1992). *Boarder crossings: Cultural workers and the politics of education*. New York: Routledge.

Griffin, D. R., Cobb, J. B., Jr., Ford, M. P., Gunter, P. A. Y., & Ochs, P. (1993). *Founders of constructive postmodern philosophy: Peirce, James, Bergson, Whitehead, and Hartshorne*. Albany: State University of New York Press.

Havel, V. (1992, March 1). The end of the modern era. *New York Times,* sec. 4, p. E15.

Jencks, C. (1986). *What is post-modernism?* New York: St. Martin's Press.

Jencks, C. (1988). *Architecture today*. New York: Abrams.

Jencks, C. (Ed.) (1992). *The post-modern reader*. New York: St. Martin's Press.

Kincheloe, J. L. (1993). *Toward a critical politics of teacher thinking: Mapping the postmodern*. Westpost, CT: Bergin & Garvey.

Kincheloe, J. L., & Steinberg, S. R. (1993). A tentative description of post-formal thinking: The critical confrontation with cognitive theory. *Harvard Educational Review, 63*(3), 296–320.

Kuhn, T. (1970). *The structure of scientific revolutions*. Chicago: University of Chicago Press.

Lather, P. (1991). *Getting smart: Feminist research and pedagogy with/in the postmodern*. New York: Routledge.

Lyotard, J. F. (1984). *The postmodern condition: A report on knowledge*. Minneapolis: The University of Minnesota Press.

McLaren, P. (1994). *Life in schools: An introduction to critical pedagogy in the foundations of education*. (2d ed.). New York: Longman.

Oakes, J. (1985). *Keeping track: How schools structure inequality*. New Haven, CT: Yale University Press.

Oliver, D. W., & Gershman, K. W. (1989). *Education, modernity, and fractured meaning: Toward a process theory of teaching and learning*. Albany: State University of New York Press.

Percy, W. (1954). *The message in the bottle*. New York: Farrar, Straus, and Giroux.

Pinar, W. F., Reynolds, W. M., Slattery, P., & Taubman, P. (1995). *Understanding curriculum: An introduction to the study of historical and contemporary curriculum discourses*. New York: Lang.

Slattery, P. (1992a). Theological dimensions of the school curriculum. *Journal of Religion and Public Education, 19*(2–3), 173–184.

Slattery, P. (1992b). Toward an eschatological curriculum theory. *JCT: An Interdisciplinary Journal of Curriculum Studies, 9*(3), 7–21.

Slattery, P., & Daigle, K. (1994). Curriculum as a place of turmoil: Uncovering the anguish in Ernest Gaines' *Pointe Coupee* and Walker Percy's *Feliciana. Curriculum Inquiry, 24*(4), 437–461.

Slattery, P., & Slattery, C. (1993). Writing children's books in a language arts curriculum. *Journal of Children's Books in Ireland, 9* (December), 7.

Spring, J. (1986). *The American high school 1642–1985: Varieties of historical interpretation and development of American education.* New York: Longman.

Toynbee, A. (1947). *A study of history.* New York: Oxford University Press.

Chapter 4

Morally Responsive Teaching

RICK A. BREAULT

Rick A. Breault is an assistant professor in the department of teacher education at the University of Indianapolis. In addition to his work in the preservice middle school program, he teaches courses in curriculum and instruction and the social foundations. His current research interests are in the area of gender equity in the classroom and teacher-held metaphors and archetypes as they relate to school reform. His university teaching was preceded by nine years of elementary and middle school teaching in both public and parochial schools.

I like persons better than principles, and I like persons with no principles better than anything else in the world.—OSCAR WILDE

Things would be so much easier if we all agreed with Wilde. In reality, there appears to be some consensus that a society that operates according to a moral compass is more desirable than one that does not. That, unfortunately, places teachers in a precarious position. Some believe they have no role in the nurturing of a moral stance and naively believe that they simply teach subject matter. Others realize that schools have always taught values and always will, sometimes simplistically and sometimes through a more complex discussion of religion, philosophy, psychology, and culture. However moral development is addressed, perhaps at no level of schooling is it more important than in the middle school.

Morals? What Morals?

Teaching can be a remarkably complex activity. Clark (1988) found that teachers encounter decision situations at 2-minute intervals throughout the day. Other research has shown that the average teacher makes 10 nontrivial decisions each hour and 1,300 decisions per day while engaging in 1,500 personal interactions (Costa & Garmston, 1987). And, as the students in the classroom become older and their problems more complex, so too do the teacher's interactions with them. Complexity in itself is not so problematic if we are well prepared for it and think carefully about it. Unfortunately, evidence shows that teachers often do not think carefully about what they do and the impact of their decisions. In fact, it would seem that many teachers view their job as simply an extended form of parenting and rely more on instinct, personal experience, informal conversation with colleagues, and trial and error to learn their craft than on more formal procedures (Banks, 1991; Book, Byers, & Freeman, 1983; Clark, 1988; Goodlad, 1984; Haberman, 1987; Lambdin & Preston, 1995; Lortie, 1975; Nias, 1989; Paine, 1990). Nowhere is the "off-the-cuff" approach more apparent than when considering the moral aspects of teaching.

A good middle level educator is preoccupied with many things—advising, teaming, interdisciplinary curriculum—each of which has implications for the intellectual development of the students. But, as important as developing the intellect might be, it is only one byproduct of a teacher's instructional decisions. During transescence, emotional and social lessons are as important as the academic ones (Davis, 1993; Havighurst, 1979). Yet teachers, especially novices, are often at a loss when it comes to moral issues, as it seems as if the only criterion for moral decisions is personal preference. However, one moral opinion is *not* as good as another, and there are principles on which the society and the profession have agreed (Bennet & Delattre, 1978; Carnegie Council on Adolescent Development, 1989; Fenstermacher, 1990; Foshay, 1993).

Schooling as a Moral Activity

There are any number of educators who have argued that public schooling is not nor should be involved in moral education (Bereiter, 1973; Bowles & Gintis, 1976; Illich, 1971; Neil, 1927). As compelling as their arguments might be, it is difficult to ignore some of the facts of school life. Whether one acknowledges it or not, there is little doubt that public education, as it has evolved in the United States, is decidedly moral (Bennett & Delattre, 1978; Clark, 1990; Dewey, 1975; Feinberg, 1990; Foshay, 1993). The purpose of this chapter, however, is not to enter into the debate over whether or not schools have any obligation to the larger society to teach values in some systematic way. Instead of looking at what some might consider the moral mission of the public schools, it may be more worthwhile to closely examine the inherently moral nature of the individual classroom and the interactions that take place there. In the process of attending to the overall moral climate of our classrooms, it seems safe to assume that we will also be attending to the character development of the students in those classrooms. I will also argue that this concern for the moral nature of the classroom is as crucial, if not more so, during transescence than at any other time.

The Moral in the Mundane

Traditional classrooms are social places that prepare us for a social existence and therefore, as Dewey (1975) argues, are moral places:

> *The school is fundamentally an institution erected by society to do a certain, specific work—to exercise a certain specific function in maintaining the life and advancing the welfare of society. . . . Apart from participation in social life, the school has no moral end in mind. (pp. 7, 11)*

If we look at a more practical, classroom level, however, the argument is even more convincing. Moral education permeates the school day, if not in specific curricular programs, then in the more subtle assumptions of what Jackson, Boostrom, and Hansen (1993) refer to as the *curricular substructure*. The materials we use, the way we arrange our rooms, the rules we set, what we say, how we say it, and even our facial expressions communicate the values that are important to us and thus become part of the implicit curriculum. Classroom actions or events may not be "moral" in themselves, but when they are "related to larger purposes, and are seen as their 'supports' and 'buttresses,' they take on moral significance" (Hansen, 1993, p. 662).

Moral education also takes place whenever we choose to act on or ignore student behaviors. A student teacher recently asked me how she should respond to a note taken from one of her eighth grade girls. In the note the girl described in sexually explicit detail what she would do with her boyfriend on the weekend. The cooperating teacher told my student to ignore the note, as the girl is already known for her promiscuous behavior. That was a moral decision. A group of middle schoolers from a different school told me how every morning two or three students smoked pot on the school bus and "the bus driver never even sees them." That is moral education of one kind or another. A local computer teacher penalizes students for cheating on his tests but distributes copyrighted disks to be taken home and copied. That too is moral education.

The moral elements of teaching are found in classrooms from preschool through graduate school, and they must be considered to have some impact regardless of the students' age. Middle school students, however, share some special characteristics that lend inordinate influence to the moral messages of the classroom. Making that influence a positive one depends on the ability of the teacher to plan for and react to the moral characteristics and climate of the classroom.

The Nature of the Beast

If a teacher could simply move through the school day knowing that any moral "lapses" would pass unnoticed or that students would willingly submit to whatever messages they were programmed to receive, concerns over the moral temperament of the classroom would be moot. Children like that might exist somewhere, but not in the typical middle school. The unsettled and exploring mind of the adolescent is open to many options, yet often closed to all advice. The paradoxical qualities of this age group make them fiercely independent and, at the same time, susceptible to rigid, cult-like influences. Even the definition of who they are is up for grabs (Erikson, 1950). As Scales (1991) observed, "In one five year period, young people can go from being sure of everything to being sure of nothing and all points in between" (p. 12). Without an understanding of the moral thinking of the students in our charge, we run the risk of responding to them at a level that is, at best, boring and out-of-touch and, at worst, confrontational and alienating.

Early adolescence is a "prime time" for moral development. Mosher (1980) identified four characteristics in particular that make the middle school mind ripe for the deliberation of values and the influence of those who would serve as models:

- A sense of idealism
- A desire to make sense of their world
- Moral concern and sensitivity, which can easily be subverted into new, exotic moralities, religion, or rigid political ideology—or into despair
- A gradual recognition of the rights and feelings of others

This developmental period also brings the onset of abstract reasoning (Piaget, 1972), the role-taking ability needed in order to see a moral conflict involving other people's rights, and the ability to perceive consequences of behavior and to delay gratification (Kohlberg, 1969; Scales, 1991; Selman, 1971). The potential for formal operations, however, while allowing students to hold many variables in their mind at once and to consider contradictory propositions, does not guarantee that those operations are under full control. Hypocrisy is a frequent byproduct of their newfound reasoning ability (Wiles & Bondi, 1993). Their intellect allows them to conceptualize fairly abstract rules of behavior, but the lack of life experience prevents the young adolescent from seeing the rules' relevance to concrete behavior. We cannot assume that since children can consider a variety of options that they can assign priorities and decide on the best choice (Romano & Georgiady, 1994; Wiles & Bondi, 1993). Throughout this time it is important for the educator and parent to realize that these traits do not necessarily reflect a lack of moral character, but rather, intellectual and chronological immaturity. This is especially true when considering the interests and needs of others. At this age most students are able to think about other people's thinking, but a strong egocentrism sometimes prevents a clear distinction between the interests of others and those of the self.

The Self and Others

The inability to distinguish between the interests of oneself and those of others often leads to the creation of what Elkind (1981) has called an "imaginary audience"—the belief that you are the center of everyone's attention and that everyone is preoccupied with your appearance and behavior. There is also a tendency to believe that what, in reality, is common to everyone is unique to them—"You don't know how it feels to . . . " . It is not difficult to see why middle schoolers are often easily offended and sensitive to any criticism of personal shortcomings. They often exaggerate simple occurrences and read much more into your comments than you ever intended. That said, although the moral implications will be discussed later, it is important to digress for a moment to look at some of the potential "side effects" of egocentrism and competing perspectives.

Running parallel with the adolescent's self-absorption are an increased role and influence of the peer group and a willingness or need to take risks. In combination, those factors can have some powerful effects. In transescence there is no greater concern than the need for peer acceptance. For many middle schoolers, meeting that need dominates their life (Romano & Georgiady, 1994). Wiles and Bondi (1993) describe five characteristics of a growing social awareness at this age level.

- The affiliation base broadens to the peer group, often resulting in split allegiance.
- Peers become sources for standards and models of behavior.
- The will of the group must prevail.
- There is a strong concern for social justice and concern for the less fortunate.
- There is a desire for direction and regulation, but they reserve the right to question or reject the suggestions of adults.

One way these elements of peer influence are commonly acted out is in the form of a "dare." Dares are important for both sexes during the middle grades (Lewis & Lewis, 1984). For boys the dares are usually in the form of testing courage, physical skills, or bravado. For girls the dare is often in the form of pushing the limits of acceptable behavior. Being challenged to tell "dirty" jokes, to partially undress, or even to have sexual intercourse are common tests. In most cases these dares are little more than posturing or, upon failure, embarrassing. When they take the form of casual sex or substance abuse, however, the innocence is gone. Such risky behaviors are compounded by young adolescents' preoccupation with self that leads to a belief that natural or man-made laws do not pertain to them (Wiles & Bondi, 1993). "*Others* will get caught. . . . *I* won't get pregnant. . . . Using it once won't hurt *me*. . . ."

Thinking about Moral Issues

The intellectual and social developmental characteristics described so far have an indirect and subliminal effect on the moral decisions made by adolescents. Equally helpful in understanding the decision-making process, however, is hearing middle schoolers themselves talk about what they value and how they think about issues of morality. In fact, hearing the students' words reminds one how little we sometimes know about our students.

When trying to understand the moral choices made by our students, it is necessary to appreciate the varying levels of reasoning ability available to them and the multiple contexts in which their choices are made. To encourage middle schoolers to "just say no" to undesirable behaviors does an injustice to the complexity of their moral lives (Kirschenbaum, 1992). Indeed, programs that rely on that approach have had limited success (Higgins, 1980; Leming, 1993; Mast, 1988). Those who wish to empower young people to make wise decisions must address the reasons behind behaviors, as well as the influence of the students' environments. Robert Coles, using data from a broad-based survey commissioned by the Girl Scouts of America, identified the "moral compasses" that guide children's decision making (Schmidt, 1990). Of the middle school students surveyed, most fell into the categories Coles called *civic humanists*, those concerned with serving the common good, or *expressivists*, those who make moral judgments based on whatever satisfies certain emotional feelings and psychological needs. Across the categories, over half of the respondents in middle school and above remained true to their general characteristics by preferring friends as a source of advice over adults. Even so, parents and family remain important factors in deciding what to value and what to worry about.

In the Girl Scout survey and in surveys of middle school students reported by Zern (1991) and Wiles and Bondi (1993), adults figured prominently both because of the high place they hold in students' values systems and because of their lack of understanding of those value systems. In two of the surveys, adults were asked to name what they thought would be foremost among the values held and moral dilemmas experienced by students. They did not do well. In the Girl Scout survey the adults expected young people to be most concerned about school violence, pregnancy, and suicide. Instead, the children put pressures related to parental expectations—good grades, preparing for the future, earning money—at the top of their list.

The Wiles and Bondi survey results were similar. Given a list of eleven commonly held values, the participants in the second survey (teachers and students in this case) were asked to list the items in order according to what they value most. Additionally the teachers were asked to rank the values according to what they believed would be the students' responses. According to the teachers' predictions, the students' top five values would be: (1) a world at peace; (2) true friendship; (3) family; (4) an exciting life; and (5) happiness. In contrast, the students' list included only two of those values. Their top five included: (1) family; (2) freedom; (3) happiness; (4) self-respect; and (5) a comfortable life.

This is more than just an interesting contradiction. Because adults are the primary moral agents in schools and the ones who develop moral education programs, the possibility that they do not really understand what motivates the moral decision making of the students in their charge could have important implications. Moreover, the surveys reviewed here indicated that other differences—social class, gender, race—might have a significant influence on the values children hold.

The Role of Gender

Boys and girls are different. Although no reference citation follows that opening statement, there is little concern that anyone will debate it on a scholarly or practical level. Nevertheless, for many years after Lawrence Kohlberg's landmark research on moral development the assumption was that boys and girls were *not* different, at least when it came to moral decision making. Kohlberg's (1968) initial research was done solely with white males, but the findings were generalized across gender, social class, and racial lines. In the past decade or so, however, Gilligan has redefined the way in which we study moral discourse.

Self, Relationship, and Morality

Adolescence is a trying time for all youth, but especially for girls. During this stage of development, girls are more likely than boys to develop psychological difficulties, respond negatively to stressful challenges, suffer from depression, and possess a poor self-image (Ebata, 1987; Elder, Nguyen, & Caspi, 1985; Gove & Herb, 1974; Pipher, 1994; Rutter, 1986; Werner & Smith, 1982). Because of this, Gilligan, Lyons, and Hanmer (1990) concluded, "Adolescence seems a watershed in female development, a time when girls are in danger of drowning or disappearing" (p. 10). Despite this apparent vulnerability, many girls enter adolescence with a strength that makes them highly resistant to outside pressures. As a result, the conflict between strength and an increasing sensitivity to the needs of others can result in the loss of any real self-identity (Gilligan, Lyons, & Hanmer, 1990).

According to Gilligan (1982), the rationale one uses in making moral decisions usually reflects one of two orientations—one emphasizing justice or one emphasizing care or relationship. The justice orientation is based on the respect and protection of the rights to life and self-fulfillment and stresses the rules and laws in society. The morality of care focuses more on the people involved, their feelings, and one's responsibility for the well-being of others (Donenberg & Hoffman, 1988). While men and women use both orientations when thinking or talking about real-life moral dilemmas, the care focus is more likely to be used by women and the justice focus used more often by men (Cortese, 1989; Gilligan, 1982; Gilligan & Attanucci, 1988; Lyons, 1983). Although there are those who question any consistent, gender-related differences in orientation preference (Ford & Lowery, 1986; Gibbs, Arnold, & Burkhart, 1984; Rothbart, Hanley, & Albert, 1986; Smetna, Killen, & Turiel, 1991; Walker, de Vries, & Trevethan, 1987; Walker, 1989), the degree to which these orientations are gender-related is less important than the acknowledgment that they exist at all, especially if the conflict between the two is indeed causing significant turmoil in young girls.

Girls in early adolescence are of special concern to Gilligan (1990) because it seems to be at around age 11 or 12 that they begin "to separate 'self' from relationship—to accept damaging conventions like defining care in terms of self-sacrifice" (p. 5). For boys, moral dilemmas involving friends and relationship usually refer to resisting peer pressure or addressing a specific incident. Girls define those same dilemmas in terms of loyalty and the fear of hurting someone, being hurt, or feeling excluded (Gilligan & Attanucci, 1988). Combine those factors with the risk-taking and exploratory behaviors typical to the age level and the temptations common to adolescents, and we start to see the inadequacy of most attempts at moral education. A one-program-fits-all approach to substance abuse or sex education is too simplistic given the diversity in our classrooms. Even if gender is the only diversity you experience among your students, important opportunities may be missed if you fail to recognize the subtle differences in their thinking and style of communication.

Gender Traits in Communication

In all but the most dogmatic approaches, discussion is an integral part of moral education. Being able to communicate your beliefs is an important part of understanding your beliefs, and communication—verbal and nonverbal—gives the only insight we have into each other. There is reason to believe, however, that not only do girls think about their moral decisions differently than boys do, but that they also talk about those decisions differently. Unless you are in a single-sex classroom, it is possible that you and your students might not be talking about the same things at all.

Tannen, a linguist, has provided one of the more concise and readable descriptions of the communication differences between men and women in her book *You Just Don't Understand* (1990). While most of the book describes differences in adult conversation, the traits she identifies are formed at a much earlier age and are pretty much in place by middle school. Her findings are relevant to the discussion here in that they support much of what Gilligan has proposed and to the extent that they can help as we more deliberately address the curricular substructure of our classrooms. Tannen's work was especially influential in the suggestions that conclude this chapter, but for now it will suffice to look at three key aspects of adolescent communication: talking about problems, competition and cooperation, and the role of status and popularity.

When boys discuss problems with each other, they tend to talk about their own trouble and dismiss those of the other boys as being insignificant or easily solved. The implication is that the friend will be comforted by hearing that the problem is not as serious as it seems and that it will probably go away soon. Talk is secondary to activity in maintaining friendships for most boys. The talk that does take place is often in the form of boasting, commands, or recounting past activities. While limited in content, however, boys' talk still plays an important role in male social structure. Boys tend to play and organize themselves in large, groups whose hierarchy is established by taking center stage, giving orders, or winning competitions. According to Tannen, "Boys monitor their relations for subtle shifts in status by keeping track of who's giving orders and who's taking them" (p. 47). Aggression and antagonism do not preclude friendship in the boys' world; instead, it often provides a good way to start interaction and determine status.

In contrast, girls will talk at length about one girl's problem. They will elaborate, support, and empathize in the course of their discussion. Conversation is the bond that holds relationships together for girls. Unlike the boys' world in which accomplishment means status, "the chief commodity bartered in the girls' community is intimacy. Girls monitor their friendships for subtle shifts in alliance and they seek to be friends with popular girls" (Tannen, 1990, p. 47). The emphasis on intimacy and trust makes the girls' community a more cooperative and communal one. Their group language tends to express preferences or make suggestions—"Let's do this" or "How about doing that"—rather than of commanding and showing superiority. Outward signs of dominance are usually counterproductive for adolescent girls as they will seldom get them what they want and need—affiliation with their peers. In mixed-sex relationships, however, the willingness to play a passive role can lead to difficulties. As Tannen explains: "Not accustomed to having others try to bend their will simply to solidify a dominant position, girls do not learn to resist others' demands on principle and don't expect others to resist theirs on principle either" (p. 154).

"Bend their will," "resist others' demands," and "principle" are all value-laden terms. For any teacher concerned with creating an equitable and moral environment in the classroom and with preparing students for real-life moral dilemmas, the preceding discussion should not have been simply a mildly interesting diversion. The implications range from planning more productive group work to helping girls respond to sexual harassment. The challenge now is to weave all the separate strands of what we know about adolescent development into an integrated and practical plan of action or, at least, a way of thinking that will improve the moral climate of the school.

Uncovering the Hidden Curriculum

That school is a very moral place should be clear at this point and, as Newsom and Newsom (1963) put it, "Teachers can only escape their influence over the moral and spiritual development of their pupils by closing their schools" (p. 160). As it is probably safe to assume that the school system as we know it will not be closing in the near future, it would seem to be to our benefit to make the moral dimensions of the classroom as much a part of our planning as our reading and math lessons. To do this, a conscious effort must be made to uncover the hidden curriculum and make explicit as much of the implicit curriculum as possible.

Finding a Common Ground

Discussions of moral education usually either come to a sudden halt or burst into an argument whenever *the* question is asked:"But whose morals do we teach?" In the public school setting the question might indeed be unanswerable—if the answers are limited to black or white choices. The options, however, are not limited to the values of white, middle-class, conservative, Protestant males or a "whatever you believe is okay" approach. There are certainly some moral issues that are highly controversial and which do come down to a decision based on personal values, but there are also a number of values and character traits upon which most people would agree. Morality should not simply imply a mental exercise or the identifying of a character trait. Transescents are still struggling with their own identity, beliefs, and newfound intellectual prowess. But morality also should not imply the simple obedience of someone else's whim. What is needed is a curriculum and methodology that teach both the values held by society and a process that encourages a thoughtful examination and acceptance of those values.

Regarding the possible goals of a moral classroom, the following principles or character traits are being widely accepted as minimally controversial:

- Respect for human life
- Commitment to the just treatment of all people
- Respect for truth and honesty
- Respect for learning and knowledge
- Freedom of thought
- Respect for all aspects of the self
- Actions that are in accord with the moral climate and ideals and that are for the good of society

It is important to remember that even generally accepted principles such as these can be inappropriate or irrelevant if presented as dogma or as more "stuff" to learn. To do so ignores the skeptical side of adolescents and does not respect their intellectual potential. Along with the content goals for moral education, there should also be some process or "ways of thinking" goals.

For the processes suggested here I have borrowed from sources as diverse as John Dewey, William Bennet, Lawrence Kohlberg, and values clarification, as aspects of the work of varying theorists have something of value to offer to the classroom teacher. The morally educated person should be able to:

- Reflect on and reason about moral issues according to a clearly delineated process of thinking
- Confront moral issues with feeling and passion
- Reflect some consistent and comprehensible relationship between moral thoughts and moral actions in daily living
- Take the place and point of view of another person as though it were one's own
- Identify and explain the value decisions made and the reasons behind those decisions

Reflection, application, clarification, empathy—these skills are not only relevant to moral education; they have implications across the curriculum and throughout life. Moreover, there is reason to believe that if those content and process goals are taught as part of a moral education "curriculum," they lose their impact.

Setting the Moral Atmosphere

If there is any area of agreement among moral education theorists and students, it is in the belief that unless whatever values or ways of thinking the school tries to instill become a genuinely integrated part of the child's life, the effort has been wasted. Middle school students, in a survey reported by Williams (1993), said that teaching moral values does not work if teachers try to "make it a big deal" or "have a separate class about it" (p. 22). Instead, more effort should be put into creating a moral atmosphere in the classroom. Adolescents are at an impressionable and vulnerable stage of development and are entitled to a trusting, secure environment in which they can feel comfortable sharing feelings and experiences (Downey & Kelly, 1978). A moral atmosphere is what provides the educational bridge between moral thought or judgment and moral action (Kohlberg et al., 1975; Lapsley, Enright, & Serlin, 1989; Power & Reimer, 1978; Power, Kohlberg, & Higgins, 1989). Deliberately nurturing such an atmosphere can also make your classroom distinctive and help provide the home base that is so important to this age group (Romano & Georgiady, 1994). Creating and controlling the moral climate is not easy, however, and to begin, one must look carefully at the role played by the principal moral agent in the room, the teacher.

The Role of the Teacher

Modeling Morality

In the survey by Williams (1993) the students said that the best way to teach values is for teachers to follow the values themselves. What makes this statement so powerful is the obvious implication that there are teachers who follow the values they teach and there are teachers who do not. The teacher's prominence in the classroom and the inherent power structure of traditional schooling put them in the unenviable position of being the judge and the judged. They are also moral models and as such have an obligation to be as considerate and understanding as possible in dealing with their students, "not because such treatment works pedagogically or has positive outcomes . . . but simply because students deserve to be treated that way" (Jackson, Boostrom, & Hanson, 1993, pp. 292–293). Furthermore, teachers should always be striving to make themselves morally educated people. "Just as it is difficult, if not impossible, for a teacher of mathematics to take pupils beyond the level of his own attainment in mathematics, so is it impossible for the teacher to help his pupil towards a morally educated state if he has not reached such a state himself" (Downey & Kelly, 1978, p. 147).

There are a number of ways a teacher can work toward being the type of moral model that will gain the respect of middle school students. Among the most important traits that must be present though, especially when working with this age level, are trustworthiness, fairness, and a genuine concern for the students' well-being and success. More specifically, William's (1993) survey again yields some helpful information. According to the students, a model teacher:

- Presents clear, consistent, and sincere messages
- Does not pull rank and is never authoritarian
- Is hardworking and communicates high expectations
- Creates environments that are nurturing and risk-free
- Is open-minded, direct, and nonjudgmental
- Is enthusiastic and committed; and
- Shows sincerity and a concern for students in his or her daily actions

To do and be all these things may seem to require a Herculean effort, but Jackson and his colleagues (1993) suggest that teachers often practice a kind of "upward hypocrisy" that helps them improve their moral stature on the job. Teachers are often forced by circumstances to behave in ways that do not reflect their innermost feelings, but this can lead to genuine change if, by acting better than they really feel, they eventually become better persons.

As important as it might be, however, the teacher's being a good, caring person is only part of the moral atmosphere of a classroom. At some point during the school day, instruction must occur, and in the course of teaching the subject matter of the curriculum, a number of moral lessons can be taught as well.

Morally Responsive Teaching

When the teacher's emphasis shifts to the teaching of subject matter, the pedagogy used must support the professed values of the curriculum and the moral model of the teacher. In the middle school, where curriculum integration and team teaching is already an integral part of the school day, taking a holistic, comprehensive approach to moral education should not be difficult. Likewise, many teaching strategies that promote moral growth—cooperative learning, democratic decision making, critical thinking—are already in use because they are pedagogically effective in their own right. Nevertheless, for them to become effective moral devices, the teacher must be able to weave content material from the various subject matter with moral thinking to create a multidimensional teaching style that I refer to as *morally responsive teaching*.

Morally responsive teaching reflects the integration of five key components: (1) knowledge of adolescent characteristics (Table 4.1), (2) subject area content, (3) consideration of desirable moral traits, (4) appropriate pedagogy, and (5) moral thinking processes. Adolescent characteristics and desirable moral traits have already been discussed in detail, and, to a great extent, subject area content is already determined for most teachers. Appropriate pedagogy implies the use of teaching styles and techniques that most effectively communicate the subject matter and are matched to the intellectual characteristics of middle school students.

TABLE 4.1 Contradictory Traits of Adolescence and Implications for Moral Education

Developmental Trait	Opposing Trait	Instructional Implications
Sense of idealism and moral concern for justice	Egocentrism; care orientation among girls	Democratic environment; narrative; discussion
Need for self-definition	Need for peer approval	Narrative; role playing
Desire to make sense of the world	Inability to distinguish between needs of self and others	Narrative; integrated studies; role playing; gender-sensitive discussion
Increased empathy and role-taking ability	Egocentrism	Narrative; role playing; field trips: Service
Increased interest in and interaction with opposite sex	Gender differences in expectations, needs and communication	Cooperative learning; gender-sensitive role playing and discussion
Onset of abstract reasoning	Lack of control over intellectual potential	Integrated studies; modeling; discussion
Dominance of peer influence	Gender differences in competition and cooperation; still concerned with parent and adult expectations; willing to experiment	Cooperative learning; role playing; narrative; single-sex groups; independent study; gender-sensitive discussion
Increased risk taking	Belief that laws do not pertain to them; need for peer acceptance	Challenging, creative curriculum Cooperative learning; narrative; discussion

As it relates to specific moral goals, appropriate pedagogy would also include cooperative learning, conflict resolution skills, community service opportunities; parent and community partners; and, most importantly, provision for systematic moral reflection.

Regardless of how many hours a student spends in school, most moral learning takes place outside of school, and teachers cannot assume that the students enter the classroom with a relatively blank slate as they might in some subject areas. The task is to start with the students' existing experiences and explore how those experiences might be converted into moral learning of the kind the teacher wants to occur. To accomplish this, the teacher needs to model and teach ways to reflect on moral decisions. The work of Lawrence Kohlberg suggests a sequence of steps as a guide (Chazan, 1985).

First, the teacher should help students focus on and confront genuine moral conflicts. In an integrated approach these conflicts could be taken from subject areas such as social studies, science, or even art. Next, the students, with the teacher's guidance, should reflect on alternative ways of reasoning about moral conflicts and resolving them. During this step the teacher should keep in mind gender-related differences in addressing moral problems, being careful not to discount one orientation because he or she holds another. The third step involves helping the students to critically reflect on the adequacies and inadequacies of their present thinking processes. After this the teacher suggests a procedure of reflection and resolution that is more effective than their current method. During these final steps the teacher should not hesitate to bring social and community concerns into the reflection process and should feel comfortable in modeling his or her own moral thinking process. Although middle school students will give the appearance of neither wanting nor listening to your model, Zern's (1991) survey of nearly 2,000 adolescents found that young adolescents do see the need for guidance in forming a perspective on moral issues and they do not see any intrinsic conflict between considering the influence of authority figures as well as peers and their own beliefs.

As with other aspects of moral education, however, it is important that moral thinking not be taught in a separate curriculum, but in the context of relevant subject matter or real-life experience. What follows is a brief description of how all these concerns might play out in the classroom. Although not intended to be a lesson or unit plan, three instructional devices are given extra attention here: the use of narrative, gender-sensitive discussion, and the development of moral imagination.

Who Did Gauguin Think He Was, Anyway?

Paul Gauguin once wrote to a friend that, "The work of the man is the explanation of the man" (in Andersen, 1971, p. 6). This sentence, as well as the life of Gauguin, struck me as an unusually rich theme for morally responsive teaching in an interdisciplinary setting. In addition to the obvious application to art instruction, Gauguin's personal life, the choices he made, and their consequences are full of moral implications that run interestingly parallel to many of the dilemmas and attitudes experienced by middle school students.

- He was convinced that his instructors in school were too stupid to perceive his gifts.
- He was idealistic in looking for innocence and directness in uncivilized societies.
- Inner conflict and searching led him to abandon his secure life for painting and Tahiti.
- He was not understood or appreciated by much of the art world and was alienated from his family.
- He led what many considered an immoral lifestyle and suffered the consequences of that lifestyle.

There are numerous subject matter connections that can be made in the study of Gauguin's paintings—historical context, geography of Brittany and Tahiti, cultural comparisons—but those possibilities are beyond the scope of this brief treatment. Instead, I will pursue the moral implications of his life and work as they might apply to a modern-day middle schooler and how they can be dealt with in class (see Table 4.2). To do so, I have identified a number of moral issues or questions relating to Gauguin's life and then developed corresponding questions that deal with the same issue but as it might relate to a young adolescent's life. Finally, several individual or group activities are suggested that will address the moral issues in a reflective, systematic way. Keep in mind the caveat that has appeared throughout the chapter. The moral questions should not be raised and discussed only in art class or only in social studies. Nor should they be presented separate from the content of other Gauguin-related lessons. They must occur as a natural outgrowth of other related topics—as such questions do in the students' real lives.

When student's confront a moral dilemma such as whether or not to shoplift an item, they do so in the context of a situation that has presented the dilemma. They are shopping with a friend, they are in financial need, they are under peer pressure. Most likely they did not just wake up in the morning and decide that shoplifting was the dilemma-of-the-day to consider. So too with the Gauguin unit. For a man to travel to Tahiti is not morally questionable in itself. The moral issues arise out of the historical context of the Victorian era, the study of his paintings of his underage Tahitian "wife," a knowledge of his previous life in Europe, and so on. Therefore, when choosing from the questions suggested in Table 4.2, consider where they would fit most logically and naturally in a larger interdisciplinary unit.

Although the content-related areas of the unit might, at times, be presented most effectively through lecture and reading, the moral aspects of the unit, because they are personal and social by nature, must be dealt with in personal and social ways (Davis, 1993). Consequently, with nearly every question there is an emphasis on the use of discussion and narrative. For these devices to be effective in raising the awareness and level of moral reasoning, however, they cannot be seen simply as talking and telling stories. Both must take into consideration the complex nature of moral decision making.

Conducting Moral Discussions
During group discussion of moral issues the teacher should keep in mind the importance of presenting what Bennett and Delattre (1979) describe as "thoughtful, considerate, and yet candid assessment of things through the guidance of an adult with a point of view thoughtfully held and presented" (pp. 7–8). It is important that the teacher take part in the discussion not as an authority figure to be obeyed, but as a member of the discussion who can model a carefully considered position and challenge others to do likewise. To prevent the teacher's position from becoming the only one considered, however, other considerations must be brought into the discussion. Students at this age are struggling with confusion between self and others, so the presentation of society's conventions and expectations can help them separate the needs of one compared to the needs of the other (Bouas, 1993). Identifying and speaking to the needs of others may be especially important to the girls in the class.

TABLE 4.2 Some Moral Themes and Questions

Theme: Action As an Expression of Belief

(Group Discussion)

What do Gauguin's paintings tell us about what he believed or how he thought?

Discussion focus: The relationship between what we think and what we do, constructive outlets for emotions

(Personal Reflection)

Which of your accomplishments or activities tell people something about you?

Narrative focus: Do your activities or interests tell others something important about you? What beliefs are important to you and how do you communicate them to others?

Theme: Self and Others

(Group Discussion)

How would you describe Gauguin's decision to become an artist and leave the "civilized" world: idealistic, self-centered, realistic, uncaring, necessary? Other ideas?

Discussion focus: Gauguin's responsibility to family vs. responsibility to himself; one's own happiness vs. responsibility for the happiness of others; duty; limits of self-interest; the responsibility of others to Gauguin

(Personal Reflection)

Describe a time when you wanted to do something for yourself but you felt as if the restrictions of or obligations to your family or school would not allow you to do it.

Narrative focus: Emphasize the accompanying feelings—guilt, resentment, cooperation; did you feel the demands were fair? What might have happened if you did what you wanted?

Theme: Standards of Morality

(Group Discussion)

Did Gauguin lead an "immoral" lifestyle?

Discussion focus: If a behavior is moral in one society (Tahiti), is it moral in another (France)? "Abandoning" his family (concept of family); sexual relations with young girls in Tahiti (sexual standards). Are the standards of his time different from those of today?

(Personal Reflection)

What do you consider to be immoral behavior in today's society?

Narrative focus: What has influenced your beliefs? Are some things immoral for you but not for others? How broad or narrow is your definition of morality?

Traditionally the curriculum has been built on either/or, conflict-oriented situations. History seems to center on war or political conflict; science often refers to competing theories that cannot coexist; in literature we speak of the conflict between characters when we study plot. To honor the variety of thinking that exists in the school, moral discussions should also focus on cooperation and relationship. Referring back to Gauguin, the teacher could encourage discussion of how the artist's choices and lifestyle addressed his own needs and how they affected the people close to him. Was he selfish? If so, in what ways? Were his family and friends the selfish ones? Did his decisions improve or hurt his family life? Would he have been happy if he stayed in France with his family? If not, what might have been the long-term consequences? These are a few questions that might address a relationship-centered perspective. Other gender-sensitive directions the discussion could take could include imagining that Gauguin was a woman and then reviewing the moral implications of "her" actions. Such imagining can play an important role in moral thinking and should not be overlooked.

Developing the Moral Imagination

Middle school students, in general, have few life experiences and influences to bring to moral deliberation and their minds have been working primarily in a concrete fashion. The imagination and fantasies that they do experience have seldom been applied to real-life problems, especially in school (Egan, 1992). Imagination, however, plays a crucial role in moral development and intellectual understanding, especially at this age. Craig (1993b) argues:

> *Using the imagination allows students to suspend judgments regarding the concrete and the abstract. Encouraging students to use their imagination permits them to look more deeply at what they know and even to form a vision of what they know that is based on imaginative interrelationships. (p. 225)*

Egan (1992) makes a similar argument for the importance of imagination in grasping and possessing intellectual knowledge. "[Imagination] is important because transcending the conventional is necessary to constructing one's sense of any area of knowledge; accepting conventional representations is to fail to make knowledge one's own, is to keep it inert rather than incorporate it into one's life" (p. 48).

Nurturing the moral imagination is not as easy as it might seem. To some extent, the teacher can do so by providing a secure, encouraging environment in which creative options can be presented and by leading discussion of moral solutions in imaginative directions. Craig (1993a) believes that theoretical discussion alone, however, is not sufficient for developing moral imagination, especially when dealing with issues of social injustice, poverty, or oppression. Instead, he suggests that students be given more direct experiences in the community that will develop a stronger connection between one's attitudes toward social justice and one's life experience. But Craig adds that, because of the complex nature of many moral dilemmas, the imaginative and intuitive appreciation required to discuss them can best be developed through the use of symbolism and metaphor found in literature and personal narratives.

Using Narrative and Story

Whenever we make moral decisions, we usually represent them to others and give them meaning by telling stories about them (Tappan & Brown, 1989). Moreover, those stories provide the only insight we can have into the complex nature of an individual's response to moral conflicts. Because the stories we hear are retrospective accounts told according to how the teller wants to depict the choices made, there is often a gap between "historical truth or reality" and the "narrative truth" (Breault et al., 1994; Lockwood, 1993; Tappan & Brown, 1989). Even so, much can be made of personal narrative and other forms of story.

Narrative, as used here, refers to stories people tell, fact or fiction, whether for personal or professional purposes. In whatever form, the story is a powerful tool because it works at so many levels. A well-written story has an emotional appeal in that it allows the reader to experience the successes and failures of a character without actually experiencing the risk (Smith & Habenicht, 1993). Because of their own need for risks and exploration, the heroism, extremes, and challenges offered through the safety of a story might be especially appealing to middle school students (Egan, 1992). Gauguin's story might well appeal to the "rebel" in young adolescents as well as to their need to find their own identity and means of expression. It might give them the courage to break away from peer influence. Or it might help them explore the sometimes painful consequences of rejecting conventions of family and society.

In stories the reader also enters the life and mind of the hero to an extent not possible in real-life moral dilemmas (Vitz, 1990). This deep involvement can work unconsciously, helping students find their own meaning or relevance in the story (Bettleheim, 1976; Coles, 1986, 1989). Gauguin's biography or letters might allow a child from a generally happy, traditional home to be rebellious for a while, or it might provide a catharsis for the student who experiences again the pain of a parent who left the family to seek his or her own life. Even if a personal connection does not occur, well-developed characters will help the reader experience the emotions of many people in many situations and thus develop a greater sense of empathy (Smith & Habenicht, 1993). To expand the moral imagination of middle school students while studying the art and life of Gauguin, the teacher could have them read other pieces of fiction or history from the Victorian era to gain a greater understanding of the responses to the artist's work and lifestyle during his lifetime.

The use of narrative should not be limited to professionally written stories. The development of a student's own stories is just as valuable, if not more so. What you think and feel influences the moral decisions you make, but the decisions you make also influence what you think and feel. Without understanding the relationship between these three dimensions—thought, feeling, and action—teachers run the risk of misunderstanding the moral processes of their students and the students themselves have less insight into their own thinking (Tappan & Brown, 1989). The writing and telling of personal stories can assist both the teacher and the student in understanding that relationship. To use personal narrative effectively as an approach to moral development, Tappan and Brown (1989) recommend considering the following three components.

1. Stories can be done in written form (journal entries, essays), but it is important that there be some sort of teacher response so that the author knows that his or her perspective has been acknowledged and so further, gradual development of authorship can be encouraged.
2. If the teacher wants to facilitate the sharing of stories with peers, narratives can be dramatized through skits, plays, or video tape.
3. Allow students to be interviewed, in addition to their written or presented stories, so they can tell their stories in greater detail. This is important because it provides a live audience in the form of a sympathetic and engaged listener. It also forces the speaker to argue for a moral perspective.

Some sort of interpretation should follow if anything is to be made of the stories, but the interpretation must avoid trying to find simplistic explanations for complex thought processes. The teacher must be careful to not assume or judge the meaning of a student's story too quickly. Nuances of voice, language, perspective, and group differences (gender, social class, cultural) can be read in a number of different ways and should be respected by the listener.

Returning to the Gauguin theme once more, the questions in Table 4.2 that relate to Gauguin's life are intended for small- or large-group discussion or role playing. In a group setting the chances of hearing more imaginative and varied responses are increased and the students are more likely to hear a higher level of thinking being modeled. The personal application questions are meant to encourage writing or responding in a narrative fashion. Here the students would be free to pursue the moral issues in a more relaxed and private setting and in a way relevant to issues in their own life. Given the time restrictions of real-life classrooms, it would be unlikely that each student could be given high-quality, reflective feedback or have a follow-up interview with the teacher. However, for moral growth to occur, some arrangement for at least occasional student–teacher dialog should be made.

Teaching for Moral Growth

Do seventh grade girls have morals? Yes, and so do sixth and eighth grade girls and boys. The problem is that those morals tend to get mixed in with the developmental hodgepodge called transescence, and it is the child who is left with little or no help to make sense of it all. For teachers to add moral education to their agenda is controversial and even impractical given their already packed schedules. Yet, for teachers to *not* add moral education to their agenda seems almost—immoral. We assume that the young learner cannot make sense out of the physical world without our help. We assume that they cannot make sense out of literature, music, or politics without our help. Should we then assume that they *can* make sense of the complex web of emotions, intellect, and sociocultural factors that make up the moral decision-making process? As Jackson and his colleagues (1993) put it, "Schools and classrooms are designed to be beneficial settings. This implies that the people in charge care about the welfare of those they serve . . ." (p. 25). All the academic "stuff" we will help the students make sense of will eventually be put to action in the real world, in a real social setting. In that world, knowledge and skills cannot remain separate from human interaction, and human interaction cannot long remain isolated from moral conflict. Morality is part of what we do as teachers. Let us learn to "do it" more intentionally and effectively.

Discussion Questions

How would you respond to the following issues?

1. Teaching in a classroom is by its nature a moral activity and so the teacher has an obligation to be intentional in developing moral reasoning in students.
2. The middle school years are especially important in and conducive to developing moral reasoning because of the intellectual, social, and emotional characteristics of the age level.
3. Gender differences play an important part in understanding and nurturing moral reasoning.
4. Morally responsive teaching does not mean using a separate "moral education curriculum." It should be taught in the context of relevant subject matter and real-life experience.

References

Andersen, W. (1971). *Gauguin's paradise lost.* New York: Vintage Books.

Banks, J. (1991). Teaching multicultural literacy to teachers. *Teaching Education, 4*(1), 135–144.

Bennett, W. J., & Delattre, E. J. (1978). Moral education in the schools. *The Public Interest, 50,* 81–98.

Bennett, W. J., & Delattre, E. J. (1979). A moral education: Some thoughts on how best to achieve it. *American Educator, 3,* 6–9.

Bereiter, C. (1973). *Must we educate.* Englewood Cliffs, NJ: Prentice-Hall.

Bettleheim, B. (1976). *The uses of enchantment: The meaning and importance of fairy tales.* New York: Vintage Books.

Book, C., Byers, J., & Freeman, D. (1983). Student expectations and teacher education traditions with which we cannot live. *Journal of Teacher Education, 34,* 9–13.

Bouas, M. J. (1993). The three R's of moral education: Emile Durkheim revisited. *The Educational Forum, 57,* 180–185.

Bowles, S., & Gintis, H. (1976). *Schooling in capitalist America: Educational reform and the contradiction of economic life.* New York: Basic Books.

Breault, R. A., Chamberlin, M. A., Dispenzieri, P., & Lagoni, C. J. (1994). Moral discourse among transescent girls. *Current Issues in Middle Level Education, 3*(2), 85–97.

Carnegie Council on Adolescent Development (1989). *Turning points: Preparing American youth for the 21st century.* New York: Carnegie Corporation.

Chazan, B. (1985). *Contemporary approaches to moral education: Analyzing alternative theories.* New York: Teachers College Press.

Clark, C. M. (1988). Asking the right questions about teacher preparation: Contributions of research on teacher thinking. *Educational Researcher, 17*(2), 5–12.

Clark, C. M. (1990). The teacher and the taught: Moral transactions in the classroom. In J. I. Goodlad, R. Soder, & K. A. Sirotnik (Eds.), *The moral dimensions of teaching* (pp. 251–265). San Francisco: Jossey-Bass.

Coles, R. (1986). *The moral life of children.* Boston: Atlantic Monthly Press.

Coles, R. (1989). *The call of stories: Teaching and the moral imagination.* Boston: Houghton-Mifflin.

Cortese, A. J. (1989). The interpersonal approach to morality: A gender and cultural analysis. *Journal of Social Psychology, 129,* 429–441.

Costa, A. L., & Garmston, R. J. (1987). Student teaching: Developing images of a profession. *Action in Teacher Education, 9*(3), 5–11.

Craig, R. P. (1993a). Social justice and the moral imagination. *Social Education, 57,* 333–336.

Craig, R. P. (1993b). Teen sexual activity and the need for the development of the moral imagination. *The Clearing House, 66,* 225–227.

Davis, G. A. (1993). Creative teaching of moral thinking: Fostering awareness and commitment. *Middle School Journal, 24*(4), 32–33.

Dewey, J. (1975). *Moral principles in education.* Carbondale, IL: Arcturus Books, Southern Illinois University Press.

Donenberg, G. R., & Hoffman, L. W. (1988). Gender differences in moral development. *Sex Roles, 18,* 701–716.

Downey, M., & Kelly, A. V. (1978). *Moral education: Theory and practice.* New York: Harper & Row.

Ebata, A. (1987). A longitudinal study of distress in early adolescence. Unpublished doctoral dissertation, University of Pennsylvania.

Egan, K. (1992). *Imagination in teaching and learning: The middle school years.* Chicago: University of Chicago Press.

Elder, G., Nguyen, T., & Caspi, A. (1985). Linking family hardship to children's lives. *Child Development, 56,* 361–375.

Elkind, D. (1981). *Children and adolescents: Interpretive essays on Jean Piaget* (3d ed.). New York: Oxford University Press.

Erikson, E. H. (1950). *Childhood and society.* New York: Norton.

Feinberg, W. (1990). The moral responsibility of public schools. In J. I. Goodlad, R. Soder, & K. A. Sirotnik (Eds.), *The moral dimensions of teaching* (pp. 155–187). San Francisco: Jossey-Bass.

Fenstermacher, G. D. (1990). Some moral considerations on teaching as a profession. In J. I. Goodlad, R. Soder, & K. A. Sirotnik (Eds.), *The moral dimensions of teaching* (pp. 130–151). San Francisco: Jossey-Bass.

Ford, M. R., & Lowery, C. R. (1986). Gender differences in moral reasoning: A comparison of the youth justice and care orientations. *Journal of Personality and Social Psychology, 50,* 777–783.

Foshay, A. W. (1993). Values as object matter: The reluctant pursuit of heaven. *Journal of Curriculum and Supervision, 9,* 41–52.

Gibbs, J. C., Arnold, K. D., & Burkhart, J. E. (1984). Sex differences in the expression of moral judgment. *Child Development, 55,* 1040–1043.

Gilligan, C. (1982). *In a different voice: Psychological theory and women's development.* Cambridge, MA: Harvard University Press.

Gilligan, C., & Attanucci, J. (1988). Two moral orientations. In C. Gilligan, J. V. Ward, J. M. Taylor, & B. Bardige (Eds.), *Mapping the moral domain* (pp. 73–86). Cambridge, MA: Harvard University Graduate School of Education.

Gilligan, C., Lyons, N. P., & Hanmer, T. J. (1990). *Making connections: The relational worlds of adolescent girls at Emma Willard School.* Cambridge, MA: Harvard University Press.

Girls at 11: An interview with Carol Gilligan. (1990). *The Harvard Education Letter, 6*(4), 5–7.

Goodlad, J. I. (1984). *A place called school.* New York: McGraw-Hill.

Gove, W., & Herb, T. (1974). Stress and mental illness among the young: A comparison of the sexes. *Social Forces, 53,* 256–265.

Haberman, M. (1987). *Recruiting and selecting teachers for urban schools.* New York: ERIC Clearinghouse on Urban Education Institute for Urban and Minority Education.

Hansen, D. T. (1993). From role to person: The moral layeredness of classroom teaching. *American Educational Research Journal, 30*(4), 651–674.

Havighurst, R. J. (1979). *Developmental tasks and education* (3d ed.). New York: McKay.

Higgins, A. (1980). Research and measurement issues in moral education interventions. In R. L. Mosher (Ed.), *Moral education: A first generation of research and development* (pp. 92–107). New York: Praeger.

Illich, I. (1971). *Deschooling society.* New York: Harper & Row.

Jackson, P. W., Boostrom, R. E., & Hansen, D. T. (1993). *The moral life of schools.* San Francisco: Jossey-Bass.

Kirschenbaum, H. (1992). A comprehensive model for values education and moral education. *Phi Delta Kappan, 73,* 771–776.

Kohlberg, L. (1968). *Education for justice: A modern statement of the platonic view.* Ernest Burton Lecture on Moral Education. Cambridge, MA: Harvard University Press.

Kohlberg, L. (1969). Stage and sequence: The cognitive developmental approach to socialization. In D. Goslin (Ed.), *Handbook of socialization theory and research* (pp. 347–480). New York: Rand McNally.

Kohlberg, L., Kauffman, K., Scharf, P., & Hickey, J. (1975). The just community approach to corrections: A theory. *Journal of Moral Education, 4,* 243–260.

Lambdin, D. V., & Preston, R. V. (1995). Caricatures in innovation: Teacher adaptation to an investigation-oriented middle school mathematics curriculum. *Journal of Teacher Education, 46,* 130–140.

Lapsley, D. K., Enright, R. D., & Serlin, R. C. (1989). Moral and social education. In J. Worell & F. Danner (Eds.), *The adolescent as decision-maker: Applications to development and education* (pp. 111–141). San Diego, CA: Academic Press.

Leming, J. S. (1993). In search of effective character education. *Educational Leadership, 51*(3), 63–71.

Lewis, C. E., & Lewis, M. A. (1984). Peer pressure and risk-taking behaviors in children. *American Journal of Public Health, 74,* 580–584.

Lockwood, A. L. (1993). A letter to character educators. *Educational Leadership, 51*(3), 72–75.

Lortie, D. C. (1975). *Schoolteacher: A sociological study.* Chicago: University of Chicago Press.

Mast, C. (1988). How to say "no" to sex. *Medical Aspects of Human Sexuality, 22*(9), 26–32.

Mosher, R. L. (Ed.) (1980). *Moral education: A first generation of research and development.* New York: Praeger Publishers.

Neil, A. S. (1927). *The problem child.* New York: McBride.

Newsom, J., & Newsom, E. (1963). *Infant care in an urban community.* London: Allen & Unwin.

Nias, J. (1989). *Primary teachers talking: A study of teaching.* London: Routledge.

Paine, L. (1990). *Orientation towards diversity: What do prospective teachers bring?* (Research Report 89-9.) East Lansing, MI: National Center for Research on Teacher Education.

Piaget, J. (1972). Intellectual evolution from adolescence to adulthood. *Human Development, 5,* 1–12.

Pipher, M. (1994). *Reviving Ophelia: Saving the selves of adolescent girls.* New York: Grosset/Putnam.

Power, F. C., Kohlberg, L., & Higgins, A. (1989). *Moral education, community, and justice: A study of three democratic high schools.* New York: Columbia University Press.

Power, F. C., & Reimer, J. (1978). Moral atmosphere: An educational bridge between moral judgment and action. In W. Damon (Ed.), *Moral development. New directions for child development* (no. 2, pp. 105–116). San Francisco: Jossey-Bass.

Romano, L. G., & Georgiady, N. P. (1994). *Building an effective middle school.* Madison, WI: WCB Brown & Benchmark.

Rothbart, M. K., Hanley, D., & Albert, M. (1986). Gender differences in moral reasoning. *Sex Roles, 15,* 645–653.

Rutter, M. (1986). The developmental psychopathology of depression: Issues and perspectives. In M. Rutter, C. Izzard, & P. Read (Eds.), *Depression in young people: Developmental and clinical perspectives* (pp. 3–30). New York: Guilford Press.

Scales, P. C. (1991). *A portrait of young adolescents*

in the 1990s: Implications for promoting healthy growth and development. Carrboro, NC: Center for Early Adolescence.

Schmidt, P. (1990, February 7). "Web of factors" said to influence children's views on moral issues. *Education Week,* pp. 1, 11.

Selman, R. (1971). The relation of role-taking ability to the development of moral judgment in children. *Child Development, 42,* 79–91.

Smetna, J. G., Killen, M., & Turiel, E. (1991). Children's reasoning about interpersonal and moral conflicts. *Child Development, 60,* 629–644.

Smith, R., & Habenicht, D. J. (1993). Stories: An old moral education method rediscovered. *Education, 113,* 541–547.

Tannen, D. (1990). *You just don't understand.* New York: Ballantine Books.

Tappan, M. B., & Brown, L. M. (1989). Stories told and lessons learned: Toward a narrative approach to moral development and moral education. *Harvard Educational Review, 59,* 182–205.

Vitz, P. C. (1990). The use of stories in moral development. New psychological reasons for an old education method. *American Psychologist, 45,* 709–720.

Walker, L., deVries, B., & Trevethan, S. D. (1987). Moral stages and moral orientations in real-life and hypothetical dilemmas. *Child Development, 58,* 842–858.

Walker, L. (1989). A longitudinal study of moral reasoning. *Child Development, 60,* 157–166.

Werner, E., & Smith, R. (1982). *Vulnerable but invincible: A study of resilient children.* New York: McGraw-Hill.

Wiles, J., & Bondi, J. (1993). *The essential middle school.* New York: Macmillan.

Williams, M. M. (1993). Actions speak louder than words: What students think. *Educational Leadership, 51*(3), 22–23.

Zern, D. S. (1991). Stability and change in adolescents' positive attitudes toward guidance in moral development. *Adolescence, 26,* 261–272.

Organization of Middle Schools—Introduction

The most overlooked aspect of the middle grades scenario is the way the educational enterprise is set up. The organizational structure of the middle school should first, and perhaps most importantly, support the unique aspects and dimensions of the adolescent. Needs such as socialization, expression, discovery, and freedom must be addressed in the structure of the community in which the educational process is housed. For example, one of the purposes of teaming is to provide a vehicle for adolescents to interact with one another. Through the effective use of teaming the organizational structure enables students to discover more about themselves and each other than would be possible in a traditional classroom setting.

Section II considers several aspects of the organization and design of the middle school and middle grades programs. A lateral or flat organizational design is emphasized to allow teachers and administrators the flexibility and discretion required by all professional educators. The need for a pluralistic power structure spread out throughout the organization is discussed from two viewpoints and the interdependency of institutional roles is approached in light of the school as a learning community. Autonomy among professionals is considered a right tied to individual expertise as well as a responsibility to both the profession and the particular values or culture of the school community.

The organizational structures described in this section have a direct impact on the health of the school in general and on the efficacy of teachers and administrators in particular. In a setting that enables teachers to engage in meaningful work, genuine fulfillment among educators results from the opportunity to hone their expertise in ways most beneficial to the adolescents they serve. A natural consequence for teachers in this context is focus on personal and professional growth and lifelong learning. To the extent that the organizational design enables administrators to provide teachers with opportunities for achievement, responsibility, and recognition, teachers more readily develop a culture that reflects a vested interest in activities that promote the enhancement of their personal expertise. It has even been demonstrated that the more teachers feel they are free to utilize their talents and skills (a sense of autonomy), the greater will be the achievement or success of their students (Ashton & Webb, 1986). Satisfaction is derived from the value of the work itself and not offered by management in the form of rewards and perks to persuade teachers to get the job done, as is often the case in inappropriate organizational settings.

Organizational redesign and renewal are a work in progress. The authors in this section stress the need for educators to be responsible for the ongoing restructuring of the middle school. Gregory Gerrick introduces the notion that the overall organizational design is directly linked to the success of the program. Sue Simpson considers options in the design of the curriculum itself in an effort to more closely link theory and practice. Lee Manning expands on these concepts in discussing the nature of the learning community in the middle school. Finally, David Kommer focuses on the aspect of teaming in its many dimensions. The status quo is never acceptable: The middle school is a dynamic organism, continuously evolving, and not a static entity that can ever become a "one best system." Renewal involves endorsing a specific value system—a unique school culture—that honors the uniqueness of the individual and the need to be part of a group. Renewal is the responsibility of each and every member of the learning community.

Reference

Ashton, P. T., & Webb, R. B. (1986). *Making a difference: Teachers' sense of efficacy and student achievement.* New York: Longman.

Chapter 5

Leadership, Organization, and the Middle School

W. GREGORY GERRICK

*W. Gregory Gerrick is Director of Doctoral Studies and Professor of
Educational Leadership at Ashland University, Ashland, Ohio. In his research,
writing, and teaching he has explored the areas of organizational design,
organizational renewal, charter schools, school choice, and doctoral mentorship.*

Effective leadership in the middle grades, and indeed in any educational context, is directly and inescapably linked to the organizational framework of a given institution. Leadership does not have to be shaped or determined by organizational structure, but that structure profoundly influences roles, behavior, relationships, and norms. Similarly, leadership is influenced, to a great extent, by the mission and philosophy of a given institution. For instance, a school that values shared decision making, teaming, and collegial relationships tends to promote a form of leadership that is participative, interdependent, and nonthreatening. The organization with which public schools must contend has increasingly been the focus of criticism in the debates of various approaches to restructuring schools. Increased emphasis on education reforms such as choice options, empowerment of teachers, and site-based management has finally challenged educators' acceptance of the corporate bureaucratic superstructure that characterizes the American public school monopoly.

In the following pages the current organization of public schools will serve as a backdrop for a discussion of principles of leadership and organizational behavior inherent to the successful and effective operation of the middle school. We live in a unique period in the history of American education: While the old order is slowly passing away, it remains, for many, the only game in town. Those beginning careers in education will participate, to a great extent, in the evolution of public school restructuring in its many forms. The contributions and involvement by these educators in this ongoing renewal of public schools will mold the schools of the future.

Organizational Structure of Public Schools

Throughout much of the twentieth century, and especially over the past few decades, public schools have evolved organizationally by adapting, compounding, and proliferating a bureaucratic corporate model in a heroic effort to become "all things to all students." As new programs are developed, whether at the national, state, or local level, new bureaucracies emerge to regulate and perpetuate these programs as the massive superstructure becomes more intricate and increasingly unmanageable. The implicit expectation that every public school must serve the individual needs of its diverse clients is impractical, unreasonable, and, in fact, impossible. Yet this is the mission of the "one best system" (see Tyack, 1974). An example of how public schools attempt to become all things to all students is the considerable number of diverse programs for special-needs students required in every school district (and often housed in each site within the district). New bureaucracies are created at the national, state, and local levels to ensure compliance with legislation for the handicapped. Money to support programs, personnel, facilities, and administration is targeted building by building within a school district, often with little regard for actual need or cost-effectiveness. While few will dispute the need, importance, and value of such programs, the practice of designating virtually each school site as a "full service institution" often stretches educational resources to the breaking point.

It is only recently that we have begun to explore seriously the innovative possibilities of organizational restructuring of this public monolith. Alternative approaches to schooling designed around specific programs and educational philosophies offer genuine choice to students and their parents without laboring under the pretense of offering the one best program or curriculum to all learners, no matter how distinct or unique their individual needs. Charter schools, increasingly popular in many states, seek to address this need. Unfortunately, within the public sector such approaches are by far the exception rather than the rule. More often than not, reformers experience roadblocks from state departments of education and local boards in their effort to waive regulations originally designed to protect the one best system from external corruption.

Because public education *is* "public," myriad players from both within education and outside the profession assert a vested interest in the direction of educational policy. The many "owners" of public education consist of elected politicians, religious groups, special interest groups, business and industry, taxpayers, teacher unions, textbook publishers, educational testing companies, and parents, to name a few. This democratic control of public education results in pressure from a number of different sources to influence the direction of educational policy. Joel Spring (1993) contends that "the major disease of the American education system is its constant propensity to change to serve the needs of various politicians and to solve economic and social problems" (p. 21).

This democratic control, according to John Chubb and Terry Moe (1990), tends to promote organizational arrangements that are highly bureaucratic.

> *In general . . . democratic authorities (and their group supporters) are driven to bureaucratize the schools in response to two basic problems that plague their efforts to impose higher-order values on the schools: hierarchical control and political uncertainty. The former is a problem experienced in all large organizations. The people at the top cannot assume that the people at the bottom will do what they want them to do, so they resort to various bureaucratic means of engineering compliance. The political uncertainty problem, on the other hand, is a trademark of democratic politics. It arises because those in authority have uncertain future rights to govern, and therefore must take steps to protect their favored policies from hierarchical control by opponents who may govern in the future. (pp. 44–45)*

Chubb and Moe conclude that public education's institutions of democratic control are inherently destructive of school autonomy and inherently conducive to bureaucracy in that the various interest groups, politicians, and so on "are motivated and empowered by their institutional setting to play the game of structural politics" (p. 47).

Restructuring: The "Already" But the "Not Yet"

It can be argued that the organizational restructuring of schools has, in many ways, already begun and will continue for decades to come. It is likely that educators entering the profession in the 1990s will spend their entire careers absorbed in the ongoing transition inherent within the organizational restructuring process. During this time of uncertainty and instability, educators must be prepared to assume the various roles of leadership characteristic of a true profession and through this, *demand*, in effect, that the organization conform to this perspective. Leadership is both the most critical and the most difficult function in the process of re-inventing public schools.

Bureaucratic Organizations

The organizational framework that characterizes schools dramatically affects approaches and decisions relating to teaching and, in particular, the way leadership is exercised. In bureaucratic organizations the structure tends to be hierarchical in that clear lines of authority are developed. Graphically organizational charts map out a vertical or "top-down" blueprint of accountability from one role to the next. The hierarchy is rigid and inflexible by design, and each member of the organization is expected to conform to recognized lines of authority. Functionally this provides an orderly chain of command and assumes that the "higher" the role, the greater the ability and expertise. In practice, however, there are dysfunctional consequences. Lines of communication are frequently blocked at various levels of the hierarchy, resulting in inefficiency, confusion, and frustration. Furthermore, experience tells us that one's position often does not guarantee expertise. Often those lower in the hierarchy (e.g., teachers in the public school bureaucracy) actually may be more influential and competent in certain areas than their superiors. This is frequently the case as new programs are initiated, developed, and evaluated.

Bureaucratic structure is heavily dependent on the use of general rules and regulations, the function of which is to ensure consistency in job performance. Often, however, the rules assume an importance in and of themselves and frequently displace the goals or outcomes they were originally intended to ensure. For example, in many universities elaborate procedures are set up to accomplish a smooth and orderly process of open registration for classes. All too frequently, individual student needs that arise during this process are routinely dismissed with the admonition that a given procedure must be observed to the letter: no exceptions. In effect, the rules have become more important than the people they were intended to serve.

Another characteristic of bureaucratic organizations is the need for specialization and the division of tasks. Functionally this provides for individuals to focus in areas of their expertise with clearly defined position descriptions. From a dysfunctional perspective, inflexibility and boredom may be consequences of finding the "right slot" for each individual in the enterprise. True professionals continually grow in their chosen field, and growth can require a change of roles within the organization. Another characteristic of bureaucracies is impersonality in relationships. Ideally, equal treatment of persons based purely on job-oriented considerations is designed to separate a person's position within the organization from his or her private life. The dysfunctional consequence is often a feeling of lack of morale and of personal isolation. Schools are "human organizations," and the needs of persons within the school must be viewed in the context of the goals of the school. Finally, the bureaucratic "career orientation" notion ensures that competence on the job guarantees a security as to one's future within the organization. Individuals advance by means of seniority and achievement. On the other hand, it is possible for tenure (as in the case of public schools) to protect an inferior teacher at the expense of a competent, but nontenured teacher.

As "human organizations," schools generally do not conform well to a bureaucratic organizational structure. Consequences of bureaucratic dysfunction have been described as communication blocks, confusion, frustration, goal displacement, boredom, lack of morale, and conflict between achievement and seniority (see Hoy & Miskel, 1991, ch. 5). These aspects are a reflection of the poor organizational fit of schools in a predominately corporate model. Schools are said to be loosely structured in an organizational sense (Weick, 1976). Behavior of educators is frequently quite distinct from the prescriptions (rules, procedures) set down by the educational bureaucracy. Educators often rely on their own preferences, judgment, and expertise in an effort to serve their students and respond to individual needs. This entails bypassing the established format of the bureaucratic superstructure. In other words, teachers tend to view themselves as professionals, having all the rights and privileges that accompany this designation. Bureaucrats, on the other hand, view teachers as workers who should conform to established rules and directives.

Professional Organizational Structure

In professionally based organizations there is not the same emphasis on "traditional" hierarchy as contained in bureaucracies. Rather than identifying expertise simply as a function of one's position in a vertical hierarchy, in a professional organization, expertise rests with those who have earned it through their acceptance of the responsibility for and commitment to their own learning, development, and growth. For professionals, knowledge is power, and in professional organizations, power tends to be spread out laterally rather than hierarchically. One's ability determines one's influence and the direction of leadership. In addition, certain professional norms or values provide the foundation for action. Autonomy in the exercise of one's practice is viewed as an inherent entitlement of the true professional. Consequently, leadership is a function of all members of a professionally oriented organization and not simply the domain of those engaged in administrative roles and responsibilities.

The process of organizational restructuring of schools is well under way, including an emphasis on teaching as a profession. Within this focus is the role of teacher as "Leader." Certainly the bureaucracy continues as the dominant organizational model for public schools. Yet there is a need to recognize the transitional nature of an organization in flux, with one foot planted firmly in a corporate and political superstructure and the other stepping gingerly into the professional experience. Not all teachers in public education are true professionals. Many, however, are and face the difficult prospect of trying to exercise professional leadership in schools that are highly bureaucratic. The bureaucracy does not easily accommodate the tenets of a professional structure. Herein lies both the difficulty and the challenge for teachers of the '90s and beyond. This evolution in transition is, in a sense, "the already but the not yet"—the promise, held hostage by the institution of the traditional past.

Autonomy

Chubb and Moe (1990) demonstrated that student academic success is a product of effective school organization. Further, "autonomy has the strongest influence on the overall quality of school organization of any factor that we examined" (p. 183). Because, as the Chubb and Moe study points out, autonomy from bureaucracy is heavily dependent on the institutional structure of school control, autonomy is high in schools controlled by markets—that is, schools with indirect control from the bottom up. This type of organizational setting more readily enables the school to exhibit professional organizational characteristics. Autonomy is usually low in public schools due to democratic control and the influence of politics and bureaucracy.

For professional teachers, autonomy means the freedom to rely on personal expertise and the expertise of fellow professionals to make informed decisions. Autonomy also means freedom from the formal authority of narrow hierarchical roles (authority based on positions or title) and a reliance on the authority of one's abilities, competence, and informed judgment. Autonomy as defined here is a threat to the specific regulations and top-down control of bureaucratic organizations. Thus, it is in the best interests of the bureaucracy to discourage discretionary behavior of staff members.

Chubb and Moe found, for example, that while private school principals are likely to be in a position to lead their organizations, public school principals are "systematically denied much of what it takes to lead" (p. 56). In terms of autonomy (that is, the freedom and flexibility to do what leaders need to do), leaders in private schools generally are not constrained by a bureaucratic superstructure dominated by multiple owners and interest groups. Because the private school is decentralized in this regard, it is generally more amenable to a professional organizational structure. Principals are able to exercise more discretion to respond to the needs of their clientele without the fear of offending a higher power. Chubb and Moe (1990) found that in these situations there was a heavy orientation toward teaching, higher interaction among professional staff, and a reflection of shared influence among teachers.

> Schools can be clear, bold, and controversial in the practices they adopt as long as they attract a specialized clientele that values what they do. They are free, in particular, to adopt whatever practices they consider most suitable to the effective pursuit of the school's mission—and they have strong incentives . . . to do just that by building an organizational team that enables a school to take advantage of the expertise and judgment of its teachers. (p. 60)

On the other hand, Chubb and Moe view the public school principal as a bureaucrat with supervisory responsibility for a public agency. Higher authorities make important decisions. This promotes a "play by the rules" and "don't rock the boat" mentality that, in most instances, rules out any bold educational initiatives. In addition,

> . . . teachers are doubly constrained in their efforts to perform their educational tasks as they see fit. First, they are required to follow rules that cause them to depart from what they might otherwise do, and thus to behave in ways that contradict or fail to take advantage of their professional expertise and judgment. Second, they are required to spend time and effort documenting, usually through

formal paperwork, that they have in fact followed these rules. The combination
may leave little room for them to do the kind of teaching they think they ought to
be doing. (p. 59)

In the public school setting, autonomy is most likely to be achieved at the building or site level and with a staff of professionals who are united in a shared vision of the purpose of their educational program. The term site-based management, currently in popular usage, assumes that meaningful change is most likely to occur at the building level rather than at the state or district level. Additional assumptions include the need for individual schools to be flexible in terms of rules and regulations and for broad-based representation of the school community in the decision-making process (Kowalski & Reitzug, 1993). True site-based management is, of course, impossible as long as the current organizational structure of public schools exists. As long as any spectre of democratic control threatens to intervene in a program at a particular school, no public school can consider itself to be totally "site-based." Again, public school professionals find themselves in an "already but not yet" situation. The more power local boards of education and central administrative offices are willing to relinquish to site-based management, the greater will be the success of teachers and principals in establishing the direction and vision of their educational program. This success comes *in spite of* and not because of the public school bureaucracy. This is, all too often, a slow and frustrating process.

Leadership and Organization

Educators cannot function outside the organization. Because all professional behavior is undertaken within the context of the organization, to fail to understand the nature of the organization is to fail as an educational leader. True leaders understand the big picture. The terms "leader" and "administrator" are not necessarily synonymous. Administrators fulfill a role within the organization, usually taking responsibility for operations and facilities in general. Leaders, on the other hand, may function in this role, but the notion of "leader" transcends any narrowly defined role within the organization. Leaders unite members of the organization in a common bond or long-term vision. In schools, leaders appeal to the expertise and values of professional educators in seeking to define a common purpose or rationale, attempting to answer the questions "What do we represent?" and "How can we focus our strengths and interests in serving the changing needs of our student population?" In a professional organization, leadership is a function and responsibility of all members of the profession. As John Gardner (1990) points out, leaders must look beyond the confines of their own particular situation and grasp its relationship to larger realities of the organization, as well as to the external environment.

In public education today we live in the "already but the not yet": We view ourselves as professionals but are not yet a true professional organization. It is essential that we understand the historical significance of our experience of ongoing organizational and curricular restructuring. It is a difficult and frustrating task to attempt the integration of principles of transformational leadership into a system that, by its very structure and purpose, opposes most forms of discretionary behavior. Transformation is a slow process wherein we must often settle for small victories. The surest way to facilitate this process is to prepare teachers and administrators as professionals who both understand current organizational constraints to restructuring and renewal and, at the same time, are empowered by their knowledge and commitment to demand leadership free of these constraints. In other words, restructuring and renewal will come from those in the "trenches" rather than from the vested interests of the public school establishment: deliberate organizational redesign evolving from the bottom up—building by building. Professional teachers are empowered to exercise leadership in transforming one site—one school—at a time.

Leadership in the Middle School

The organizational structure of the middle school is a good fit for the type of leadership and professionalism discussed here. Small size, integrated curricula, individualization of instruction, and teaching teams provide teachers and administrators a wealth of opportunities to "reinvent" the traditional school to accommodate particular needs and interests of students. Leadership in the middle grades focuses on professional growth, collaboration, motivation, inspiration, and vision. Leadership emerges as situations call for specific abilities and competencies of the professional team. Individuals or groups of individuals function in interdependent relationships providing direction and action as situations warrant. Effective middle school leadership is dynamic, collegial, and rooted firmly in service to children and to the profession.

Effective middle school leaders possess a clear understanding of the characteristics and needs of young adolescents and consistently translate that understanding into a vision of an appropriately organized and effective middle school program (George et al., 1992). Further, leaders are able to organize staff members, students, programs, time, and the school building itself to create a unique and effective learning environment. In addition, effective leaders act as change agents in the process of organizational restructuring. Finally, leaders engage teachers, parents, students, board members, and central office staff in shared decision making in the continued long-term maintenance and improvement of the school.

One example of organizational restructuring in the middle school is the attempt to move from a fragmented, disjointed, subject-by-subject curriculum to an integrated interdisciplinary approach. Related subjects such as American history and American literature may be linked together in longer blocks of time. Instead of the traditional 40- or 45-minute class period, this double blocking of courses allows students to put concentrated effort into fewer courses each day, with more time spent in the double block class. This extended time promotes greater interaction among students and teachers and allows for a fuller exploration of topics. In addition, the professional educators within the middle school will seek to define their goals for students by means of a collaborative mission statement and incorporate general learner outcomes as they design a curriculum consistent with the unique developmental needs of their students.

Edward Pajak discusses this notion in combining the ideas of Peter Senge and H. A. Giroux in that both conceive of leadership as an empowerment of self and others through cooperative effort, an intellectual activity that helps group members transcend superficial understanding, the collective application of knowledge to practical problems, and a commitment to making the future somehow better than the present (Pajak, 1993). James McGregor Burns (1978) sees leadership among professionals as transformational. Such leadership "transforms" a teacher's and administrator's perceptions and beliefs from being self-centered to focusing on the larger picture and the good of the educational enterprise itself. Leadership must focus on the true purpose of the school and the relationship between the school and the larger community.

The School as Community

Thomas Sergiovanni and Robert Starratt (1993) believe that schools should be understood as learning communities. True learning communities are defined by values, norms, and beliefs that bond people in a common cause. When viewing schools in this way, professional educators are concerned with what the community represents; with relationships among parents, students, teachers, and administrators; with shared values, purposes, and commitments that bond the community; how members of the community will work together to embody these values; and what kinds of obligations to the community members should have and how these obligations will be enforced (Sergiovanni, 1992a). In this perspective, teaching is seen as a vocation, a calling, a ministry of service rather than as merely a job or even a career. Defining the school and teaching in this way suggests that there is an ethical or moral responsibility to the profession.

Collegiality is inherent in viewing the school as a learning community. *Collegiality* refers to the "existence of high levels of collaboration among teachers and between teachers and principal and is characterized by mutual respect, shared work values, cooperation, and specific conversations about teaching and learning" (Sergiovanni & Starratt, 1993, p. 103). This highly professional atmosphere strengthens the feeling of a common sense of purpose within the learning community. Team teaching and mentoring relationships succeed when all parties involved appreciate the value of collegial relationships. On the other hand, collegiality cannot be imposed on teachers by a well-intentioned principal or supervisor. Formal procedures to foster collegiality rarely have lasting impact. True collegiality is rooted in what Sergiovanni calls professional virtue: It is valued for its own sake; it implies connectedness to a community that provides one with the right to be treated collegially and the obligation to treat others collegially; and, finally, it represents interpersonal relationships characterized by mutual respect (Sergiovanni, 1992b).

Roland Barth (1990) observes:

A healthy institution is one characterized by relatedness with other people and gratification from others and from the work itself. If these are among the benefits of more collegial relationships among adults in schools, collegiality may indeed be closely related to the time-honored purposes of schools. And the task of developing collegiality may be integral to the task of improving schools. (p. 31)

In this spirit, professional collaboration at the middle grades level enhances the opportunities of teachers and administrators to experiment with new techniques and approaches they might not have attempted on their own. If the school is a true community, efforts at innovation go beyond simple teamwork. The commonality of values and beliefs shared by the staff provides the basis and rationale for shaping practice that is both appropriate for given situations and clientele and is the product of the shared expertise of the building's professional educators. A genuine sense of teacher empowerment drives the educational enterprise and a motivation to service underlies one's commitment to the profession.

Sergiovanni and Starratt (1993) define teacher empowerment as indicating a moral basis for teacher autonomy and professionalism. They view "power" as a power to be and a power to do. The power to be oneself is the most unique power each person possesses. Power, however, is given for the benefit of the community. One exercises the power to be oneself only in relationship to the community. In other words, "You can be yourself only in relation to others, to other selves whom you value as they value you" (p. 57). Leadership within the context of the school as community *enables* professionals by enlarging the power to be themselves—the power to act as reflective decision makers in their areas of expertise. When the goals of the school are linked with the needs and talents of educators in the context of a shared purpose, authentic empowerment is both possible and viable.

Instructional Leadership

When asked to name the most important facet of principalship, many, if not most, principals respond that curriculum development and instructional leadership are most essential. Yet, in the day-to-day activities of the principal, administrative concerns dealing with the management of operations and facilities tend to occupy an inordinate amount of time. The attention a principal is able to devote to curricular and instructional concerns is often severely compromised by the demands of discipline, scheduling, record keeping, attendance, the state department of education, the physical plant, meetings, budgets, routine paperwork, and the like. Balancing administrative tasks with the responsibilities of leadership is one of the most difficult challenges faced by the typical middle-level principal.

It has been demonstrated that effective schools (i.e., schools with clear academic goals, strong educational leadership, professionalized teaching, and ambitious academic programs) have principals who are more likely to exhibit an above average level of dedication to teaching (Chubb & Moe, 1990). Leaders in high-performance schools "tend to show a greater propensity to know what kind of school they want, to value innovation and new ideas, and to keep the school apprised of where it should be going" (p. 86). In other words, those effective principals are leaders who communicate and promote a definitive vision for their schools. Instructional leadership drives this vision, and commitment to the profession nurtures the development of staff within the context of a dynamic culture serving a diverse community of learners.

Implicit within the definition of the instructional leader is the expectation of a broad-based expertise. Effective leaders must be competent in the areas of curriculum and course of study development, teaching models, content areas, sequencing of course objectives, lesson and unit planning, instructional methodologies, various learning styles, formative and summative evaluation, and diverse approaches to staff development. It goes without saying that ongoing and focused professional development on the part of the educational leader is a lifelong commitment. Teachers and other education professionals who assume responsibility for their own continuing education have a right to expect this level of expertise in program and building leaders. Professionals are not impressed with formal authority as a basis for leadership. In other words, leaders who rely on the position they hold in a bureaucratic hierarchy as justification for their decisions rather than their earned expertise (functional authority) are generally not viewed as credible leaders by their colleagues.

Often educators are prone to focusing on one particular instructional strategy, teaching model, or methodology as being a "best approach" to teaching and attempting to apply this solution to any and every instructional problem that arises in practice. For example, at this writing, cooperative learning models are extremely popular and are increasingly adopted by teachers for use in virtually all learning contexts as a panacea or best instructional method. Certainly, cooperative learning models can be effective in a variety of learning contexts provided the teacher has carefully studied the rationale, implementation, implications and potential problems of using a cooperative approach. But human nature often gravitates toward a "best method" solution for situations that are often complex and influenced by a diverse set of variables. This "bottom line" mentality is evident when educators seek simplistic solutions for multifaceted problems.

Instructional leaders need to exercise great caution to avoid the temptation to endorse one best approach to teaching. All models, taken together, enhance one's practice, but none is truly an exact fit. All models become part of the mix in enabling the teacher to view the big picture of how best to practice in a given context. It all comes down to the teacher functioning as a decision maker in attempting to link the most appropriate method to the situation at hand while, at the same time, drawing from the teacher's own experience in practice to adjust or modify his or her theoretical constructs. It is the function of the instructional leader to promote this decision-making process by engaging in reflective practice with teachers. Donald Schon (1983) uses the term "reflective practice" to refer to the process of professionals intuitively reflecting on their practice as it happens, drawing on experiences that parallel the situation at hand. The teacher evaluation process offers both teachers and instructional leaders the ideal opportunity to reflect together on specific teaching episodes from the teacher's perspective and, in hindsight, to offer feedback linking appropriate models and ideas with the teacher's own reflection-in-action.

Teacher Evaluation

The relationship between teachers and the instructional leader within the context of teacher evaluation often determines the success or failure of this process. An open, trusting, collegial relationship enables teachers actually to take responsibility for their own evaluation—to take the initiative in their own professional growth and development. Clinical supervision, as described by Morris Cogan (1973), is a process that views teacher evaluation as growth-oriented and focuses on an ongoing commitment to improvement of teaching. With clinical supervision the anxiety of simply having one's teaching graded by the principal once or twice a year on the basis of objective criteria and rating scales is eliminated. Instead of trying to work up to the evaluator's expectations (or general standards), teachers take control of the evaluation process by closely working with another instructional leader—a colleague—in a climate of mutual trust and respect. The focus is on the continued improvement of basic teaching skills and on broadening the knowledge and utilization of teaching models and methodologies.

Clinical supervision (one of several approaches to staff development) is a cyclic process and is especially helpful for those in their first few years of teaching as well as those wishing to focus on particular aspects of classroom effectiveness. The teacher and a trusted colleague (principal, supervisor, mentor, master teacher) plan lessons and units together. Outcomes, strategies, anticipated problems, and content are discussed over time. Prior to an actual observation of in-class instruction, a preconference is held during which the teacher and evaluator discuss which aspects of the lesson will be examined and the nature of the data to be collected. Following the classroom observation a postconference is held during which teachers and evaluator compare their impressions of what actually occurred and whether these outcomes match the teacher's original intentions for the lesson. As evaluation is formative or ongoing, the process continues as teacher and evaluator resume planning the next unit or lesson and examine new strategies or techniques.

While it is the responsibility of the educational leader to monitor instruction from the standpoint of adherence to general standards and predetermined lesson objectives, the leader's duty to promote the professional growth and development of staff must never be abdicated. This is a good example of how the leader's administrative responsibility and commitment to the profession are bound together. An educational leader is more than a mere administrator responsible for predetermined standards and the day-to-day operation of the organization. The leader is concerned with growth of both the school and its professional staff. The leader is both inspiration and motivation in the transformation from teachers who simply work in a school to professionals sharing a common set of values for the purpose of a higher commitment to the learning community.

Summary

Schools are in a period of ongoing organizational restructuring that, in all probability, will last for decades to come. To be effective, leaders in education must understand the organization, where it has been and where it is going. Understanding the organization means accepting the fact that the current corporate bureaucratic model adapted for public schools is a bad fit: inappropriate for professional educators. The multiple ownership of America's public schools (democratic control) promotes a highly bureaucratic organization that destroys school autonomy, thus denying professional educators much of what it takes to lead.

Public schools are organizations in flux; the restructuring process has begun in earnest. The role of the educational leader will continue to emerge within the context of an emphasis on teaching as a profession. Autonomy is most likely to be achieved at the building level, and the middle-level school lends itself well to this renewal. The true educational leader will unite a staff of professionals in a shared vision of the higher purpose of their educational program. Leadership empowers professional teachers to engage in the systemic transformation of one building at a time.

Professional educators are concerned with what the learning community represents—with its organizational culture. Teaching is undertaken in light of its ethical and moral dimensions—as a vocation, a calling, a ministry of service. Collegiality strengthens the common sense of purpose among professionals within the learning community.

Instructional leadership entails a broad-based expertise. Lifelong learning, commitment to the profession and the promotion of professional growth and development in staff define the true educational leader. Leaders promote a vision of what education should be, help to define a set of shared norms or values among the professional staff, and pursue higher-order institutional and personal goals. The ultimate purpose of leadership is nothing less than the organizational renovation of the educational enterprise.

Discussion Questions

1. Assuming that a radical restructuring of the public school bureaucracy will not occur any time soon, how can middle grades educators function as true professionals in spite of the current organizational structure of the public schools?
2. In addition to integrating the curriculum and employing various types of block scheduling of classes, in what other specific ways could educators rede-

sign the middle grades program to address the needs of a given population of students? How do collegiality and teacher empowerment contribute to this effort?

3. What are the advantages of developing a relationship with a trusted colleague for the purpose of working together to improve your own classroom instruction? What can be gained through this process that is usually not forthcoming in traditional classroom evaluations conducted by the principal alone?

References

Barth, R. S. (1990). *Improving schools from within.* San Francisco: Jossey-Bass.

Burns, J. M. (1978). *Leadership.* New York: Harper Torchbooks.

Chubb, J. E., & Moe, T. M. (1990). *Politics, markets and America's schools.* Washington, DC: Brookings.

Cogan, M. (1973). *Clinical supervision.* New York: Houghton Mifflin.

Gardner, J. (1990). *On leadership.* New York: The Free Press.

George, P. .S., Stevenson, C., Thomason, J., & Beane, J. (1992). *The middle school—and beyond.* Alexandria, VA: Association for Supervision and Curriculum Development.

Hoy, W. K., & Miskel, C. G. (1991). *Educational administration: Theory, research, practice* (4th ed.). New York: McGraw-Hill.

Kowalski, T. J., & Reitzug, U. C. (1993). *Contemporary school administration.* New York: Longman.

Pajak, E. (1993). Change and continuity in supervision and leadership. In G. Cawelti (Ed.), *Challenges and achievements of American education: 1993 yearbook of the Association for Supervision and Curriculum Development* (pp. 158–186). Alexandria, VA: Association for Supervision and Curriculum Development.

Schon, D. (1983). *The reflective practitioner: How professionals think in action.* New York: Basic Books.

Sergiovanni, T. J. (1992a). *The moral dimension in leadership.* San Francisco: Jossey-Bass.

Sergiovanni, T. J. (1992b). *Moral leadership: Getting to the heart of school improvement.* San Francisco: Jossey-Bass.

Sergiovanni, T. J., & Starratt, R. J. (1993). *Supervison: A redefinition* (5th ed.). New York: McGraw-Hill.

Spring, J. (1993). *Conflict of interests: The politics of American education* (2nd ed.). New York: Longman.

Tyack, D. B. (1974). *The one best system.* Cambridge, MA: Harvard University Press.

Weick, K. (1976). Educational organizations as loosely coupled systems. *Administrative Science Quarterly, (21),* 1–19.

Chapter 6

Interdisciplinary and Interthematic Curriculum Designs

SUE SIMPSON

Sue Simpson has been a teacher at the elementary, high school, and university levels, but the majority of her teaching experience is at the middle level. She is currently a curriculum consultant, a reviewer for the National Middle School Journal, *and newsletter editor for the Ohio Alliance for Arts Education.*

Interdisciplinary instruction for middle grade students is not new, nor is it fully realized. Historically the professional literature provides definition and structure to middle school curriculum theory; but in reality, practice has only sporadically followed theory. The interdisciplinary/interthematic approaches outlined in this chapter demonstrate how middle level educators can put theory into practice.

Beginning with the Eight Year Study (1930–1940), developmentally appropriate curriculum methods have been considered for teaching adolescents through integrated approaches (Aiken, 1942; Reinhartz & Beach, 1983; Vars, 1991). Pressure and influence exerted by strong departmentalization structures or "discipline-field" (Jacobs, 1989) academicians, plus the sociopolitical developments of the late 1930s and early 1940s stymied efforts to move toward broad-based, integrated education (Wraga, 1992). By the 1960s, another study, *The Integration of Educational Experiences*, examined the implications for educational objectives, methods, curriculum organization, extra class experiences, and administration of inte-

79

grated instruction. Interdisciplinary teams were identified as a key ingredient and a basic requirement of any middle school environment. But once again, history and politics hampered emerging efforts to recognize and create a developmentally appropriate middle level curriculum. For example, the launching of Sputnik in 1957 fostered an emphasis on specific content area courses, particularly in math and science, that devalued interdisciplinary curriculum approaches.

In spite of the shift in national priorities, the middle school movement has survived mainly through the determination of individual teachers and administrators who persevere in the belief that traditional programs fail to meet the needs of early adolescents (Brazee, 1991). By 1977, fifteen states had 100 or more middle schools; several states had over 200. By 1982, middle schools (those with fifth or sixth through eighth grade populations) numbered over 5,000 (Reinhartz & Beach, 1983).

The idea of interdisciplinary teaching also survived. As of 1988 (Epstein & MacIver, 1990), 42% of the middle grade students were being taught by interdisciplinary teams. More recently, George and Shewey's *New Evidence for the Middle School* (1993) reflects the growing trend of the integrated curriculum. Of those schools included in the study, 63% felt that "interdisciplinary curriculum and instruction involving teachers from a variety of disciplines has contributed to the long-term effectiveness of [their] middle school program" (p. 103).

But just as the label *middle school* fails to guarantee the existence of a true middle school philosophy in operation, the term *interdisciplinary teams* fails to guarantee that interdisciplinary instruction exists within those teams. The "wished-for" and the "reality of" an integrated curriculum often differ.

Types of Interdisciplinary Instruction

Over the past forty to fifty years, the idea of an integrated, cross-curricular program for middle level students has manifested itself in a variety of organizational structures and instructional designs (Beane, 1993; Erb & Doda, 1989; Fogarty, 1991; Horton & Sheathelm, 1991; Jacobs, 1989; Merenbloom, 1991; Vars, 1991; Wraga, 1992). For this text, integrative or interdisciplinary curriculum indicates two or more teachers working cooperatively to develop and create educational opportunities. Jacobs (1989) defines interdisciplinary as "a knowledge view and curriculum approach that consciously applies methodology and language from more than one discipline to examine a central theme, issue, problem, topic, or experience."

Integration comes in many forms. The terms *integrative, integrated, interdisciplinary, multidisciplinary,* and *holistic* seem to be used interchangeably (Vars, 1992), and *transdisciplinary,* a relatively new descriptor, should probably be added. It is sometimes described on a four-level continuum moving from pre-integration activities to a thematic unit developed by two or more teachers planned around a common theme or problem (Erb & Doda, 1989). Or it may be classified by type, from a simple Type I, in which two teachers develop a cooperative unit to be taught during a shared time slot, to a more complex Type III, in which a number of resource people work together to develop a unit that extends the school into the community (Horton & Sheathelm, 1991). The leveling of integrative structures has its roots in the work of Wright (1958), who defined them by types, A to D.

Type A   Each subject within a common block of time is taught separately, sometimes with, other times without aligning or correlating the content.

Type B   Subjects within a time block are presented around a central theme tied to one or more of the subjects.

Type C   A "predetermined" problem is posed, and students are usually given a choice of activities, materials, and/or approaches to use in solving the problem.

Type D   The students and the teachers determine the problem or focus of the study.

Most current definitions of integrated instruction evolved from these four types.

The verbal guises of interdisciplinary instruction are, as Jacobs (1989) describes it, "cumbersome" at best. Vars (1993) defines *interdisciplinary/cross-disciplinary* as the larger, umbrella concept of "any curriculum that deliberately links content and modes of inquiry normally associated with more than one of the scholarly disciplines" (p. 18). He then sorts the various types into two major categories: content-centered designs and student-centered designs:

- Content-centered: Multidisciplinary content and modes of inquiry from various disciplines applied to a common theme, topic, or problem; usually accomplished by either correlation or fusion.
- Student-centered: Core curriculum focus directly on needs, problems, and concerns of students with subject matter and skills brought in as needed; sometimes called transdisciplinary.

In order to provide a common base of reference, the Vars's language or terminology is preferred, as it provides classification labels that appropriately indicate the basic differences in integrated curriculum.

Content-Centered

Correlation of Curriculum

There are basically two types of content-centered approaches. Probably the most commonly used is what Vars refers to as correlation. In this design, teachers of different subjects recognize a commonality or relatedness from one subject area to another. Determination of the topic or theme that reflects the common thread is generally made by the teachers who cooperatively plan but independently teach the unit. Correlation designs are usually a "once in a while approach" or a "You do your thing; I'll do mine" system of instruction. Traditional delivery of content by individual subject area teachers in separate classrooms may be temporarily suspended "while implementing an interdisciplinary unit" (Maute, 1992). A typical example is a social studies/language arts theme based on the Civil War or "the '50s" or a science/math focus on understanding measurement. Teachers determine the terminology to be used, who will give what assignments and projects, and the overall timing of the unit. They create a calendar outlining when each will teach selected activities. A film may be shown in social studies, for instance, that complements a novel being read in the English/language arts class, or the use of standard measurement systems may be emphasized in science, while in math classes students explore how measurement applies to a problem-solving task.

Correlated versions of interdisciplinary instructional units (IDU) abound. Most state middle school journals include at least one in each issue. In addition, state and national conference break-out sessions offer numerous presentations in which classroom practitioners share successful IDU ideas. One example of a correlated unit comes from a Canton, Ohio, area team of teachers who developed an interdisciplinary project called The National Football League. Each subject area teacher included separate activities related to the topic.

Social Studies

Using maps, locate all the NFL cities and explain the divisions.

Using stations in the library, answer history/geography trivia about the NFL.

Science

Identify the NFL team mascots by traits, classification, and why the mascot is appropriate to that team.

Label the mascot names on the map created in social studies.

Reading

Develop an explanation of appropriateness for nonanimal mascots.

Label the mascots on the map created in social studies.

Create a crossword or word search using the cities, states, and mascots of the NFL.

English

Develop a brochure for the Hall of Fame.

Maintain a journal.

Identify and locate the home towns of the twenty-eight NFL quarterbacks.

Write a short biography on one of the NFL players.

Mathematics

Explain time zones—using one weekend, find the starting times of all the games (home team) and figure the time of day in the opposing team's city.

Driving distances.

All

National Football Hall of Fame field trip.

At Eastwood Middle School, Pemberville, Ohio, a mystery-problem–solving thematic unit entitled "Who Kidnaped Cupid?" is used every other year in early February. Borrowed from a similar unit done at Winston Park Junior High School in Palatine, Illinois, where only math and science are involved, the Eastwood version adds history and other curricular areas, as well. Forensics, interviewing techniques, "news reporting" with "live" video, "Wanted" posters, and a study of Cupid from Greek mythology immerse the students in the unit, connecting many of their classes to a shared theme (Pollick, 1992).

Typically a correlated unit idea comes from one or more teachers who enjoy working together and who see a need or opportunity to pull together two or more content areas into a common learning experience. These teachers form a plan and recruit other staff members who commit to some part of the plan. For a few days, perhaps even a week or more, they deliver instruction based on the theme. What is done in each class relates to the site-wide theme, but most of the activities are also directly related to the specific content area classes.

Correlation designs motivate students at a time in the school year when students' interest ebbs (Kerekes, 1992). Yet there are powerful connections that may be made through correlated units. Inherent, however, in the correlated model are some limitations:

- There are only a few skills or knowledges in a discipline field that relate to any other set of skills or knowledges in another discipline field.
- Integrated teaching is a diversionary, "play-like" experience. It is a way of "cheering us up" or rejuvenating our interest in "real" learning. But "real" learning occurs best in the content area to which it really belongs.
- Integrated instruction is not as goal-oriented and accessible as regular content area instruction. When working toward education goals and standards to be measured, we work through the content areas.

For many middle level students the interdisciplinary unit is the only available form of connected curriculum experience offered. This is, however, the type of interdisciplinary instruction with which many teachers and administrators are most comfortable, and it has the potential of whetting appetites for more integrative instruction. In addition, the interdependency and shared workload appears to motivate reluctant and insecure faculty to dabble in new instructional approaches. If it is the appetizer that prompts future use of more long-term, more student-empowered interdisciplinary structures, it serves a valuable purpose.

Fusion of Curriculum

The other content-centered approach is called "fused." Curriculum becomes fused when teachers develop a unit "focusing on central concepts and values" (Vars, 1992), and they unify or fuse the objectives and content of both subject areas for a more sustained period of time. The combined material is taught cooperatively and interchangeably. This blending strengthens the relatedness and relevance of the two areas. This approach also goes by terms such as *unified studies, combined, complementary,* or *webbed curriculum.*

Fusion represents the blending of content areas. Disciplines come together as one. Again, a fusion of content usually occurs between two or more amicable teachers who feel secure in the discipline of their teaching assignment and see the value of connecting learning experiences to real-life situations. Mutual or common components in previously separate curriculum areas become evident, and teachers eliminate unnecessary duplication of some elements, yet strengthen or reinforce others by building a strong foundation, gradually increasing the complexity or intensity.

As an illustration of fusion, Levy (1992) offers a basic approach to a fused plan on Chinese culture. This plan could be broadened to a study of a combination of cultures. As suggested by Jacobs (1989), focus questions or key issues give direction and a solid base to learning experiences. For example, "How is daily life in China different from ours? What major contributions of the Chinese culture affect us?" No matter who is delivering or facilitating the day's instructional activity, students and teachers alike have a sense of where things are headed. Instruction and learning have a shared focus; learning becomes primary, and the content becomes secondary.

In Shelburne, Vermont (Compton & Hawn, 1993), interdisciplinary study occurs in multi-age groups in one of three teams: the Technology Team, composed of math, science, practical arts, and living arts (consumer/home economics); the Humanities Team, composed of language arts, social studies, art, music, and physical education; and the Communications Team, composed of foreign language, keyboarding (typing and computers), math, and physical education. The teams meet two afternoons a week for 12 weeks, with every student having the opportunity to experience each team every year. Collectively, the three teams select an annual theme, such as "A Limited Earth," and each team experience explores that theme with different focus questions. For example, the Technology Team might focus on natural resources and alternative energy sources. The Humanities Team might compare life in Vermont with life in China. The Communications Team might investigate all the ways people communicate.

The level of cooperation and flexibility team members bring to this type of instructional plan is critical to the success of the approach. Together teachers lay out the unit's major components: content, skills, and applications based on "What do we want students to know and be able to do?" These decisions drive the assessment approaches, materials, and resources needed.

The relevance and excitement that a fused approach generates represents the system's greatest "good." The learning activities tend to be student-centered, and the students' instructional needs are usually identified and addressed quickly. The old cliché "two minds are better than one" holds true and makes the planning and delivery of instruction richer.

However, any time a group, even a group of two, tries to work together, aspects of the program become more complicated and require cooperation. Using the strengths of each team member is the key. Vars (1993) warns to avoid giving "the impression . . . that English, for example, is merely a 'handmaiden' of social studies, or that art is just brought in to add a little variety." Themes should be selected that are concrete in nature, such as "World Conflict" or "Families and Tribes." Abstract themes such as "Systems" or "Patterns" are difficult for early adolescents to grasp as motivating ideas or as topics that are personally relevant.

Student-Centered

Core

Core curriculum, a totally integrative design, should not be confused with "core of the curriculum," the courses required of all students or the common learning in general education (Vars, 1992). A true core curriculum has two basic characteristics. First, the experiences fit adolescents' emotional, intellectual, academic, physical, and social needs. Second, the educational experiences are cross-curricular; they weave together a range of disciplines.

Core design, when based on a preselected topic or theme that the teacher or teachers see as an adolescent need or concern (Vars, 1987, 1991, 1993), is much like Wright's Type C design. Teams representing distinct subject areas may allow for student choice and input while also permitting teacher control of the selection of material and determination of activities or assignments. Capelluti and Brazee (1992) offer a model that presupposes that many teachers have some experience in developing interdisciplinary instruction. They suggest to select a theme based on student concerns, create a short description of the curriculum, develop a brief description of the problem, elicit student-generated questions, determine the goals, list all possible activities, develop a time line, generate a list of resources and materials, determine responsibilities of team members, and document reflections on the experience.

Numerous authorities (Arnold, 1991; Beane, 1990a, 1990b, 1992, 1993; McDonough, 1991; Toepfer, 1992; Vars, 1992, 1993) urge broad core curriculum visions. When students are "given" or assigned a topic, the message is "See what you can do with MY idea" (Price, 1993). A true core curriculum encourages students to identify the problems and concerns they will explore (Vars, 1992, 1993); it validates what students see as important (Stevenson & Carr, 1993).

In addition, the core curriculum avoids segmented, departmentalized, and discipline-field boxes or compartments. The core curriculum is dynamic, and as it evolves it encourages exploring, creating, and envisioning relationships between diverse concepts. Investigation of issues takes precedence over finding the right answer (McDonough, 1991). Students become problem solvers and information synthesizers rather than isolated trivia recall artists (Arnold, 1991). Genuine core curricula unite all aspects of instruction, including instructional strategies, organizational arrangements, integrated content, and the cultural environment (McDonough, 1991).

When students are part of the planning and development of the unit, core design parallels Wright's Type D approach (Wraga, 1992). Many advocate that true integration is realized only with core design (Arnold, 1991; Beane, 1991; McDonough, 1991; Rubin, 1993; Taylor, 1994; Toepfer, 1992). The study or solving of the problem, in turn, is "free of any concern for the pretense of subject divisions" (Wraga, 1992).

Because the core approach evolves, the following example outlines approaches to implementation rather than specific descriptions of core structures.

Core curriculum blooms from the seeds of student needs and interests. What we teach and how we teach often appear to be a matter of what best fits the adults involved rather than what best fits the young people we serve (Beane, 1992, 1993; Brazee, 1991; McDonough, 1991). The adolescent is frequently seen as confused and uncommitted to issues beyond the latest fads and fashions. This view is contradicted by McDonough (1991), who surveyed 500 students from rural to urban environments. The results of the survey reflect students' deeper concerns and interests.

Based on typical student concerns, Beane (1991, 1993) suggests considering themes such as: self-identity, human relationships, environment, wealth/poverty, war/peace, cultural diversity, racism, and freedom/interdependence. Some themes can be explored on a personal level but are also relative to more global issues. Student populations and school/community environments vary; each has its own unique needs and goals.

Erb and Doda (1989, 1991) suggest that beginning with the desired outcomes and how they fit into the evaluation process is the most logical approach. This also avoids fragmentation, in which, due to efforts to relate the topic directly to some aspect of each discipline, the unit fails to provide strong connections to larger goals and content (Erb, 1991; Jacobs, 1989). Erb (1991) proposes the following steps for preservice teachers, but they work equally well with veteran teachers:

1. Organize teachers into curriculum planning teams having three to five members, all with different academic backgrounds.
2. All curriculum planning teams complete a personality inventory that enables them to see the individual preferences and attributes of team members.
3. The instructor/professor defines basic parameters of a curriculum development activity, for example, length of unit.

4. The curriculum team plans the activity "backward" with goals/outcomes identified, and culminating activities with the following characteristics:

   - Require students to produce something tangible and observable.
   - Require students to integrate skills and information from various content/subject bases.

5. Select the theme, based on an understanding of adolescent development. It must be "significant . . . and sufficiently broad to include all academic areas relevant to the inquiry" (Erb, 1991, p. 27). Have the planning team create a grid. Along the left-hand side, list anticipated adolescent questions or concerns; across the top, list social issues and trends. By identifying adolescent concerns that intersect social issues or trends, the planning team can pinpoint themes to pursue.

6. Brainstorm and web in a list-group-label process *all possible* resources, activities, skill/concept strands, and materials that relate to the theme.

7. Limit or narrow the focus by using guiding questions (Jacobs, 1989) or unifying objectives (Erb & Doda, 1989).

8. Organize the actual experiences:

   - Grouping of students—whole group, small group, individual
   - Evaluating and grading of activities/products—checklist, letter grades, or "weighted" values
   - Accountability—daily/weekly; individual group
   - Facilities and materials—checking material and equipment in and out; space allocation and assignment

9. Develop a written account of the aspects of the unit as outlined here.

10. Share the end product with peers and other educators; possibly present some of the components in a demonstration lesson with adolescents who volunteer to participate.

Similarly, Thornton (1993b) describes how three sixth grade teachers worked together to build a core curriculum. As a group, they established a shared philosophy about how students learn and the nature of the curriculum content. They discuss, for example, how to teach children emotionally, socially, and intellectually; the role of the teacher in the learning process; and the degree to which students will be involved in deciding what and how they will learn.

From this philosophical base, Thornton and her colleagues developed two lists of desired outcomes. One list is a skills list, including such things as decision making, communication, and accessing information. The second list is an attitudes list, including such things as respect of self and others, a sense of self, and an appreciation for change. These two lists provide the basis for the assessment and the team's grade card.

After the students share their personal concerns, correlations can be made between their concerns and broader societal issues (Brazee & Capelluti, 1993). The key is to recognize the students as genuine people seeking intellectual answers to authentic issues. Beane (1992) suggests that students individually identify questions and concerns, identify mutual questions and concerns in small groups, and meet as a whole class to select one theme, brainstorm for possible activities, and list knowledges/skills they might need to carry it out.

The realization of an authentic interdisciplinary curriculum rests, to a large degree, on the elements previously presented: validation of students as thinking, concerned human beings, teacher awareness of early adolescent needs and current issues and trends, and administrative support that allows building principals and teacher teams to have the time and freedom to meet the needs of the students. When these elements are in place, the focus can be appropriately placed on the ingredients or components of the actual interdisciplinary plan.

Team Planning of Instruction

Most models for interdisciplinary units focus on how to write units, not on how to teach (Brazee & Capelluti, 1993). However, plans for integrated instruction do exist. Dahlberg (1990) provides a framework for teachers that places the students at the center of learning. The focus is on strategies for learning; the students explore, monitor, construct, apply, and evaluate their thinking. For example, Hoffman's (1992) I-Chart is a natural integrative tool. Students negotiate key questions to be explored, and each student or group investigates all questions by exploring a variety of resources. The information found is recorded on the I-Chart (Inquiry Chart); then the findings are analyzed. In addition, Hoffman suggests how large group aspects of this process can gradually become small-group or individual pursuits. In Tomlinson's (1993) piece on independent study, another scaffolding approach is offered in which students gradually move toward more self-guided learning. The premise is that perceptive teachers know that not all students are independent learners, but that with guidance, students can be nudged toward greater independence. For those lacking an appropriate level of personal control, the teacher exercises a high degree of structure. This includes some student determination of direction, short-term deadlines (or dividing the task up into chunks easily realized in a short period of time), and opportunities to complete things during school time rather than as homework. The other two stages leading to independence are structured independence and shared independence. Models such as these help the team members see how all of the content areas can filter into the overall instructional plan and provide necessary support to students.

There are so many forms of interdisciplinary curriculum that the task can become overwhelming (Erb, 1991). The team should decide on the goals and objectives and then pick or modify the model that seems most appropriate. Being patient and persistent in the process is important; Lounsbury (1992) believes that "few teams reach their potential during the first two to three years—some never do" (p. 2). Rubin (1993) supports this view: "It is not that schools should avoid dealing with specific disciplines; rather, they also need to create learning experiences that . . . demonstrate a relationship of the disciplines, thus heightening their relevancy" (p. 4).

The five principles proposed by Arnold (1985) represent the criteria for integrative instruction success:

1. The curriculum must help students make sense of themselves and of their world.
2. Methods and materials must be geared to the developmental levels of the students.
3. Knowledge—consisting of thinking, feeling, and doing—must be emphasized over simple information and isolated skills.
4. The curriculum must focus on concrete and real-world experiences.
5. The curriculum must be taught by teachers who are knowledgeable human beings who trust their own judgments and instincts enough to rise above the rules and models.

A bibliography of published team interdisciplinary units is purposely omitted from this chapter. State affiliate journals and the *National Middle School Journal* often contain articles relative to successful interdisciplinary units. There are also numerous books available to provide ideas for units. As useful as these may be, none of the units may fit your situation, your students, or your goals. The most effective units are those designed or adapted by teachers to fit the individual characteristics of specific students. There are only two prerequisites to interdisciplinary curricular success (Erb, 1991): (1) Know your clientele—learn and clearly understand what makes the early adolescent tick, socially, emotionally, psychologically, and physically; (2) prospective interdisciplinary teachers must be intrinsically driven lovers of learning who "study and reflect on some major societal trends . . . [and] have a sufficient passion for, and knowledge of, some area of human inquiry such as those associated with the liberal arts disciplines" (p. 27).

Professional organizations representing many of those liberal arts disciplines may provide the impetus for curriculum change. The National Council of Teachers of Mathematics and the National Science Teachers Association are two major examples of subject area groups developing curriculum frameworks that represent a new, integrated view. These frameworks urge the inclusion of the traditionally separated strands within the discipline field. For example, geometry, algebra, and data analysis should be taught in an interrelated way at every level, kindergarten through high school; life science, physical science, and earth science complement each other and should be taught at every level, kindergarten through high school. Whole language and integrated language arts pervade the publications of the National Council of Teachers of English. The International Reading Association reflects a similar philosophy. All of these frameworks urge more integration, more student self-selection, hands-on involvement, and more relevant, real-world applications. Whether schools have teaming or not, all schools already are or will soon confront the issue of integrated instruction (Lounsbury, 1992).

Summing Up

Integrative curriculum has been recognized and valued to varying degrees through most of this century. When compared to traditional curriculum organization patterns, it is valued for providing increased flexibility for teachers and students, increased levels of understanding, improved attitude and attendance, as well as healthier teacher/student relationships.

Whatever the type of integrated instruction employed, two elements make it authentic (Beane, 1991, 1993): (1) Integration implies wholeness and unity, and (2) it allows young people to come face to face with relevant questions and meaningful experiences. These questions should be ones that students genuinely want answered. The quest for personal answers to genuine questions is a true revision of standard school practice. Traditionally students learned the content teachers dictated and thought what teachers wanted them to think. Enfranchising students to follow their curiosity and to reflect on what they are learning empowers both teachers and students to focus on issues of personal importance.

The current curriculum revolution raises issues about the nature of teaching. If teaching is a dynamic and moral profession, we must strive to change in response to the evolving nature of our students and the demands of our society.

Discussion Questions

1. Develop a chart that lists three different types of interdisciplinary instructional approaches down the left side of the paper. Label three columns across the top with the categories: Distinguishing Feature, Benefits, Weaknesses. Fill in the grid with the appropriate information. Which of the three do you believe is most beneficial for students? Why? Which of three would be easiest for you to use in your classroom? Why?

2. What about interdisciplinary instruction seems particularly appropriate for middle level students?

3. Locate a school and team using interdisciplinary units of some type. Observe or interview a team member; identify the type of interdisciplinary plan the team seems to be using (and support your view with specific information). Discuss what you consider to be the strengths of this team. What strengths would you bring to this team if you became a member?

References

Aiken, W. (1942). *The story of the Eight Year Study.* New York: Harper.

Arnold, J. (1985). A responsive curriculum for emerging adolescents. *Middle School Journal, 16*(3), 14–18.

Arnold, J. (1991). Towards a middle level curriculum rich in meaning. *Middle School Journal,* 23(2), 8–12.

Beane, J. A. (1990a). *A middle school curriculum: From rhetoric to reality.* Columbus, OH: National Middle School Association.

Beane, J. A. (1990b). Rethinking the middle school curriculum. *Middle School Journal, 21*(5), 1–5.

Beane, J. A. (1991). Middle school: The natural home of integrated curriculum. *Educational Leadership, 49*(2), 9–13.

Beane, J. A. (1992). Turning the floor over: Reflections on a middle school curriculum. *Middle School Journal, 23*(3), 34–40.

Beane, J. A. (1993). A middle school curriculum: From rhetoric to reality (2d ed.). Columbus, OH: National Middle School Association.

Brazee, E. N. (1991). Warning: These ideas may be hazardous to your (mental) health. *Middle School Journal, 23*(2), 56–58.

Brazee, E. N., & Capelluti, J. (1993). Focus on middle level curriculum integration: Getting out of the blocks. *Journal of the New England League of Middle Schools, I*(1), 25–29.

Capelluti, J., & Brazee, E. N. (1992). Middle level curriculum: Making sense. *Middle School Journal, 23*(3), 11–15.

Carnegie Council on Adolescent Development (1990). *Turning points: Preparing American youth for the 21st century.* Washington, DC: Author.

Compton, M. F. (1984). Balance in the middle school curriculum. In J. H. Lounsbury (Ed.), *Perspectives: Middle school education 1964–1984.* Columbus, OH: National Middle School Association.

Compton, M. F., & Hawn, H. C. (1993). *Exploration: The total curriculum.* Columbus, OH: National Middle School Association.

Dahlberg, L. A. (1990). Teaching for the information age. *Journal of Reading, 34*(1), 12–19.

Epstein, J. L., & MacIver, D. J. (1990). *Education in the middle grades: National practices and trends.* Columbus, OH: National Middle School Association.

Erb, T. O. (1987). What team organization can do for teachers. *Middle School Journal, 18*(4), 3–7.

Erb, T. O. (1988). Focusing back on the child by liberating the teachers. *The Early Adolescent Magazine, 2*(3), 10–18.

Erb, T. O. (1991). Preparing prospective middle grades teachers to understand the curriculum. *Middle School Journal, 23*(2), 24–28.

Erb, T. O., & Doda, N. M. (1989). *Team organization: Promise, practices, and possibilities.* Washington, DC: National Education Association.

Fogarty, R. (1991). *Integrate the curricula.* Palatine, IL: Skylight.

George, P. S., & Oldaker, L. L. (1985). *Evidence for the middle school.* Columbus, OH: National Middle School Association.

George, P. S., & Shewey, K. (1994). *New evidence for the middle school.* Columbus, OH: National Middle School Association.

Golner, S. J., & Powell, J. H. (1992). Ready for teaming? Ten questions to ask before you jump in. *Middle School Journal, 24*(1), 28–32.

Heath, I. A., & Wagner, C. L. (1995). Developing research skills in a cooperative content integrated middle school civics program. *Current Issues in Middle Level Education, 4*(1), 38–52.

Hoffman, J. V. (1992). Critical reading/thinking across the curriculum: Using I-Charts to support learning. *Language Arts, 69,* 121–127.

Horton, K., & Sheathelm, S. (1991). Interdisciplinary units made easy. *The NELMS Journal, 4*(1), 23–24.

Integration of educational experiences. (1958). *The fifty-seventh yearbook of the National Society for the Study of Education.* Chicago: University of Chicago Press.

Jacobs, H. H. (Ed.) (1989). *Interdisciplinary curriculum design and implementation.* Alexandria, VA: Association for Supervision and Curriculum Development.

Kerekes, J. (1992). The interdisciplinary unit—it's here to stay! In J. H. Lounsbury (Ed.), *Connecting the curriculum through interdisciplinary instruction.* Columbus, OH: National Middle School Association.

Levy, P. S. (1992). Webbing: A format for planning integrated curricula. In J. H. Lounsbury (Ed.), *Connecting the curriculum through interdisciplinary instruction.* Columbus, OH: National Middle School Association.

Lipsitz, J. (1984). *Successful schools for adolescents.* New Brunswick, NJ: Transaction Books.

Lounsbury, J. H. (Ed.) (1992). *Connecting the curriculum through interdisciplinary instruction.*

Columbus, OH: National Middle School Association.

Markle, G., Johnston, H., Geer, C., & Merchtry, Y. (1990). Teaching for understanding. *Middle School Journal, 22*(2), 53–57.

Maute, J. (1992). Cross-curricular connections. In J. H. Lounsbury (Ed.), *Connecting the curriculum through interdisciplinary instruction.* Columbus, OH: National Middle School Association.

McDonough, L. (1991). Middle level curriculum: The search for self and social meaning. *Middle School Journal, 22*(2), 29–35.

Merenbloom, E. Y. (1991). *The team process: A handbook for teachers* (3d ed.). Columbus, OH: National Middle School Association.

National Middle School Association (1993). *Middle level curriculum: A work in progress.* Columbus, OH: Author.

National Middle School Association (1995). *This we believe.* Columbus, OH: Author.

Pollick, J. (1992). An interdisciplinary Cupid kidnapping. *Ohio Middle School Journal, 19*(2), 10–14.

Price, P. (1993). *Breakout sessions presentation on choice: Critical thinking through reading and writing process,* The Ohio Council of Teachers of English and Language Arts, Spring Conference, Worthington, OH.

Reinhartz, J., & Beach, D. M. (1983). *Improving middle school instruction: A research-based self-assessment system.* Washington, DC: National Education Association.

Rubin, S. E. (1993). Resource-based education: It's like inviting kids to a buffet instead of a sit-down dinner. *The NELMS Journal, 6*(1), 8–13.

Sizer, T. (1984). *Horace's compromise: The dilemmas of the American high school.* Boston: Houghton Mifflin.

Stevenson, C., & Carr, J. F. (Eds.) (1993). *Integrated studies in the middle grades: Dancing through walls.* New York: Teachers College Press.

Thornton, H. (1993a). Educational change and implementation. *Ohio Middle School Journal, 20*(1), 11–14.

Thornton, H. (1993b). Educational change and implementation. *Ohio Middle School Journal, 20*(2), 2–7.

Toepfer, C. F., Jr. (1992). Curriculum for identity: A middle level educational obligation. *Middle School Journal, 23*(3), 3–10.

Tomlinson, C. (1993). Independent study: A flexible tool for encouraging academic and personal growth. *Middle School Journal, 25*(1).

Vars, G. F. (1987). *Interdisciplinary teaching in the middle grades.* Columbus, OH: National Middle School Association.

Vars, G. F. (1991). Integrated curriculum in historical perspective. *Educational Leadership, 49*(2), 14–15.

Vars, G. F. (1992). Integrative curriculum: A deja vu. *Current Issues in Middle Level Education, 1*(1), 66–78.

Vars, G. F. (1993). *Interdisciplinary teaching: Why and how.* Columbus, OH: National Middle School Association.

Wraga, W. C. (1992). The core curriculum in the middle school: Retrospect and prospect. *Middle School Journal, 23*(3), 16–23.

Wright, G. S. (1958). *Block-time classes and the core program in the junior high school.* Bulletin 1958, no. 6, Office of Education. Washington, DC: U.S. Government Printing Office.

$$C \quad h \quad a \quad p \quad t \quad e \quad r \quad \mathbf{7}$$

Building a Sense of Community in Middle Level Schools

M. LEE MANNING

M. Lee Manning is Associate Professor of Curriculum and Instruction at Old Dominion University, Norfolk, Virginia. A former language arts teacher in the fifth through seventh grades, Manning presently works with preservice teacher education students preparing to teach in the middle school. His major areas of interest include effective middle school practices, multicultural education, and communities of learning.

People for centuries have experienced the need for a sense of community and have realized the benefits of considering themselves a part of a genuine community. Throughout history, people have gravitated toward living and working in communities because they have recognized the positive effects on individuals and on the group collectively. While understanding the need to maintain individuality, people also realize a basic need to consider themselves functioning members of a group, to feel regard for other community members (and vice versa), and to feel a degree of concern for the welfare of the group as a whole. Recent scholarly writing (Graves, 1992; Sergiovanni 1994a, 1994b; Westheimer & Kahne, 1993) has provided considerable insight into communities, their purposes, and their development. These writings have offered definitions, rationales, defining characteristics, principles, and suggestions for developing true communities.

Several indicators suggest that the late 1990s and the twenty-first century will be times for middle level educators to develop communities in such a way that young adolescents feel a sense of belonging: additional insights into communities and how they work; our increasing knowledge of the early adolescence developmental period, which suggests 10–14-year-olds need a sense of community; and a growing movement in schools to instill closer relationships. This chapter defines "a sense of community" by examining various definitions, proposes a definition for "middle level school communities," and suggests ways educators of young adolescents can build a sense of community in our schools.

Building a Sense of Middle Level School Community

Both *This We Believe* (National Middle School Association, 1995) and *Turning Points: Preparing American Youth for the 21st Century* (Carnegie Council on Adolescent Development, 1989) urge middle level educators and students to develop a sense of community. For example:

> *A good middle school is a healthy community composed of persons of differing ages, roles, and responsibilities. (National Middle School Association, 1995, p. 19)*
> *The student should, upon entering the middle grade school, join a small community in which people—students and adults alike—get to know each other well to create a climate for intellectual development. Students should feel that they are part of a community of shared educational purpose. (Carnegie Council on Adolescent Development, 1989, p. 37)*

Middle level educators and students need to understand that while benefits of communities far exceed the efforts expended to build such a culture, the task of community building will be a difficult process. Offering a warning to "the faint-hearted" (Sergiovanni, 1994a, p. xix) that community building takes courage; Sergiovanni (1994b) adds, "There is no recipe for building community. No correlates exist to implement. There is no list available to follow, and there is no package for trainers to deliver" (p. 218).

Although some middle schools function as effective communities, educators might be more accurate to say they are involved in the process of community building rather than saying they have genuine communities. Each community should be considered an evolving process that begins with a state of mind (Sergiovanni, 1994a). For transformation from "individuals" to "communities" to occur, potential community members, both educators and young adolescents, should be linked by unified action that includes shared values, conceptions, and ideas. Middle level educators should consider community building to be a slow process that develops in stages (Graves, 1992). Progress might appear to be nonexistent, and then, evidence that educators and young adolescents are becoming a community might surface. Community builders might suffer setbacks when acts of selfishness, racism, or sexism occur. The impact will undoubtedly hurt the progress of the community, but the commitment of community builders will determine future progress. Many people in contemporary society long for a sense of community, yet, when asked to define "community," offer hazy ideas and concepts of community and how to achieve it. In reality, they all have a reasonable idea of what community means, but when they are pressed to place defining characteristics on the term, only vague and often abstract definitions surface (Graves, 1992).

Defining Characteristics of a Community

The following definitions of community, though general, are useful:

- "A process marked by interaction and deliberation among individuals who share common interests and commitment to common goals" (Westheimer & Kahne, 1993, p. 325)
- "An inherently cooperative, cohesive, and self-reflective group entity whose members work on a regular face-to-face basis toward common goals while respecting a variety of perspectives, values, and life styles" (Graves, 1992, p. 64)

Additionally, several defining characteristics can be offered for school communities or a sense of community.

1. Communities are socially organized around relationships and the felt interdependencies that nurture them.
2. Communities empower educators, students, and others by emphasizing individuals' commitments, obligations, and duties toward the school.
3. Community members connect to each other because of interdependencies, mutual obligations, and other emotional ties.
4. Communities are collections of individuals bonded together by natural will and who are together bound to a set of shared ideas and ideals.

Sergiovanni (1994a) suggested that a key to the understanding of community is the concept of collective conscience, defined as collective moral awareness, mutual obligation, and involvement in collectivity. Such involvement has three elements: duty, attachment, and self-determination. For example, in a community:

1. People feel a duty to others—they have self-discipline to work toward the welfare of the community.
2. People feel an attachment, a sense of membership, to the community that includes commitment and identity.
3. People feel a sense of self-determination that involves knowledge, understanding, and a rational sense of awareness regarding their duty and attachment to the community.

Looking specifically at schools, Sergiovanni (1994b) viewed democratic communities as schools and classrooms embracing teachers as well as students. Defining characteristics in democratic communities include teachers and students sharing ideas and leadership roles, forming authentic relationships with each other and among themselves, and being willing to better know themselves and their community members and being open to new ideas. Adults' roles in democratic communities include a responsibility to ensure that relationships with each other and with learners model the best that active citizenship has to offer, to teach learners the values of democracy and the skills of active citizenship, to show learners how these values and skills lead to the development of standards and codes for living together, to teach students the obligations of citizenship to the common good, and to teach community members to feel a responsibility for caring for one another (Sergiovanni, 1994a).

Simply having an organization does not mean that a sense of community exists. In a genuine community, members interact in a spirit of peace, feel comfortable expressing feelings, consider themselves accepted by other members, listen to others with empathy, support others unconditionally in nonthreatening situations, and feel a sense of synergy that makes the community highly productive (Canning, 1993). Other essentials include members feeling a sense of belongingness and respect, focusing on common goals, and being a self-reflective group (Graves, 1992).

Definition of a Middle Level School Community

The preceding definitions lend some credence to Graves's (1992) assertion that scholars often define communities in vague, hazy, and abstract terms. Still, even with limitations any definition may have, a definition of community in middle level schools should be proposed.

A community or a sense of community in the middle level school is a continuing, evolving process whereby young adolescents and educators interact and work collaboratively in an atmosphere of trust, belongingness, and respect toward shared common interests and commitment to common educational and developmental goals.

While this definition suffices for this chapter and for many middle level schools, definitions of communities may vary with schools and educators—one school might emphasize the process of community while another might place emphasis elsewhere, for example, on collaboration or respect. One essential point deserves to be emphasized: Building a middle level school community involves both educators and young adolescents; a sense of community flows from educators to students and vice versa.

Rationale for Communities

Why do communities exist? Why are communities needed? Communities may serve several purposes: caring, learning, inquiring, and being professional, collegial, and inclusive. People have a basic human need to belong to others and to feel part of a group that works toward common goals, each forsaking some measure of individuality to work toward a common goal. Communities can provide this sense of belonging and give the feeling that people will work collectively toward agreed-upon and shared goals. Without this sense of community, people risk feelings of alienation—they feel cut off from others, whether "others" be peers, friends, family members, or acquaintances. Communities can serve learners in several specific ways, such as helping students meet their needs today as well as guiding them to become tomorrow's caring and active citizens. Unless students feel a sense of value and place, they run the risk of drifting further away from school life (Sergiovanni, 1994a).

Another rationale for building a sense of community includes the need for schools and classrooms to be interdependent, cooperative communities in which students and teachers learn and work in a more comfortable and inspiring environment. Teachers expect peers to support and assist them in educational efforts; collaboration occurs in the development of both methods and curricula. While improving the educational environment for both teachers and learners is a logical and sound argument for building a sense of community, middle level educators recognize that young adolescents often come from disturbing family and neighborhood environments. Also, television viewing often inculcates an individualistic perspective and violent nonrational solutions to problems (Graves, 1992). A comfortable, inspiring community offers an alternative view.

While learners of all levels benefit from being integral members of a caring culture, an even stronger case might be offered for young adolescents needing a sense of community. What is it about young adolescents and their lives that makes them need communities? What societal and demographic changes suggest middle level schools need to build a sense of community, and does the middle school concept lend itself to this need? Obviously, preparing a convincing rationale for building a sense of community in middle level schools requires consideration of these and other questions.

Answering the question "What is it about young adolescents and their lives that makes them need communities?" requires an examination of several psychosocial and cognitive developmental characteristics. Young adolescents undoubtedly benefit from caring and concerned individuals in their middle level school: Many have just come to an unfamiliar and probably larger school; many face the challenge of new teachers and new peers; and many often feel lost or anonymous. Rather than fostering feelings of anonymity and alienation (Manning, 1993) during an already difficult developmental period, a caring culture can provide young adolescents with a sense of closeness, of familiarity with others, and of being a member of a group.

Perceptive middle level educators readily recognize how young adolescents' development relates to community building. Becoming more concerned and aware of the treatment of others, young adolescents perceive the value of living and learning in a true community.

- Young adolescents can make choices about behavior toward individuals and groups.
- Young adolescents can determine characteristics and traits they want in friends.
- Young adolescents can develop personal attitudes toward other people and institutions.
- Young adolescents can perceive differences among people and eventually develop attitudes toward others' differences.
- Young adolescents can consider their judgments about people and institutions.

Table 7.1 offers an overview of selected developmental characteristics and how communities can address each characteristic.

Addressing how societal and demographic factors illuminate the need for a caring culture requires a look at elements such as changes in family life, increased cultural diversity, and violence, just to name representative examples. Middle level communities address these selected factors as they provide young adolescents with feelings of physical and psychological safety and with awareness that significant adults and other young adolescents know and respect them.

Family life has undergone several changes that have the potential for affecting young adolescents and their educators. Factors such as the increased divorce

TABLE 7.1 Young Adolescent Development and Communities of Learners

Young Adolescents Experience . . .	Communities Can . . .
Changes in self-esteem	Help young adolescents feel better about themselves and their abilities to cope in middle schools through increased socialization
Shifts in allegiances from parents and teacher to peers	Teach that allegiances do not have to be either/or situations—caring community members want to care for, interact with, and support others
Increased desire for friendships and social interaction	Convey similarity between friendship making and community building
Changes in reasoned moral and ethical choices about behavior	Help young adolescents realize the rightness and wrongness of events and make choices about behavior toward individuals and groups
Engagement in social analysis and making judgments about people and institutions	Help young adolescents engage in social analysis of how people treat others and why and consider personal and social injustices and wrongs

Source: Manning, 1993, 1995.

rate and one-parent homes can be addressed by middle level communities. Also, in many cases both parents work, thus leaving less time for interacting with their young adolescents. While many one-parent homes provide excellent care and loving relationships (and some two-parent homes do not), communities in middle level schools can provide caring and nurturing that some young adolescents do not receive at home.

Census reports document the steadily increasing diversity among Americans. School-age (5–19 years) Native Americans number 769,000; African Americans, 10,715,000; Asian Americans and Pacific Islanders, 2,339,900; and Hispanic Americans, 8,636,000 (U.S. Bureau of the Census, 1992). The European American population totaled 112.4 million in 1990. In 1900, 85% of immigrants came from Europe; in 1990, only 22% came from Europe (U.S. Bureau of the Census, 1993). Population reports do not provide the number of school-age European Americans. Middle level communities can make significant contributions to help all people, regardless of ethnic and cultural backgrounds, feel accepted as a part of the social fabric.

Incidents of aggression and violence are increasing at alarming rates in our schools. The U.S. Department of Justice reports that three million crimes, or about 11% of all crimes, occur each year in public schools (Sautter, 1995). According to *Turning Points,* "Where petty theft from lockers and occasional fights were once problems, today assaults, carrying of weapons, drug transactions, and robberies are constant worries in schools" (Carnegie Council on Adolescent Development, 1989, p. 65).

While violent assaults on students and teachers grab media attention, the majority of aggressive acts are less extreme, such as bullying, verbal/physical threats, shoving, fist fights, and other simple assaults. Similarly, most aggressive acts in middle level schools consist of fighting and simple assaults, with males involved three times as often as female students (Carnegie Council on Adolescent Development, 1989). Teenagers more frequently are victims of crime than any other age group, and a quarter of the crimes committed against them take place in or near schools (Gable & Manning, 1996). Middle level communities can provide young adolescents with havens of safety and security, especially when community members demonstrate peaceful attitudes and behaviors. In such communities, participants feel close to each other and concerned with each other's physical and psychological well-being.

The question "Does the middle school concept lend itself to the need for a sense of community?" also can be answered in the affirmative. In fact, several aspects of the middle level school concept lend themselves to a caring culture: advisor-advisee programs that encourage young adolescents feeling part of a small group and in which educators and young adolescents work collaboratively to discuss problems and concerns; cooperative experiences that provide opportunities for learners to explore areas of interest (such as community relationships) and that allow educators and learners to learn from one another; positive school environments, which are the heart of both the middle level school movement and communities and which promote an atmosphere of trust and respect; and inter-disciplinary teams and teaming, which encourage small groups or clusters of teachers and young adolescents to work together toward agreed-upon and common goals.

The Middle Level School Community

Middle level educators might ask, "What should middle level communities be like?" and "What characteristics should we strive for?" While communities differ, just like people and schools, middle level educators can still develop a picture of what their communities need to represent, especially when they want communities reflecting the middle level school philosophy. Therefore, in determining characteristics, middle level school educators need to concentrate on questions such as "What do we want our community to be like?" "What basic characteristics should underlay our communities?" and "What values will we emphasize in our community?" Genuine communities in middle level schools should strive toward and instill a sense of:

- *Pervasive and genuine caring* for young adolescents and educators, both individually and collectively
- *Student-centered educational philosophies* that reflect the importance of learners as well as curricular areas and instructional techniques
- *Need to work together,* both to achieve academic integrity and to develop interpersonal relationships
- *Being known* by others and knowing others
- *Togetherness* whereby young adolescents do not feel anonymous and isolated from friends and educators
- *Responsibility* for others' welfare and vice versa
- *Respect* for self and others
- *Fairness,* both in attitudes and actual treatment, without a hint of exclusivity
- *Safety,* both physical and psychological
- *Trustworthiness* among young adolescents, teachers, and administrators
- *Humor,* the ability and willingness to consider others, oneself, and situations humorously (as long as others are not hurt)
- *Collaboration and cooperation* whereby young adolescents learn and their educators work in harmony rather than competition
- *Positive school and class atmosphere, climate, and culture* in which young adolescents feel good about themselves, their educators, and their interactions with others
- *Order and purpose* in all aspects of the school day
- *Optimism and high expectations* for self and others

This list provides middle level educators with goals to work toward; however, middle level educators, after examining their own individual schools, can undoubtedly suggest other traits and characteristics. A complete list probably does not exist—possibilities grow as educators consider potentials in their own communities.

Assumptions Underlying Communities

Building a sense of community in middle level schools undoubtedly requires several assumptions, all of which contribute to caring cultures continuing to evolve even when educators feel pessimistic about progress. Also, the assumptions potentially form the building blocks on which educators build communities. Assumptions in one school might not hold true in another school; therefore, each middle level school needs to determine its assumptions, especially those that have the potential for making the desired community a reality.

Westheimer and Kahne (1993) proposed two assumptions that they consider valid, especially when educators expect organizational changes (e.g., site-based management, magnet schools, house systems) to result in community building. First, educators know how to create genuine communal relationships. Second, educators actually want to seek such communities. Such might not always be the case, especially when educators emphasize individualism and autonomy.

Other assumptions have been proposed by Barth (1990) and Sergiovanni (1994a). Sergiovanni took assumptions from Barth's (1990) *Improving Schools from Within:*

Assumption 1: Schools have the capacity to improve themselves if the right conditions exist.

Assumption 2: When the need and the purpose are evident and when the right conditions exist, adults and students alike learn, energize, and contribute to the learning of the other.

Assumption 3: School improvement is an attempt to identify what schoolpeople should know and be able to do and to devise ways to get them to know and do it.

Selected Principles of Effective Communities

While communities differ, writers still have been able to suggest principles that contribute to communities being effective. Middle level educators need to consider their own individual schools and classrooms to determine whether basic principles are being met. Three selected principles of effective communities are:

Principle 1: Communities serve a meaningful purpose (Scoble, 1987).

Principle 2: Communities depend on support, motivation, and direction from one another (Westheimer & Kahne, 1993).

Principle 3: Communities accept and celebrate differences and various forms of diversity because differences provide resources that improve the quality of group interaction (Graves, 1992).

Middle level educators and young adolescents building caring cultures should consider these three principles as a beginning point. Administrators, teachers, and students need to discuss their purposes in forming a community, their progress in the community-building process, and where they want to evolve. Such dialogue will likely result in acceptance of these three principles as well as the selection of other principles unique to the respective community.

Planning Middle Level School Communities

Several writers (Canning, 1993; Graves, 1992; Sergiovanni, 1994a) have offered general information on building school communities. Graves (1992) suggested several stages for faculty, administrators, other school staff, parents, and students engaged in the community-building process.

Stage 1: Forming the Community—Who Are We?

People naturally want to know their place within the community. During this stage, people find their role by asking questions such as "Who are you?" and "Who am I?" Community members need to offer opportunities for students to get to know one another under circumstances that maximize enjoyable interaction while creating opportunities for information exchange and problem solving. When first building communities (or when new community members enter), such activities include whole-group mixers, icebreakers, and get-acquainted activities. Activities should be relevant and authentic (rather than games) and should involve learning information such as names, interests, skills, and experiences.

Middle level schools can take several directions toward forming communities (Graves, 1992):

- Choosing a name, motto, or logo that can be displayed on a banner or tee shirt (an attempt to "define" the group)
- Creating events to celebrate group unity such as celebrations of member or community achievements
- Using unifying daily classrooms or school rituals
- Collaborating on events such as field trips, parties, and cooperative adventures
- Keeping an ongoing record of community life, such as a scrapbook or a photograph album
- Building in bonding experiences at least twice yearly, such as a retreat, a camp-out, a family math night, or a school-wide carnival
- Fostering ownership of the community physical environment by involving members in exploring, organizing, and improving the school and classroom

Educators in middle level schools have a "head start" on community building because advisor-advisee programs and exploratory programs already provide ideal opportunities for teachers and students to become acquainted. Likewise, effective middle level schools offer commitments to positive school environments, an essential key to effective caring cultures. Last, interdisciplinary teaming, another form of community, provides a sense of togetherness or closeness among students and educators.

Stage 2: Exploring Community—What Can We Do Together?

As community members begin to feel accepted and to value one another, they begin to explore their purpose as a group (Graves, 1992). Questions include "What do we want to accomplish as a community?" "What group goals should we adopt?" and "What is our purpose?" Community members can form deeper connections and learn to communicate in ways that convey empathy for others' feelings and respect for others' opinions. Activities for this exploring stage include establishing rapport and effective communication, perspective-taking activities such as role plays and role reversals, and teaching of cooperative skills necessary for collaborative tasks.

During this stage, community members explore possible goals, standards, procedures, and expected outcomes. For example, activities might include jointly establishing class and school rules, group responsibility for chores of the community and rotation of leadership, regular community meetings for posing issues and solving problems, and frequent celebration of accomplishments (Graves, 1992).

During the exploring stage, middle level schools can take several directions. Specific activities for involving educators and young adolescents include collaboratively deciding on school projects, working together to ensure that teams or clusters function smoothly, deciding on extracurricular activities, practicing communication skills during advisory sessions, discussing possible exploratory topics, and talking about ways to make schools more positive and humane. The list is limited only by educators' and students' commitment to community building and their willingness to take risks.

Stage 3: Functioning Productively—How Can We Do Our Best?

Stage 1 and Stage 2 might suggest "all is well" and that a sense of community is a reality; however, based upon the belief that community building is a process rather than a finished product, educators continually have to refine and determine how improvements can be made. Hurdles, internal resistances, and obstacles continually challenge community members to propose adequate responses (Graves, 1992).

As the challenges mount, the participants may become immersed in unconstructive bickering and other unproductive behaviors such as ignoring others' feelings and opinions, forming alliances and excluding members, and trying to solve problems alone without shared leadership. The only solution lies in learning to solve conflicts, listening to others' points of view, and commiting to achieve an adequate balance. Strategies to promote productive functioning include using role playing in small and large groups, building cooperative skills, using interpersonal structures that ensure participation and rapport, and learning techniques for conflict management and resolution strategies (Graves, 1992).

The hectic demands on middle level educators—teaching young adolescents, working in interdisciplinary teams, planning advisories and exploratories—undoubtedly can strain community relationships, both between and among students and educators. Specific strategies for the middle level school include cooperative learning, social skills training, and group interaction processes for students. Educators can use their interdisciplinary teams as a mechanism to understand others' perspectives as well as to decide on appropriate goals and objectives and strategies for reaching agreed-upon directions. In team meetings or in community-building activities, educators can determine problems to be addressed, decide on obstacles and hindrances, and reach a consensus on constructive action to address bickering and disagreements.

During team planning time, one team of teachers sought to improve the allocation of duties. In essence, too many team duties and responsibilities had shifted to one person, who felt overwhelmed. The team discussed the situation and divided responsibilities in a more equitable fashion. Ironically, when the one teacher shared her feelings that she felt responsible for too many duties, others shared that they had felt somewhat left out of the process by not having significant roles. They felt the one teacher considered them incapable of successfully conducting the tasks. These teachers used their interdisciplinary team as a mechanism to solve a problem that could have weakened the community. Instead, the team's sense of community grew stronger.

Stage 4: Providing Outreach—How Can We Help Others?

As a community perfects its skills of working collectively, one of its celebrations to acknowledge its successes can be to provide services to other communities. Providing outreach helps others and rewards those who have succeeded. For example, the classrooms of successful teachers can serve as demonstration sites for others new to the district. Students can present one or more of their cooperative ventures such as a cooperative game, a radio show, an art project, or community service project. Such outreach activities strengthen class and school identity by providing unity experiences and the impetus for heightened cooperative efforts. During this outreach stage, communities must be sure that their own work continues; outreach should not occur at the expense of the community.

Middle level school educators can take several directions to provide outreach to others. First, working as peer counselors, young adolescents can work with students from other middle level schools that are in more preliminary stages of community building. Often students are more successful with students than are adults, especially in new ventures in which students might feel uncomfortable. Second, educators can provide inservice workshops and play consultative roles to assist other educators in their community-building activities. For example, a group of seventh grade educators who have implemented an effective interdisciplinary team can help struggling teams. Outreach can be extended even further as educators and students offer their expertise to professional associations and student groups, respectively. Such outreach can also include teachers working with civic groups; students from an effective community such as a cooperative learning team can offer their help to a science or drama club.

Facilitating Strategies

Several facilitating strategies that contribute to effective team building are (Canning, 1993):

- Setting ground rules such as strongly encouraging full attendance at all meetings, confidentiality, right to pass when a member does not want to voice an opinion, no discussions that are exclusionary or have the appearance of being exclusionary, and no deprecating jokes
- Frequent reiteration of the community's goals and purposes
- Meetings with opportunities for all members to speak to share information relevant to the group
- Use of various techniques to facilitate the articulation of members' feelings and to examine the community's interactions and process of development

Communities Reflecting the Middle School Concept

Effective communities in middle level schools reflect the concepts and philosophical beliefs espoused in *This We Believe* (National Middle School Association, 1995), such as a comprehensive guidance and counseling program (i.e., advisor-advisee programs); opportunities for exploration (e.g., community mentor programs); positive school environments; interdisciplinary teaming; cooperative planning among educators and young adolescents; and range of organizational arrangements that promote a sense of community, such as heterogeneous grouping, cooperative learning, peer tutoring, and peer mentoring. In many aspects the middle school philosophy and a sense of community are synonymous—both represent student-centered orientations, both attempt to "bring out" the best in all people, and both strive for mutual benefit and the pursuit of common goals and mutual obligation.

Community can be reflected in advisor-advisee and exploratory programs in several ways. Possible topics to reflect upon include: people feeling a part of a caring culture; advisor-advisee sessions and exploratory programs modeling effective communities; and issues such as how people can improve, the building of close interpersonal relationships, people's roles in a democratic society, basic human needs to be a part of a group, the dangers of alienation, the importance of trust and respect, and the creating of new and dynamic relationships. Middle level educators can assess individual young adolescents, school strengths and weaknesses, and progress of communities to determine appropriate topics to be addressed. The important aspect is to consider how the advisory and exploratory program can be vital parts of the community (and vice versa).

Also, middle school curriculum, organizational practices, and behavior policies should reflect an appreciation of community and its contributions. Educators cannot teach and promote the concept of community yet continue to plan in isolation, ignore young adolescents' needs, and practice exclusivity. For example, the curriculum needs to reflect the benefits of shared concerns and working together (such as contributions of groups), organizational strategies that emphasize group approaches such as cooperative learning and peer helpers, and school policies such as young adolescents having a voice in school rules. Traditional school practices such as teaching competition and individualism at the expense of collaboration, homogeneous grouping practices promoting exclusivity, and school policies solely written from educators' perspectives will not promote caring cultures.

Dilemmas and Challenges Often Associated with Building a Sense of Community

To this point, only the positives of building a sense of community have been discussed. Perceptive readers surely have asked, "Is community building this easy?" "Are there difficulties?" or "What obstacles face community building?" The answer to these questions is "Yes, community builders face challenges." However, the nature of genuine communities is such that dilemmas and challenges can be addressed. Table 7.2 examines several dilemmas and possible solutions.

Other dilemmas undoubtedly exist, depending on the individual schools and community members. Educators building communities need to assess their own situations to determine dilemmas and then use resources and expertise to address the dilemmas. The key to overcoming or at least addressing the dilemmas and challenges is the commitment to make communities a reality.

Middle Level Communities of the Future: Prospects and Possibilities

Three indicators suggest middle level communities have a bright future, limited only by the commitment and dedication of the community builders. First, the middle school concept (actually closely akin to the concept of caring cultures) continues to be refined and respected. Second, the concept of "community" and of "a sense of community" are being better understood, both the values as well as the implementation process. Third, the 1990s have seen a wealth of information on cooperation, collaboration, and the values of working collegially.

What communities might middle level schools have? Again, the extent to which middle level educators build communities depends upon their dedication and commitment to the process. However, several distinct possibilities exist. Indications suggest there might be genuine commitments to community and to the community-building process. These communities can reflect the middle level

TABLE 7.2 Dilemma and Possible Solutions

Dilemma	Possible Solution
Equating community and individual freedom	Convince others of the values accrued from a sense of community
Conflict with traditional values such as achievement resulting from competition	Convince others a community can be more productive in terms of achievement and relationships
Becoming exclusionary	Preventing cliques by building firm identities within communities
Dealing with turnover among community people	Making new teachers and students feel welcome to the community, offering meaningful roles, and ensuring new members feel accepted
Considering community a diversion from school purpose or assuming community feelings develop automatically	Explain similarities among schools and communities and how school conditions improve

Sources: Scoble (1987), Westheimer & Kahne (1993), Graves (1992).

school concept (and vice versa) and can demonstrate genuine respect for cultural, ethnic, social class, gender, and handicapping conditions.

Summary

Throughout history, people have had a notion of what communities mean, the importance of people feeling commitment to others, and how people can accomplish more collaboratively than when working in isolation. Definitions of "community" and "building a sense of community" have been hazy and nebulous, but increasingly educators are developing a clearer notion of what communities mean and how communities are developed. Middle level educators know definitions, defining characteristics, assumptions, principles, and challenges. The growing body of writing on communities and community building, increased knowledge of and commitment to the middle level school concept, and the recent interest in and emphasis on collaboration and collaborative efforts suggest a bright and unlimited future for building caring cultures. As with all school efforts, the actual success of communities will depend upon young adolescents' and middle level educators' determination to make communities a reality.

Discussion Questions

1. In the transformation from individuals to communities certain elements must be present. What is it that prompts educators to set aside their own personal

needs on a regular basis to work toward common goals for some greater good? Are all educators capable of this self-sacrifice?

2. Often middle school communities provide caring and nurturing that some young adolescents do not receive at home. To what extent do you think middle school communities are able to make a substantive difference in the lives of young people whose family experiences are less than desirable?

3. Communities promote a feeling of responsibility for caring for other members of the group. Do you believe communities may also promote a feeling of responsibility for learning?

References

Barth, R. (1990). *Improving schools from within*. San Francisco: Jossey-Bass.

Canning, C. (1993). Preparing for diversity: A social technology for multicultural community building. *The Educational Forum, 57,* 371–385.

Carnegie Council on Adolescent Development (1989). *Turning points: Preparing American youth for the 21st century*. Washington, DC: Author.

Gable, R. A., & Manning, M. L. (1996). Facing the challenge of aggressive behaviors in young adolescents. *Middle School Journal, 27*(3), 19–25.

Graves, L. N. (1992). Cooperative learning communities: Context for a new vision of education and society. *Journal of Education, 174,* 57–79.

Manning, M. L. (1993). *Developmentally appropriate middle level schools*. Wheaton, MD: Association for Childhood Education International.

Manning, M. L. (1995). Addressing young adolescents' cognitive development. *The High School Journal, 78*(2), 98–104.

National Middle School Association (1995). *This we believe*. Columbus, OH: Author.

Sautter, R. C. (1995). Standing up to violence. *Phi Delta Kappan, 76,* K1–K12.

Scoble, F. (1987). On community. *Independent School, 47*(1), 5–7.

Scoble, F. (1988). School as community. *Independent School, 48*(1), 35–39.

Sergiovanni, T. J. (1994a). *Building community in schools*. San Francisco: Jossey-Bass.

Sergiovanni, T. J. (1994b). Organizations or communities? Changing the metaphor changes the theory. *Educational Administration Quarterly, 30*(2), 214–226.

U.S. Bureau of the Census (1992). *Statistical abstracts of the United States: 1992* (112th ed.). Washington, DC: Government Printing Office.

U.S. Bureau of the Census (1993, September). *We the American . . . foreign born*. Washington, DC: Government Printing Office.

Westheimer, J., & Kahne, J. (1993). Building school communities: An experienced-based model. *Phi Delta Kappan, 75*(4), 324–328.

Chapter 8

Developing Teams: Good News for Teachers

DAVID KOMMER

Dave Kommer has been involved with middle level restructuring in California and Ohio. His experience includes development of interdisciplinary teams at two middle schools in Southern California, and he is currently consulting with middle schools in Ohio. His research interests focus on middle grades issues with work on school uniforms, networking between middle schools, and multi-age teaming. He currently teaches at Ashland University in Ashland, Ohio.

There you are, sitting through another boring faculty meeting, when your building principal mentions that your school will begin implementing some middle school changes. Just what you needed, right? You are already up to your eyeballs in work, and this sounds as if it will be another load of straw piled on the camel. He begins to talk about how the students will be organized into interdisciplinary teams in all of their core classes. The teams will consist of four teachers—mathematics, science, language arts, and history—who will share a group of about 120 students.

Through the panic you start asking yourself questions. You wonder how the schedule you have earned after so many years in the building will be affected. You wonder which of your colleagues scattered about the teacher workroom today will be your teammates, and you mentally note those you couldn't possibly work with. When will you find time to meet with your teammates? "There are already too many meetings," you say to yourself.

After these initial questions surface with no immediate answers, you begin to add to the list. What exactly is a team, anyway? How will you know if what you are doing is right? About this time you are overcome with anxiety, and the rest of the meeting is a blur.

As an administrator in two schools that were transformed through the development of teams, I have seen enormous changes result. Leading teams of professionals through the process was both rewarding and challenging, as the previous scenario might suggest. The good news is that teachers become more effective and professionally charged through teaming, but the journey is not an easy one.

Nothing is more central to restructuring middle schools than interdisciplinary teams (Erb & Doda, 1989). They are the soul of any school that begins to structure the secondary setting according to the developmental needs of adolescents. However, the reorganization into teams has an enormous effect on teachers as well as students. Even teachers who see the obvious benefits to students can resist the changes teaming might make in their teaching. After all, they have spent years perfecting their craft, and becoming a team member will certainly alter their normal role.

So what is the benefit to teachers as they move into interdisciplinary teams? How should the team formation process begin? How can they best prepare themselves for this new role? What can they expect each year as they develop effective teams?

Getting Teams Started

There are some critical issues that need to be addressed before teaming will succeed. Teaming is a difficult enterprise. Learning a new way to function will be difficult for the staff. There will even be times when things will go so badly that they may wish for the good old days. When old, comfortable methods are abandoned for new ones, however, everyone needs to remember that for a while they are working in an area unfamiliar to them. It may easily bring a staff to exhaustion within a year if care is not taken.

Planning time is the first critical issue. Teams must have separate team planning time (Stevenson, 1992). The more time a team has to meet and work collaboratively, the more effective the team can become. A master program must be developed that gives teachers a team planning period in addition to the normal personal planning periods. Many schools move into teaming by simply giving team teachers the same conference period. That is a formula, if not for failure, certainly for very limited success.

When I was principal of a small school with little program flexibility, the district allowed us to build in planning time by "banking minutes." We extended student instructional time by 20 minutes 3 days a week and shortened 2 days by 30 minutes. The teacher contract day was not disturbed. It would have been preferable to have team time on a daily basis, but this was the best we could do. Suggesting a program like this will determine if buses run your schools or if instruction does. We had wonderful support from both transportation and food services, who were also affected by our novel schedule.

A great deal of effort is required to find ways to build in this collaborative time in the face of shrinking resources. It is unlikely that districts will readily support the additional staff members needed to create a team planning period. Too many schools expect teachers to support the team concept by working beyond their contractual day. Even if this time is compensated, it is unfair to teachers (Raywid, 1993). Besides the time banking mentioned here, another suggestion for finding team time is to schedule larger groups of students in some classes to release team teachers. Some schools have moved to a service learning component that may also free up teachers for planning time. Still another way is to have mini-courses taught during the first few hours of each Friday, using all adults on the campus to teach some hobby or interest to groups of students. Because all adults will be involved, a rotational planning period could be arranged for team teachers (Raywid, 1993). The point is that schools must creatively find ways to "make time" for collaborative planning.

The luckiest middle schools will receive the support needed from their central office to give teachers both personal and team planning time every day. As a budget item this is difficult for many districts. As a bargaining unit issue it is also difficult, as elementary and high school teachers may not see why the middle school staff is given both periods. As any team teacher can attest, the extra time is not free time for longer breaks in the lounge. The time provided for teachers will make a huge impact on the effectiveness of the middle school program. Much public relations work is needed to convince boards, superintendents, and union leaders that this time will benefit the middle school students.

Team Formation

How the teams are formed is a critical issue that far too often is overlooked. The reason it is overlooked is usually because factors such as the size of the school, the certification of the teachers, and the history of special programs at the school will often decide who will be teamed with whom. Whether a school has the luxury of forming teams from a willing pool of teachers or is forced to put teachers together, several things must be kept in mind.

Looking first at the best of all worlds, how will you sort out a large staff into effective teams? Let me suggest some approaches. One way to shake a staff into teams is to simply have them sign up for a slot on a team. Suppose a large chart is posted in the teachers' lounge with the teams listed and lines drawn below in each of the subject areas. Teachers simply sign up for a team.

Typically much discussion will be carried on before anyone signs up. Teachers will begin to organize themselves with their friends. This may work, but potential dangers lurk. Teacher friends may have developed that particular bond for the reasons that may hinder the development of an effective team. Friendship is usually based upon commonalities—likes, dislikes, methods of approaching issues, temperament, and so on. Strong teams must have a degree of diversity in order to function well. Also, an administrator must be aware that there is some diversity of teacher ability level. It is not wise to get all of the school stars on one team; talent needs to be spread around. In fact, this is one of the real benefits of teams, as strong teachers are able to encourage and support less able or new teachers (Barth, 1990).

As a middle school administrator, I used a system called a sociogram to form teams. With a sociogram, teachers rank the teachers in other departments according to those with whom they would like to work, those with whom they can work, and those with whom they cannot work (Fogarty & Stoehr, 1995). Once an administrator has this data (which must be absolutely confidential), he or she can avoid teaming teachers with colleagues with whom they are uncomfortable. Of special concern would be the teacher who might not be chosen by any teachers. Administrators must preserve the dignity of all in finding a team that can bring out the best in all the team members.

Smaller schools, of course, do not have the luxury of such choice. Often, once teachers have selected their preferred grade level, their subject area will dictate team composition. While this sounds as if it may lead to disaster, the lack of choice often makes it successful. All teachers want to do a good job, and they are used to doing it under less than optimal conditions. Once placed in a team and given proper training and support, they will try to make it work.

Small schools can also effectively team if they break the core subject paradigm. Teams in the same school can have different subject configurations. One team may have the four core academic areas, but another team may have a math-science teacher teamed with a social studies and a language arts teacher. It is also possible to have one of the traditional core subjects outside of the team and substitute a physical educator, art, music, or another elective teacher.

Whereas creative teaming may prove successful, sharing teachers between teams is a recipe for failure. The shared teacher seldom feels like a part of either team. Loyalties are divided and very little bonding results. Students also feel that the shared teacher is "not one of them." If the master schedule appears to require a teacher or two shared between teams, the schedule should be revisited with a look into a more nontraditional team such as just described. Be sure that each team teacher shares the same students, and that no student is allowed to float in and out of the team. All team students must be completely a part of their team. Whether or not teachers have a choice as they become teams, there must be great attention paid to preparation before they can function as a team.

Team Building

Teaming is a whole new task for teachers. It is not simply the sum of four or so teachers; it is a new entity. Teaming requires learning new ways and, perhaps, even unlearning some old patterns of behavior. Training is a key element that cannot be overdone. This training should address issues beyond interdisciplinary teaching and team structures. The "people part" of teaming, the ability to work together, should be stressed as an avenue to efficient and effective team building (Merenbloom, 1991).

Whether a great deal of time is spent carefully selecting teams or whether school size, program, or credential patterns determine the selection, a considerable amount of time and effort should be spent on the team-building process. Starting teams out on the right foot requires following several essential steps.

Can you get your staff to a retreat setting during the summer prior to teaming? This is a great way to start, away from classrooms, parents, and phones, although pulling it off is difficult. Marshaling resources and getting a summer commitment from teachers may make the retreat a challenge, but give it a try.

No off-site retreat? Other initial team-building functions might occur at weekend get-togethers at various staff homes or evening work-ins complete with catered meals. Getting together in a relaxed collegial setting in whatever way is possible, is essential. A neutral site with a professional setting is a requirement. Often local banks or other businesses have such rooms that schools can use. At any rate, do not simply arrange teachers into teams and expect them to function. Try as they might, the teachers will run into many problems, and without a process to resolve them, they will return to old departmental patterns.

The agenda for the initial meetings should cover a range of activities, both fun and introspective, that will help teachers learn more about themselves and their teammates. Some suggestions would include personality inventories, learning style preference activities, or left-right brain preference inventories that might encourage open discussion about personality differences. Consult with the district psychologist or staff developer for suggestions for these inventories. Even typical icebreaker games are important for setting the mood. All of these activities will allow teachers to talk about their philosophy of teaching. Additionally, they will be able to talk about their own working preferences—are they neat or sloppy, planners or last-minute people, detail-oriented or big-picture folks? Remember, try to compose teams with a good mix of types. A team of detail fanatics might not have the creativity of dreamers, while a team of dreamers will have great ideas but no follow-through.

By identifying individual strengths and personality idiosyncrasies, the teachers can begin to place themselves and their teammates into meaningful categories. Greater understanding will foster greater team cohesiveness, and roles and responsibilities will begin to emerge from these sessions. It is time well spent. Keep in mind, too, that team building is also a process, not an event. After the retreat the staff will need to revisit these lessons from time to time.

Many teachers begin a whole new approach to their careers as a result of this staff building. Teachers who were comfortable in their isolated classroom worlds, who may have been hesitant to peek out beyond familiar walls, afterward never want to return.

Examples of this abound, but I am reminded of a teacher who came to my school from the elementary level. As we began to talk about middle school transformation and teaming, this teacher began to think about returning to the elementary school. Statements such as "I can just finish out my career with a class of thirty sixth graders" seemed to indicate that I wasn't going to get much out of this teacher. However, when the next year began, the teacher was still on my staff, having decided to give these newfangled ideas a try. After the first year a convert had been made. The remaining years of this teacher's career will be a more enriched experience because of the close working relationship developed with the team members. I believe nothing else could have motivated this teacher to undertake such growth experiences so late in a career.

Middle schools are definitely about connecting. The literature is rich with references to students connecting to each other, to curriculum, to teachers, to the school, and to themselves. But teachers have a chance to connect as well. This connection is one of the most professional and positive outcomes of the change to middle school (CCAD, 1989).

Effective Teaming through the Years

The First Year

What can teachers expect in the first year of interdisciplinary teaming? Well, first of all, lots of work and little self-satisfaction. Harsh, I suppose, but things will look up. First-year teams are burdened with the bulk of the organizational work, which is tedious and time-consuming. At times it will seem that no progress is being made. Teams try one system, evaluate it, abandon it, and try another over and over until they find the best one for their collective personalities and styles.

What should administrators expect the first year? Typically teams develop a working vision, develop common practices and procedures, and create a team discipline program. In short, they learn to work together. Nothing else should be required. Both teachers and administrators must realize that the entire school will be involved in a process they have never tried and know little about. In any endeavor, including sports, writing, and hobbies, the first step in the process yields many failures and small victories—teaming is no different.

Teams will travel through several phases on their way to becoming effective (George, 1982). All teams will go through four phases: (1) organizational concerns, (2) community issues, (3) instruction, and (4) governance. There will be some crossover between the phases, especially the third and fourth, but they are distinct levels through which every effective team passes. It will take time to get through all the stages. In fact, Stevenson (1992) asserts that the process will take 3 to 5 years. Professional educators hear that but do not really believe it. Let me reiterate it: Becoming an effective team will take 3 to 5 years of consistent work.

The first phase is the organizational stage. During this stage, teachers are learning to work with one another and to handle disagreements. During the initial team-building sessions, team teachers should create a vision that is shared by all members. Teachers must decide what the team is all about. A significant amount of time should be spent on setting goals (Stevenson, 1992). Once developed, the team goals should be shared and announced with everyone—students, parents, other teams, and administration. Some teams print the vision and post it in the team rooms. Others create banners that hang in hallways by team rooms. The vision should not be created and filed away; it should be shared and lived.

Common procedures need to be developed. These include such items as how to accept late homework, what the tardy policy will be, how papers will be headed, and the dozen or so other things that teachers had taken so much for granted prior to forming teams. While these may seem innocuous, many an argument has erupted even at this stage. I had more than one team that worked to establish these rules through some rancorous discussions. Finally, after what appeared to be agreement, one of the team members decided not to follow the procedure. This cannot occur, and it points out the type of working relationships that must develop. Rest assured that these problems can be resolved, and usually teams are stronger for working through them. This is also useful practice for later on when more intense decisions need to be made.

A big task in organizing teams is developing a common discipline program with identical consequences. The good news is that teaming will make classroom management more effective and efficient for all teachers (Erb & Doda, 1989). One of the problems middle schoolers face after they leave the elementary school is that their teachers seem to have slightly different rules and procedures. A consistent discipline plan will eliminate the need for students to constantly remember specific rules for every teacher. The rules are the same as they move throughout the day. They are clearly stated and posted in each room and reinforced in exactly the same way by each team teacher. A word of warning here. As the teams begin to discuss these common rules, teachers must commit to standing by them. This is no small matter. Too often I have seen teachers agree to the rules during the planning meetings but refuse to enforce them later or create new ones when the students arrive. This will confuse the students and undermine the efforts of the team.

Student and parent conferences take on a whole new element with teams (George, 1991). The one-on-one conferences of the past often put teachers in a defensive mode. Students were convinced that the teacher just didn't like them or, worse, was out to get them. Even parents might adopt this attitude. Picture, instead, the team conference. Four teachers discuss the student in a rational and comprehensive way. They do not "gang up" on the student, however. The team structure takes the teacher's personality out of the situation. The task at hand of finding a plan of action to lead the student to greater success proceeds efficiently.

For parents, teaming is also a great benefit. Trying to keep up with their child's progress with seven teachers is a difficult and daunting task. However, contacting one of the team teachers will allow the parent to check progress in all of the team classes. Because of the ease in dealing with teams, parent contact at the middle school usually increases. This increase is just one of the happy side effects of teaming and middle level restructuring. Teams can also capitalize on this parent involvement by getting them to assist with student projects, field trips, and other activities.

Establishing a team identity is another task for beginning teams. A team name is essential. This can be a fun task for team teachers as they find a name that will embody their vision. Naming teams should not be left up to the students. There are several reasons for this. First, when students arrive at school, they join an established identity. They instantly begin to feel a part of something. If the team is nameless, students have to create the identity, and that takes time. Second, students might want to become a little more creative than teachers or administrators want. I remember a team that insisted on letting the students name their team, and the students voted on a theme taken from a current rap song. The voting process itself left some students feeling that they had "lost" in the selection process, and they only slowly accepted the name. The name that was chosen also became a challenge to other students, and several fights occurred between members of the different teams.

In addition to a team name, many teams expand the theme with logos, mottos, team colors, cheers, and handshakes. Team shirts are another idea that gives character and identity to teams. Providing incentives for students to wear their shirts will help to quickly establish a sense of identity among students. Some incentives might include a team shirt day or providing a homework pass or other prize for students who wear shirts on scheduled days. Of course, teachers must wear the shirts, too.

Team colors can also be an important part of their identity. In one school we had the door frames of all the rooms for each team painted with the team colors. It was great way to establish territory as well as identity. Of course, I think it goes without saying that team colors must stay away from local gang colors.

Related to the issue of team identity is the need to build in celebrations for team members. In all aspects of our society, celebrations and rituals are important. Teams are no different. Celebrations can be wonderful opportunities to build student self-esteem and confidence. Ranging beyond the normal recognition for honor students, awards can be given for grade improvement, homework completion, helpfulness, cheerfulness, and so on. There is no limit to the creativity that can be developed. Team celebrations also become the basis for traditions that will establish the team's identity for years to come.

The team identity issue, while essential to effective teams, must be monitored closely. Without vigilance, team identity can erode into school-sanctioned gangs. Teachers must be on guard against this aberration of teaming. In one middle school where I served as the team coordinator, we had one team with all of their classes in a hallway together. By about January, any student from another team who had the nerve to enter this hallway did so at some peril. Needless to say, we had to step in to counsel students about these attitudes.

It is preferable to head off these problems before they arise. Students need to be taught that their team is unique, but not superior to other teams. Social and noncompetitive activities between teams are also effective ways to build a sense of pride in one's team in conjunction with an appreciation for other teams.

I have also seen team teachers who developed an attitude of superiority. This, too, is destructive to the whole premise of teaming. Teachers jealously guarding their good ideas so other teams will not try them is one indicator of this attitude. In fact, one of the pitfalls of teaming is that while it breaks down traditional isolation, it may also break down faculty cohesiveness as bonding occurs between teammates. School administrators need to be sensitive to this and provide opportunities for school staffs to meet together, have fun together, and maintain a sense of connection to the entire school.

Problems between teammates are also likely to occur during this crucial first year, especially if teams were formed as a schedule expedient, with little teacher input into team formation. During my first year as an administrator in charge of teams, there was a particularly difficult situation in which one teacher simply could not agree with three others who wanted to prescribe more student-friendly rules than she did. Initially they seemed to agree, but students began to complain that they could not use special passes in all classes. The team met and tried to resolve the problem, but they arrived at an impasse. They tried to ignore the problem and work around it, but it left a growing disaffection between them.

About 3 months into the school year the teachers came repeatedly into my office complaining about each other. The three felt that the other was not living up to prior agreements; the lone teacher felt that the three were against her. It created so much stress for her that she was often in tears relating how the situation was adversely affecting her home life and her relationship with her husband. It was a serious situation and an example of the worst possible scenario.

I wish that I had some magic wisdom for those attempting to team when things get this bad. Unfortunately, I have none. I met with the team and tried to facilitate the process to reach an acceptable compromise. Nothing worked. Finally, the solution was to move the disheartened teacher to another team whose teachers had a philosophy closer to hers.

Once again, this story is used to illustrate the worst possible scenario involved in creating effective teams. Not all teams will become this dysfunctional. For teams that seem to have no problems like this, I advise that discussions about priorities and practices are necessary. The functional team is not one that has no problems; it is the one that learns how to deal with them. The first year is the best time to test the systems set up to deal with issues.

It may be necessary at the end of the first year to replace team members. This provides an opportunity for the teams to feel empowered to control their own destiny. The process to replace the team member must include the remaining members. My early experiences as an administrator were quite eye-opening. One team, after interviewing a prospective candidate, was reluctant to decide on a replacement. They seemed to prefer that the administrator stay in control of hiring. Another team, after interviewing several candidates, asked me to leave the room as they debated about the candidate they wanted. In both cases, it was important that the teams be in complete control of hiring their teammate.

The Second Year

The second year will get better, as things begin to fall into place. Organizational systems that did not work last year should be modified or abandoned. During year two, teams should move to George's second phase, which he describes as "community." By this time, teachers should feel that they are team teachers first and subject teachers second.

During the community phase, teams begin to form themselves, students, and parents into a more cohesive group. The vision and purpose described in those early heady days will begin to take shape during this year. It is a much better time for the professionals who put in so much time and effort the first year.

The identity of the team begins to soar during this year. Because teachers are more comfortable with the concept and have some valuable experience with it, students are able to easily identify with the team and take more pride in being part of it. There is less of a sense that we are all finding our way with nobody really knowing what to do. By this time the team logo has a history; the cheers and rituals are part of a developing tradition. This is sensed by the students.

This is not to say that teams are fully functioning by any means. There is a long way to go, but the worst is definitely over. The second year is a time to experiment with flexible schedules and regrouping of students for more effective instruction. It is a time to develop relationships with resource personnel. This year will involve more team activities or field trips, some instructional, others team-building activities. Team meetings will be refined this year. This is a good time to start using early meetings to become as familiar as possible with the students. Developing a working relationship with teachers outside the team will take on greater importance this year. There might even be attempts at interdisciplinary instruction.

By this time the team should be comfortable with trying alternate schedules. In fact, many teams try some scheduling changes during the first year, although I have never seen a team that used them consistently that year. Making arrangements to show an instructional film for the entire team during part of the block time is relatively easy. This process might gather the team students in the auditorium or multipurpose room during their first team period to view a 90-minute film. During the remaining two periods of the team schedule, the classes are cut to half of their normal length so that four classes can meet in the time reserved for two. One of the real advantages to teaming is the ability to make these accommodations to the instructional program. The days of taking 3 days to view a film 30 minutes at a time will be gone. It can now be shown to every student at one sitting.

Another effective scheduling technique the teams can arrange is the single testing period. If the math teacher, for example, wants to give a test to all of the team students, the teachers might agree to all give the test during the first team period to all students. By regrouping students a little, it is also possible to free up the math teacher to float from room to room to serve as a resource and answer student questions. Gone will be the days of taking an entire day to test, while wondering about test validity as the student grapevine spreads the test information throughout the day.

More complicated scheduling may also be tried during year two. Grouping and regrouping students for instruction may take place. This is a way to effectively teach gifted students, who should be heterogeneously mixed into the teams.

However, there are times when these students might be pulled out for a special activity working with one teacher. The remaining students will be divided among the other teachers and given a different special task or project.

That type of regrouping is a way to deal with not only gifted students, but also inclusion students; students falling below minimum standards; and students working on special projects, such as science fair or history day projects. The only requirement is the commitment on the part of the team teachers that while one teacher works with the small group, the others are willing to take the larger group and create a special activity for them.

Another aspect to scheduling that begins to develop in this year is the placement of students into classes. Traditionally middle grades teachers had students assigned to their classes, and only an administrative action could transfer a student into another class. Teaming allows teachers to have full control over how students are scheduled into team classes. I have seen teachers after the first 2 to 3 weeks seated around a huge table using index cards or small bits of paper to redistribute students into classes to improve their instructional chances. This is an extremely effective technique.

I have also seen teams that regroup their entire classes each quarter just to keep it interesting and give students the chance to mix with other students in the team. Once teachers are empowered to control their student assignments, they enjoy the new flexibility.

Another example of using the block schedule to team advantage involves rotating classes through the day. Secondary teachers often complain that students at certain parts of the day are harder to teach. Sometimes during the first period of the day, students are still tired and sluggish. Lethargy sets in after lunch, and by the end of the day they become hyperactive. The team block allows teachers to adjust—for instance, meeting first period early the first day of the week and later each remaining day. All of the other periods also rotate through this schedule. As a result, teachers get to see students at their best at least some of the time.

Team meetings will become more effective the second year. The first year was a time to experiment with all of the meeting issues. Deciding leadership issues might take some time. Will one teacher remain team leader, or will the job be rotated? What will agendas look like? Many agenda formats will be tried. Keeping on task will become a concern. Rambling may characterize early team meetings, but soon team members will want to find a way to get the work done more efficiently.

Most importantly, teammates must find a way to resolve conflicts. The first year will likely progress on a great deal of good will, and conflicts will be hidden. While there certainly will be issues, some team members will not bring them up, not wanting to make any waves. By year two, however, conflict avoidance needs to be minimized. In order to do so, team members need to find ways to disagree without making personal attacks. I worked with a team that refused to plan any activities because one team member was uncooperative, and none of the others was willing to bring up the issue and deal with it. When teams are in the community stage, they must overcome these problems.

This second year is also a time to develop a more reliable working relationship with resource personnel, such as administrators, special education teachers, psychologists, and outside child service agencies. New teams will feel as if they are inundated with student problems. I believe the reason for this is that students no longer fall as easily through the cracks in a team structure. In the traditional model, teachers often overlook the deep-seated difficulties students experience until much later in the year. By the time resources begin to be employed, the school year is running down.

In a team arrangement, teachers identify student problems early. They begin to marshal their own resources immediately with student consequences, conferences, and contracts; parent conferences; special educator assistance; and counselor or administrator conferences. If these fail to work, then more resources need to be provided. In our case, we were unprepared for this new reality, and the first year was not productive. We began to plan for this during our second year and brought outside agencies into the loop to support children.

Working with these agencies is a new role for most teachers. It can be both a rewarding and a frustrating experience. Agencies such as child services are usually very willing to meet with teachers in support of students. Social workers often have information about the child's background that can be helpful for the teachers in dealing with the student on a daily basis. However, these agencies, with large caseloads and few resources of their own, often cannot do much to help monitor a child's behavior and success. Nevertheless, it is in the best interest of the student and the team to continue to develop these relationships and find new ways to reach students and help them achieve.

The Third Year

According to George, after developing a sense of community, the team enters into a third phase that places a priority on interdisciplinary instruction. The third year is also the time that teams should take on a greater role in school governance, George's (1982) stage four. By now the mechanics of teaming are second nature. While there is always going to be refinement, teams are comfortable in the organizational issues, and an established team community exists. Procedures should be working smoothly, celebrations and rituals are becoming traditions, and working relationships with other adults in support of students are underway.

The exciting part of this stage of development is the opportunity for teachers to grow professionally. Teaming is in reality a form of peer coaching. While teachers do not necessarily come together for the purpose of improving their own instructional delivery, that is exactly what happens.

Peer coaching has always depended on teachers spending time discussing curricular and instructional issues. The problem was that teachers did not have the time to do it; therefore, widespread acceptance of peer coaching did not occur in traditional schools. Unlike traditional staffing structures, teams have the time to carry on these discussions.

The strength of peer coaching rests not in the advice teachers may give to one another. The strength lies in the sharing that occurs as they plan together, share materials, and watch one another deal with students (Showers & Joyce, 1996). That is an inherent quality of teaming.

While teams might have experimented with interdisciplinary instruction in the first 2 years, they had other, more pressing tasks to master. By this time, however, this practice needs to be implemented. Teaming is only a structural beginning. The ultimate goal is to combine the talents of teachers and students through effective instruction. Teaming stems from the notion of meeting student needs, so instruction must also focus on those needs. Fogarty and Stoehr have listed ten ways to integrate curricula (1995). I have taken several as examples.

Using "Skill of the Week" activities is a good way to test the waters. All teachers are concerned with the level of basic skills students have. Following directions, locating information, setting up a notebook, writing complete sentences, reading for details, reading for the main idea, listening for main ideas, sequencing, taking notes, drawing conclusions, predicting outcomes, distinguishing between fact and fiction, outlining, comparing, and speaking are skills all teachers can emphasize in their classes. By coordinating these skills so they are taught in all team classes during a single week, teachers give students a significant dose of each.

Another relatively easy way to begin interdisciplinary instruction is through parallel or shared teaching. In this arrangement, teachers list their units for the entire year. By comparing the lists, teachers can see that they may be teaching similar or related units, but at different times of the year. A simple rearrangement can bring these units within the same time frame. Teachers can again support each other, with each responsible for some parts of the curriculum. They can also reinforce the same concepts for students. One of the benefits of this approach is that instruction can be made more streamlined as less becomes more in each subject area classroom.

Using themes is another way to integrate the team curricula. Teachers can web each subject around a broad theme. Technology, family, diversity, folk tales, oceans, and space travel are examples of themes that might apply to all subject areas. The list of possible themes is endless. By generating a significant question around the theme, the unit can be enriched for the learners. An example might be "Is diversity a source of strength for the United States?" The social science teacher can provide lessons on immigration and the contributions immigrants have made to our social fabric. The language arts teacher can cover one of a myriad of books written by or about immigrants. The science teacher can show how immigrants and minorities have expanded our scientific knowledge. The math teacher can teach concepts such as graphing, charting, percentages, and population trends in comparing the rates of immigration throughout American history.

Building curriculum in an integrated way is another new role for teachers. Although some teachers may lack skills in curriculum development, preferring to let experts do it, integrated teaching opens up new dimensions for teachers. The strengths and subject area expertise each teacher brings to the team can be used in new and challenging ways.

For teaming to be successful, teams must be empowered to create their own destiny. If teams feel that they cannot implement the plans they make for lack of authority, they will soon lose momentum and cease working. Teams give visionary administrators the structure and ability to move to greater site-based decision making.

Team teachers have become more aware of the complex nature of school management through their team activities. The task of organizing a field trip will make teachers more sensitive to issues such as budget, transportation, food services, parent involvement, communication, and supervision. Team teachers learn more about school management than they thought they ever wanted to know.

Many schools organize their leadership councils with representatives from individual teams. Having one member from each team, unified arts, physical education, and administration brings a cross-pollenization that improves decision making. While representing their individual constituencies, all the teachers add to more thoughtful decisions on important issues. Collegial decisions made by empowered teachers tend to be better decisions, and implementation of these decisions is also more effective (Barth, 1990).

Areas of governance that are done well through teams include master scheduling and budgeting. By the time teams are functioning smoothly, student programming should become a team responsibility. Team input should be a key element in placing students into teams for the upcoming years. Because teams have complete control over their students for the team periods, they should be empowered to schedule students for the best interest of the student and the team. For example, teams soon learn the strength of being able to separate students who together act as behavioral catalysts. Such room changes no longer need to come from the main office.

School budgets are traditionally closely guarded by school principals. After all, the principal is ultimately responsible for financial allocations. However, if teams are given a per student allotment for team purposes, teachers become experts in the budgeting process as well. Giving teams a budget also will increase their ability to plan activities that improve instruction and build a sense of community.

The knowledge learned by team teachers is a valuable resource for any administrator who is wise enough to tap it. When this resource is utilized, not only are decisions likely to be better, but staff morale will also improve (George, 1982).

The Developmental Process

Teaming is critical to successful middle schools. All teams will go through a developmental process, and the teachers themselves and their administrators must be aware of the nature of this growth. Expectations beyond what is possible by either will lead to frustration and burnout. While all teams will go through phases of development, they will do so at different speeds. Some teams will begin to try integrated instruction early on, while others will wait until other matters are settled.

While this chapter speaks to yearly development, it should not be considered a complete recipe for team development. Unlike kitchen recipes that call for a systematic addition of the ingredients, team ingredients may often be added at different times. What teachers and their administrators must be wary of is the "we can do it all" syndrome. Teachers and administrators must be patient with their progress.

Some Final Thoughts

For over 30 years, middle schools have used teaming as a keystone of restructuring. As an administrator and a university professor, I have seen teachers and schools renewed by the development of teams. The question that now needs to be answered is "Where do we go from here?" In my view, the next logical extension of interdisciplinary teams is the creation of multi-age teams.

Creating a "house" arrangement with students spanning several years is an effective way to accelerate team development. Imagine that your team has students from three grades—one-third from sixth grade, another third from seventh, and the last third from eighth. The eighth graders have been with you for 3 years, while the sixth graders are new to the team.

This arrangement helps in many ways. First, it creates a continuity for the student through the middle school years. As the literature stresses the need for students to be connected to school and known well by the adults on campus, the multi-age team concept seems to be an effective model (CCAD, 1989). Teachers would have students for their entire middle school tenure and be able to know the students' strengths, weaknesses, and moods.

This continuity also makes it possible for the senior students to serve in the role of mentor to the younger ones. New students coming into the team would be "shown the ropes" by older ones. The time it would take for students to learn the team rituals would be minimized. Traditions would be carried on more easily. A side benefit is that student mentors may enjoy the leadership opportunity.

This house team would allow teachers to group and regroup for a more developmental instructional program. At times it would be best to have students arranged chronologically, at other times in a cross-age grouping. Because the middle school's years are characterized by such wide developmental diversity among students, this type of team would allow teachers to narrow the spectrum among the grade levels represented.

School year beginnings and endings become much smoother in a multi-age team (George, 1991). Teachers need to invest less time in orienting students to team procedures, rules, and rituals, because as many as two-thirds of them have been in the team for 1 or 2 years. As suggested, the new students can benefit from the experience and direction of older students.

Any teaming situation seems to reduce discipline problems, but the multiage team makes discipline even less of a problem. Positive parent relationships are allowed to develop more fully over the years, and conferences take on a more productive function (George, 1991).

Of course, the multi-age team has curriculum consequences. Because teachers have the students for 2 or 3 years, and because students will be taught in a cross-age setting, the current curriculum must give way. In fact, one of the strongest reasons to institute such teams may be to shake the current curriculum model now present in middle schools. It is time for middle level educators to ask the question "What should be the middle school curriculum?" (Beane, 1990).

The multi-age team would demand that teachers have a multiyear curriculum. After a student enters the team, that year's curriculum would not repeat until the student has moved on to high school. Teachers would have the opportunity to write a curriculum more responsive to the developmental needs of the learners.

Teaming is the keystone of middle school restructuring. Teaming means new roles for teachers and administrators. Accepting new roles is a difficult process, but experience shows that teachers like the results. Comments from team teachers such as "I have never worked so hard or been so satisfied in my career" are common. When asked if they would like to revert to traditional ways of teaching, middle school teachers overwhelmingly respond negatively. Teachers like teaming.

Discussion Questions

1. If you were to become a member of a middle school team, what attributes would you bring to the team?
2. If you were to become a member of a middle school team, what would concern you about working with a group of fellow teachers?
3. List five benefits you believe are associated with teaming.

References

Barth, R. S. (1990). *Improving schools from within.* San Francisco: Jossey-Bass.

Beane, J. A. (1990). A middle school curriculum: From rhetoric to reality. Columbus, OH: National Middle School Association.

Carnegie Council on Adolescent Development (CCAD) (1989). *Turning points: Preparing American youth for the 21st century.* Washington, DC: Author.

Erb, T. O., & Doda, N. M. (1989). Team organi-zation: Promise—practices and possibilities. Washington, DC: National Education Association of the United States.

Fogarty, R., & Stoehr, J. (1995). *Integrating curricula with multiple intelligences: Teams, themes and threads.* Palatine, IL: IRI/Skylight.

George, P. S. (1982). Interdisciplinary team organizational phases. *Middle School Journal, 13*(3), 10–13.

George, P. S. (1991). Student development and

middle level school organization: A prolegomenon. *Midpoints Occasional Papers.* Columbus, OH: National Middle School Association.

Merenbloom, E. (1991). *The team process: A handbook for teachers.* Columbus, OH: National Middle School Association.

Raywid, M. A. (1993). Finding time for collaboration. *Educational Leadership, 51*(1), 30–34.

Showers, B., & Joyce, B. (1996). The evolution of peer coaching. *Educational Leadership, 54,* 12–16.

Stevenson, C. (1992). *Teaching ten to fourteen year olds.* New York: Longman.

Practices in the Middle Grades—Introduction

Previous sections of this book provide a philosophical and organizational foundation for effective school practice. The initial chapters, for example, discuss how adolescents develop emotionally, physically, and cognitively. In later chapters an overview of the importance of teaming and building a sense of community is provided so the reader will understand the importance of appropriate organizational structures. Administrative and organizational considerations are addressed to highlight the essential role administrators play in developing a sound middle school program. The stage is now set to examine how philosophical considerations and organizational patterns influence what teachers do in the classroom.

Section III illustrates how foundational considerations play out in classroom practice. The chapters are included for a variety of reasons. First, some topics are selected for their potential to bring together the total curriculum. Both the language arts and the visual arts, for example, can be catalysts for integrating a variety of subjects, as all disciplines use forms of communication to foster reflective thought. Social studies performs a similar function. Curriculum units that bring together a variety of subjects frequently develop around social studies themes. These themes enable teachers and students to work together in the teams suggested earlier in this book.

Technology is another vehicle for connecting a variety of subject areas. It would also be a serious omission to dismiss the value of technology to enhance instruction and to motivate student learning in all subjects. The technology chapter offers a teacher's view of how technology enriches the lives of teachers and students.

A second consideration for selecting chapters is the inclusion of areas traditionally omitted from the discussion of middle school programing. To this end, the chapter on gifted education discusses the particular needs of this select population. Every school in America has gifted students in its classrooms, but these students are frequently excluded from the discussion of middle school practice. In addition, the chapter gives insight into how to meet the intellectual and emotional needs of all adolescents.

The voice of the adolescent easily falls within the category of viewpoints normally excluded from middle school textbooks. In perhaps the most thought-provoking chapter, students describe *their* middle school experience. In many cases the statements support the views of the authorities in this book. At other times, in true adolescent fashion, they contradict these same authorities. Their comments provide an insightful view of middle school life. The ideas and subjects discussed in Section III have generalizations applicable to all areas of the curriculum. Concepts such as providing choices for students, allowing open exploration of ideas, or providing avenues for expression of diverse views are essential to success in any subject. Section III demonstrates that adherence to the foundational guidelines for middle school programs creates viable and exciting possibilities for students and teachers alike.

Chapter 9

Language Arts in the Middle Grades

CARL WALLEY

Carl Walley is an Associate Professor of Education at Ashland University, where he teaches courses in curriculum development and language arts. He has served in education as a teacher, principal, and curriculum consultant. His previous publications addressed integrating language arts and instituting democratic processes into the school curriculum.

In recent years many elementary school classrooms joined a quiet revolution in language arts instruction. Beginning on their first day of formal schooling, kindergarten children are reading, writing, and enjoying the pleasures of exciting literacy events. Subsequent teachers provide extensive time for children to participate in authentic literacy activities. For example, a typical second grade student in a literature rich classroom will read hundreds of books by the end of this pivotal year. In addition, these same children will create numerous self-authored books complete with a title page, table of contents, illustrations, and "about the author" sections. Children coming from these classes are familiar with the structure of stories, many genres of literature, and a wide range of book titles and authors.

Due to the symbiotic relationship between reading and writing, these same students are also more familiar with composition methods than students in previous generations. To illustrate, in a second grade classroom, students might write every day, and many of the books read during the year are composed by classmates (Routman, 1988). The books they write commonly contain narration, rhythmic language, and dialogue, and they have experimented with writing from various points of view. As part of this creative process, they have interacted in writing groups, reader's response groups, and peer- and teacher-led conferences. They have experienced the social nature of reading and writing.

Through these socially rich literacy events, students discover how expository texts are structured and information is embedded into print. This insider's view enables them to comprehend other formal language presentations such as published textbooks. Their familiarity with writing also gives them a comfort with composition that was unusual in previous generations. These students view writing as a standard school practice rather than an anomaly or threatening event.

In past generations, children read books, but the body of literature they encountered in reading class was largely narrative. As a result of this narrow focus, children experienced difficulty when they read more formal and content-driven texts in the upper grades (Farnan & Kelly, 1993). In recent years, however, the typical student's literary palate has been filled with both narrative and expository text. In addition, they understand the structure of these literary forms because they compose books and reports using both registers. The teachers in these classrooms also know that the world of children's literature provides an extensive array of books to aid understanding in all subject areas.

A cornerstone of the literacy movement is children's literature. Using beautiful illustrations combined with rich and informative narration, teachers effectively instruct on topics as far-ranging as the inner workings of a volcano to the atomic bomb drop on Hiroshima; from the place of mathematics in everyday life to a tortured and vivid view of life on a nineteenth-century slave ship. The breadth and depth of current literature for children provide a wealth of material for daily use in elementary school classrooms. Correspondingly, their understanding of concepts and events is more extensive than that of typical students in previous decades. The picture being painted is of students entering the middle school classroom with broad and insightful understandings of literacy-related areas (Feirsen, 1997). This presents exciting possibilities for middle grades teachers. Instead of teaching students the basics of composition or the structure of texts, middle school teachers can capitalize on the knowledge these children bring to the middle grade classroom. Literature designed for children and adolescents also supplies materials that explain complex concepts and add interest to every discipline. The use of literature encourages students to see the relationship that exists among all areas of the curriculum (Walley & Walley, 1995). This expansive view of school subjects encourages students to think beyond the surface-level facts of the material. As they read, discuss, and write about literature, the students make connections between concepts and ideas, as well as develop questions and opinions of their own. In this way, they participate in creating the curriculum they are studying (Whittin, 1994). Students entering the middle school classroom have experienced the excitement inherent in using authentic literature as part of the curriculum. These literacy understandings can enhance teaching in every subject.

This literacy revolution has not spread to every elementary teacher, all classrooms, and each student in America's elementary schools. Nor is every student as enthusiastic and competent as suggested here. But many are, and to assume that nothing has happened in the literacy world in recent decades is a restrictive view of present-day curricula and instruction that limits possibilities for all middle school students. This chapter explores foundational issues teachers may use to capitalize on middle school students' refined literacy skills.

Literacy in the Middle Grades

Language arts programs in the middle grades should build on the literacy foundation established in the elementary grades. One of the essential facets is an environment that encourages meaningful language learning. Myers and Hilliard (1997) list three elements of an effective language arts program. First is the immersion of students in reading, writing, speaking, and listening activities. Too frequently the language arts are divided into discrete subjects with the emphasis placed on language mechanics. This approach leads to an artificial picture of how language works and places barriers in the way of meaningful language activities. On the other hand, when teachers immerse students in integrated language activities, they write in response to what they read, discuss what they write and have read, and learn to listen to and value the literacy efforts of their peers.

The second facet involves encouraging students to take risks. This requires the development of open interactions between students and teachers. Because adolescents have a fragile self-image, they must have a classroom environment that encourages honest interactions and is free from ridicule and destructive criticism. An additional aspect of risk taking is modeling by the teacher. As the teacher shares his or her own writing and engages in honest inquiry about pieces of literature, the students begin to mirror the same behaviors. In addition, the teacher engaged in modeling behaviors is demonstrating to students that the teacher trusts them to accept him or her as a fellow learner and that the teacher, too, desires acceptance and respect.

The third element focuses on developing clearly understood communications as opposed to concentrating on language rules. This implies helping students address language mechanics deficiencies in the context of seeking clarity in their compositions and oral presentations (Myers & Hilliard, 1997). Too frequently the language arts curriculum has centered on the instruction of grammar and punctuation rules divorced from meaningful writing experiences. Effective language arts instruction, on the other hand, concentrates on improving the quality of the messages students write. For clarity, students must apply the language rules that teachers have traditionally struggled to teach through drill and lecture. Now, students learn these rules as they write authentic pieces that express their heartfelt thoughts and feelings.

Environmental Factors

The foundation for language development is built around literacy-rich materials, immersion in literacy events, and effective teacher modeling (Cambourne, 1984). An essential material used in successful language arts programming is literature designed for children and adolescents. In most ways, authentic literature also meets the social, academic, and creative needs of adolescents. Ruddle and Ruddle (1995) state five goals for a reading program, and most of these goals are addressed through literature:

1. To provide students with a range of literature experiences that build and extend the students' knowledge base, including an awareness of people and other living things, events, and ideas outside their life experience.
2. To bring students' prior knowledge, life experience, and values into sharper focus through active comprehension by examining and contrasting the many aspects of life represented through literature.
3. To provide students with aesthetic pleasure through the joy of language, and to encourage the appreciation of life experience by isolating, magnifying, or contrasting "slices of life" for aesthetic observation.
4. To develop students' self-understanding through insight into their own behaviors as they encounter a broad range of human behaviors. In addition, they may correlate their personal life experiences to the personalities they encounter in literary works.
5. To develop student's awareness of language as a powerful means of human expression.

The list of goals supplied by Ruddle and Ruddle meshes with key factors of effective middle school programming. First, language arts is a socially embedded curriculum area. Numerous authorities (Irvin, 1997b; Johnson & Johnson, 1989; Lounsbury, 1991; Myers & Hilliard, 1997; National Middle School Association, 1982) assert the value of peer interactions for middle school students. Martin (1993), for example, endorses the importance of developing positive social interactions with peers. Language is a social construct; therefore, by involving students in meaningful language activities, teachers accomplish both curricular and social-emotional goals (Irvin, 1997b). As an illustration, incorporating peer editing strategies into the instruction of composition provides students with an opportunity to meet on a common ground of purpose that transcends physical, emotional, or academic differences. These students have a chance to become acquainted and accepted in a socially constructive atmosphere. As they examine their writing, the students build on their life experiences and extend their understanding of themselves and others.

In other language arts situations, such as a literature response group, students read books together, write in response to literature, and help one another develop intelligently written pieces (Short, Harste, & Burke, 1996). As they work together, they learn to cooperate and appreciate the opinions of others. They see their contributions being discussed and accepted by peers, and, consequently, students gain self-confidence and develop insight into how groups function effectively. In classrooms in which students discuss common readings, they develop important social skills such as self-expression and listening (Irvin, 1997a). These students acquire interpersonal skills, and they delve deeper into the curriculum content than if they merely read the material and composed a report in isolation from the views of others.

Students who have experienced the benefits of sharing and discussing their work constructively and honestly are open to exploring the strengths and weaknesses of their work. Through open discussion of written pieces with teachers and fellow students, they learn how to give constructive criticism to other writers and how to accept meaningful suggestions from peers. In this way, instead of being discouraged and embarrassed about their written efforts, the students learn to celebrate their growth in composition skills.

Elements of Effective Middle Grades Programs

Manning (1993) asserts that an essential element of middle grades education is the application of basic skills students learned in earlier grades. The inclusion of reading and writing groups into the language arts program provides an opportunity to apply prerequisite learnings and to enrich students' understanding of language use through application. Rather than sitting passively as the teacher explains how and when to apply language rules, students learn the rules through authentic literacy experiences as they read, write, and discuss literature. Because they are more cognitively advanced than in the elementary grades, adolescents gain increased insight into the language skills they learned through the elementary curriculum. For example, as they write and discuss their writing with peers, they extend their knowledge base and develop a clear appreciation for the purpose of language conventions such as grammar, punctuation, and sentence structure. In the elementary grades they may have been shown when to use commas or exclamation marks. In the middle grades these basic understandings take on new meaning as they write original pieces and discuss how to add emphasis or precision to what they are writing.

The language rules encountered in earlier grades become clearer as they struggle for clarity of meaning and attempt to mirror the quality of writing they experience in the literature they read. For decades, teachers have struggled to teach adolescent students rules for grammar and punctuation, usually with discouraging results. This effort to instill an understanding of language mechanics has depended on direct instruction of surface-level language needs. In a typical class the teacher presents the rule; the students memorize the rule; the students use the rule on a teacher-developed test; then the students ignore the rule when they write. As an antidote to this timeless problem, Myers and Hilliard (1997) assert that language mechanics should be taught in the social context in which real language use occurs. In addition, they state that teachers should avoid using "transitional terminology" that intimidates the student and obscures the message that the teacher is trying to convey. Instead, teachers should encourage students to discuss with one another why a message is clear or unclear in peer editing sessions. The insight they gain from peers about language helps to improve their language arts skills and develops the independence they need to continue writing.

A second factor in an effective middle school curriculum involves the development of personal interests (Manning, 1993). Adolescents are exploring their place in society, and they seek avenues to express their individuality. The world of the adolescent is a world of contradictions. One striking observation is how adolescents assert their individuality by mirroring peers or cultural icons. These students are experimenting with various roles to explore unique interests, mannerisms, and ways of solving life's problems. Through a language arts program built around literature, students discover characters, personalities, and situations that are like themselves or like the people they wish to be (Sutherland, 1996). Middle school students can use literature to vicariously explore new personality types or experiment with problem-solving strategies. These models may differ from their previous images of effective strategies or from those of peers in their immediate surroundings. Literature helps reveal possible solutions to life's problems and exposes them to careers and mannerisms outside their immediate environment.

The intellectual and social diversity prevalent in a typical middle school classroom is another reason to use literature and individual investigations in the curriculum. Middle school classrooms may contain children from rural, urban, or suburban homes and children from Asian, Appalachian, African American, Hispanic, Native American, Eastern European, or other backgrounds. The list is endless, and the average classroom is a microcosm of our evolving American culture (Ruddle, 1993). The single textbook, a one-size-fits-all approach to school curriculum, is of limited value when teachers attempt to make the curriculum relevant to the mix of children in the contemporary classroom (Walley & Walley, 1995). Authentic literature, however, is rich in its diversity and complexity. There are approximately 3,500 new titles added to the list of literature printed for children and adolescents each year (Sutherland, 1996). These extensive resources enable teachers to present an array of materials applicable to any school curriculum. Students may focus on a determined concept or topic through a variety of literature corresponding to the range of abilities, backgrounds, and interests present in the classroom; everyone can study together through individually selected materials. Using literature, just one facet of the modern language arts program, presents the possibility of making the middle school curriculum accessible and interesting to students as it simultaneously broadens their knowledge of other people, ideas, and areas of study.

The development of a sense of personal responsibility is the third aspect of a successful middle grades program. One language arts method that develops sound understandings of language arts skills and also fosters individual initiative and responsibility is the literature circle (Raphale et al., 1995). The literature circle is a student-directed group designed to encourage discussion of books and literacy-related issues. A common feature of the literature circle is exposure to a variety of literary forms, such as trade books, poetry, expository texts, articles, and magazines. Traditionally content area disciplines used textbooks to present information. Authentic literature, on the other hand, provides an array of materials in a variety of forms appealing to the broad range of learners in a typical classroom. Teachers and students alike may discover that a carefully chosen poem, for example, provides greater insight and information than an entire chapter in a drily written textbook.

Literature circles also provide opportunities for students to interact with peers and to structure lessons and discussions around common readings. Daniels's (1994) description of literature circles gives insight into how this approach helps students assume responsibility for their own learning:

> *Literature circles are small, temporary discussion groups who read the same story, poem, article, or book. While sharing common readings, each group determines the portion of the text to be read each day, and each member assumes specific responsibilities in the upcoming discussion, and everyone comes to the group with the notes needed to perform that job. The circles have regular meetings, with discussion roles rotating each session. When they finish a book, the circle members plan a way to share highlights of their reading with the wider community; then they trade members with other finishing groups, select more readings, and move into a new cycle. Once readers can successfully conduct their own wide-ranging, self-sustaining discussions, formal discussion roles may be dropped. (p. 18)*

The teacher's role in literature circles is to coordinate students' efforts and to teach them how to function in a group. In addition, the teacher helps students synthesize common understandings about language arts concepts and assume responsibility for their own learning. Daniels lists twelve features of literature circles that foster new levels of personal responsibility for language learning:

1. Students choose their own reading materials.
2. Small temporary groups are formed, based on book choices.
3. Different groups read different books.
4. Groups meet on a regular, predictable schedule to discuss reading.
5. Students use written or drawn notes to guide both their reading and their discussion.
6. Group meetings are designed to be open, natural conversations about books, so personal connections, digression, and open-ended discussions are welcome.
7. Discussion topics come from students.
8. Students play a rotating assortment of task roles.
9. The teacher is outside the group and performs a facilitative function.
10. Evaluation is by teacher observation and student self-evaluation.
11. A spirit of fun and playfulness is present.

12. When books are finished, readers share their books with classmates and new groups are formed around new book choices.

This system emphasizes student control over processes used to explore and discuss literature. Lifelong learning is frequently presented as a goal for middle grade students (Manning, 1993). One aspect of lifelong learning for students is assuming responsibility for applying skills through personally chosen topics. In this way, they become active participants and problem solvers in their own projects. For example, a group of students exploring a Civil War topic would read appropriate books, discuss the contents of the books, and develop common understandings from what they read. As a result of their research, they would discover information new to them and develop insights into the feelings, thoughts, and actions of people living during this historic period. The importance of effective communications skills becomes apparent as they search for ways to relate their understandings to classmates. Literature circles encourage students to develop intellectual curiosity, discover unique ways of studying self-directed questions, and reflect on what they are learning. By taking charge of what and how they will learn, these students are becoming the independent learners that schools desire.

Another facet of personal responsibility hinges on providing students with choices about what they will learn and how they will acquire knowledge. Traditionally schools treat the content of the curriculum as a static commodity to be acquired by passive students (Walley, 1991). The teacher efficiently dispenses knowledge, and students, in turn, absorb this information and repeat it back at required times. In this paradigm the content of the curriculum and its predetermined outcomes disregard the students' prior knowledge and interests.

Organizational Structures

The typical school day is tailored to match this restricted view of curriculum. Instruction comes in 50-minute blocks, and each subject is isolated in content and approach from all other subjects (Canady & Rettig, 1995). Each discipline is treated as a separate entity, and the teacher is viewed as an isolated subcontractor on the educational assembly line. Thus, the language arts classroom is organized to dispense the curriculum in bite-size pieces. This approach leaves little opportunity for students to reflect on what they learn and to explore ideas in depth. More importantly, they are discouraged from drawing conclusions and personal insights from what they are learning. Due to the assembly line organizational structure, students are required to absorb what they are taught, learn in the way the teacher dictates, and think the way the system demands (Wills, 1995). The only valued knowledge is that of the teacher or the textbook. Choice, a key variable in helping students develop their personal and intellectual personalities, is left out of the school day.

This restrictive structure, additionally, discourages teachers and students from making connections between subject areas and topics. Teachers are so isolated in their classrooms and within their disciplines that Lortie (1976) described teachers as individuals living lives of isolation, much like prisoners in cells. Students, too, are "prisoners of time" (National Education Commission on Time and Learning, 1994), retained when they are unable to adjust to dictated learning and time requirements structured around discrete subjects. This is unfortunate, as authorities (National Association of Secondary School Principals, 1993; Vars, 1991) stress the value of having students understand the relationship between principles and concepts that transfer across curricular lines. Numerous studies (Ashton & Webb, 1986; Lee & Smith, 1993; Warren & Muth, 1995) have indicated the benefits of integrated curriculum structures on student achievement, attitudes, and behavior. In addition, integrated approaches have shown positive benefits on teacher expectation of student learning (Ashton & Webb, 1986) and on teachers' perceptions of themselves as professionals (Gatewood et al., 1992; Warren & Muth, 1995).

The indication that integrated approaches are beneficial for students is predictable. It is unlikely that students could appreciate the common threads connecting areas of the curriculum when it is fragmented into discrete subject areas and when their teachers have little opportunity to share ideas. In opposition to regressive approaches to curriculum and instruction, the integrated language arts structure uses a fluid organizational pattern for both how the curriculum is organized and what is learned. This dynamic structure may take several forms.

One form honors the consistency of the traditional language arts classroom by maintaining the integrity of language arts areas such as reading, writing, and instruction of language conventions (Glatthorn, 1994). However, instead of each area being treated as an isolated unit taught in separate time blocks, elements of the language arts are woven into a seamless fabric of language instruction. The value of this approach is that instruction mirrors how we experience language in daily life. We read as we write; correspondingly, the material we read influences the content and forms for what we write. Furthermore, how we express ourselves and take in information is facilitated by following language conventions for spelling, language mechanics, and composition. Students want to learn the rules for grammar and punctuation because they realize that clear communication hinges on following established language rules. When the language arts are introduced and reinforced in an interactive context, students experience enjoyment from learning in ways that enrich their lives and give them a feeling of personal authority.

The essential element of this approach is to provide a relatively large amount of time for instruction, usually about 90 minutes (Canady & Rettig, 1995). Within this time block the teacher and students determine the degree of emphasis placed on each language arts area. Equivalent blocks of time are provided for mathematics and either social studies or science. (The social studies and science blocks are usually rotated by unit or semester.) Subjects such as physical education, music, art, or electives meet for 90 minutes every other day. This dynamic structure allows instruction to fit what is needed by the students and the teachers. In addition to extended learning and enrichment times, this schedule enables teachers to meet and know smaller groups of students (Canady & Rettig, 1995). One day the majority of the time may be spent discussing literature; another day brings an emphasis on composing responses to what is being read. The instruction of literary or composition skills is integrated into the day as needed.

Another pattern of integration uses language arts as a vehicle for enhancing instruction in other subjects. This approach brings together two or more areas with the objectives of one discipline providing the primary instructional focus (Glatthorn, 1994). Science objectives, for example, may form the central organizational structure. The content and skills for language arts are taught by applying these skills as the students study science. This method gives purpose for the use of language arts skills. In particular, it fosters reinforcement of language conventions the students learned previously. Situations are also created in which students must confront language issues in order to clarify their ideas. They eagerly learn new language skills because they see an immediate value to what they are learning.

In addition, study of the core subject is enhanced through insights gained from reading and writing. Careful planning, however, is needed to ensure that necessary language arts instruction occurs. The language arts may easily become the neglected stepchild of the primary discipline. The demands of teaching science concepts, mathematics processes, or social studies content could easily displace the need to instruct students in language arts skills. Therefore, when time is allocated for direct teaching, it is imperative to provide a portion of the schedule for instruction in reading and writing. This method requires that teachers become familiar with the content and instructional approaches appropriate for a variety of disciplines, including the language arts. The versatility required of these teachers is a limitation for some, as they feel unprepared to teach a variety of subjects to the degree required for middle school students.

To overcome the insecurities of teachers unaccustomed to integrated approaches, professional development opportunities must be provided for practicing teachers to adjust to new organizational patterns. Professional development opportunities need to be offered for teachers to help them understand methods for developing integrated curriculum units, authentic assessment methods, and ideas for working cooperatively with colleagues. Teachers also need regularly scheduled discussion times to process alternative teaching methods and to give and receive support from colleagues (Walley, 1989).

One approach that addresses this limitation is team teaching. When teachers from a variety of disciplines are combined into one team, students are presented with the necessary curriculum in an integrated manner. In this way the central focus is on the core subject, but language arts content is taught by a knowledgeable teacher. Each person on the team assumes primary responsibility for the direct instruction of a particular area, and together the teachers reinforce and monitor the application of the content of all subjects. Thus, a balance is maintained across all subject areas, and students have the opportunity to use language arts skills in the content areas. Research (Ashton & Webb, 1986; Goodman, 1979) indicates that middle grade teaming improves student achievement, productivity, and self-esteem. In large measure these improvements may be due to the organizational changes that occur when teaming is implemented. The structure of teams inherently leads to more democratic organizational arrangements among teachers, who, in turn, replicate these collegial patterns with their students (Walley, 1991).

Erb (1992) states that two elements are essential for effective teaming. The first is the establishment of common planning time for teachers. Members of teams must have time to discuss mutual concerns about students and curriculum issues. The second consideration is shared students. By having a group of students as part of the team, teachers may view students from multiple perspectives and develop unique understandings about the students' strengths, weaknesses, and problems. Common planning times and shared responsibility for a set of students help create a productive work environment for teachers and for students (Erb, 1992).

A third method of integration unites multiple subject areas around a central theme or project, for example, "Families." This approach enables students and teachers to connect the curriculum around a motivating theme and to demonstrate how each discipline enhances understanding about a subject (Wills, 1995). Many issues related to other forms of integration (e.g., scheduling blocks of time) are present in this method. In addition, careful planning by teachers and students is required to ensure that time is used productively. It is easy for students to participate in an interesting maze of activities but fail to connect those activities to specific curricular understandings and objectives. For instance, students may create an engaging dramatic presentation about their grandparents and yet not learn to write and punctuate dialogue or develop a deeper understanding about the social and historical importance of family in American life. These connections must be encouraged through teacher-led discussions, instruction, and supervised practice.

The effectiveness of this approach is enhanced by carefully monitoring the instruction of curricular objectives from each subject area. One authority (Glatthorn, 1994) suggests developing a calendar for the year that establishes a cycle of themes. Based on the themes, the teachers define the central objectives and assessment means for each theme. The teachers maintain a record of which objectives were taught and the degree of understanding each student gained from the unit. Together the teachers develop a report of student progress for parents and students.

Evaluation

With all methods of integration, systems are required to monitor student progress and to create records for what students learn. Teachers following traditional curricular structures adhering to linear organizational patterns have a built-in system for knowing what was taught by previous teachers and what they should teach. Their curriculum is organized in a continuum that follows an ordered progression (Wills, 1995). In addition, tests are available to assess the degree of student understanding of objectives on the continuum. The price for this organizational scheme is diminished relevance of the curriculum for many students, limitations on student and teacher creativity, and a lack of real-life value contained in the curriculum. The use of test scores also creates an illusion that the score represents all that a student knows about a subject and includes all that a student learned in a course. The teach/test system provides only one avenue for students to demonstrate the depth and breadth of their knowledge. Many students possess understandings about what they have learned that are beyond what can be displayed through objective testing (Farr, 1996). The restrictions of a linear curriculum structure and associated tests deter students from demonstrating the intensity of their understanding of a subject.

Whenever teachers integrate subject areas and make learning more participatory for students, evaluation methods must also be developed to assess projects as well as cognitive understandings (Stiggins, 1997). If teachers attempt to evaluate students' knowledge solely through traditional approaches, such as quizzes and chapter tests, before long the students will focus on minute subskills rather than applicable understandings. Correspondingly, if the total accountability for what is learned is made through evaluation of products, students may disregard incremental understandings and subskills that are prerequisites for later work. Integrated approaches require assessment methods that gauge learning across subject areas and that also determine the degree of understanding students have acquired about the relationship between these subject areas. This balance enables teachers to determine both the degree of students' understanding about specific skills and their ability to apply knowledge in real-life contexts.

Ruddle (1993) provides a set of principles designed to guide the development of balanced assessment measures (p. 206):

1. *Focus on learning*—the essence of effective assessment is encouraging and assisting students in their quest to learn. In order to accomplish this goal, assessment should focus on what students know and reward students for their efforts.
2. *Be equitable*—assessment should be fair and sensitive to the diversity that exists in most classrooms. Therefore, assessment should provide for multiple ways of demonstrating knowledge and be sensitive to multiple interpretations of information.
3. *Create congruence between district aims and assessment methods*—if a district values "critical thinking," "problem solving," and "cooperation," the assessment means should honor these aims as well as more traditional assessment goals.
4. *Recognize limitations of assessment means*—no one assessment method can evaluate the depth and breadth of students' knowledge. Multiple means are required to determine students' understanding of basic information and their ability to apply this knowledge in authentic situations.
5. *Reduce competition and increase cooperation*—assessment should increase student confidence, help them establish learning goals, and develop curiosity about learning. These aims are frustrated if the primary focus of students' efforts is "beating" their peers for a grade.
6. *Include students in the assessment process*—one way to increase student motiva-

tion for learning and to assume responsibility for their academic progress is to include them in the evaluation process. By giving students a voice in the assessment process and some choice about the means that will be used, teachers can gain a perspective on what students value in the curriculum and what they perceive about their performance.

7. *Use consistent reporting methods*—the reporting method should be developed to provide reliable assessment for all students. Parents and students need to believe that the appraisal is the same for every member of the class.

Many of the elements listed by Ruddle may be addressed through performance assessment measures. In the past, effective teachers sought to evaluate student achievement through correction and evaluation of written compositions, with a major focus on application of grammar and punctuation rules. Current practice offers an array of methods to assess students' command of all language arts skills and to identify their understanding of reading and writing processes. Three of the methods that teachers may use are portfolios, anecdotal records, and scoring rubrics.

Farr (1996) asserts that performance assessment is most effectively put in place through portfolios. The portfolio has become a common practice in integrated language arts programs. Essentially the portfolio is a longitudinal documentation of the students' language arts experiences. Papers and projects are entered into the portfolio regularly; however, the portfolio is more than a clever scrapbook of student papers. As Farr (1996) states, "Papers must be added frequently; others can be weeded out in an ongoing rearrangement and selection process; most importantly, the whole process should involve frequent self-analysis by the student and regular conversations between the teacher and the student" (p. 208). The portfolio is an organic document that grows and evolves in a way that mirrors the student's language arts experiences.

The primary reason for maintaining a portfolio is to foster thoughtful reflection by the student and to enlighten the teacher about what is being learned. This introspection helps students, with the aid of the teacher, to develop individual learning goals. The empowerment of students over what they will learn and how they will represent their language development encourages academic responsibility. This creates motivated students who care about what they are learning.

As the language arts program discussed in this chapter incorporates the use of language arts skills in a variety of subject areas with a team of teachers, methods are required to include subject area teachers in the assessment process (Miller, 1994). One method of doing this is through anecdotal records. This involves the creation of an efficient record-keeping system that quickly records observations and insights about students' learning experiences (Block, 1997). The system may vary widely from teacher to teacher. Some teachers record entries on index cards throughout the day, others prefer to spend a few minutes at the end of each day recording thoughts and observations in a log for later reference. No matter what the system, the use of anecdotal records helps create a total picture of each student's progress. In addition, seemingly incidental observations may reveal patterns of behavior that have deeper meaning than when viewed as isolated events. The contents of anecdotal records provide a picture of each child's performance that is useful when discussing the student's performance with other teachers, with the student, or with parents.

In addition to the students' daily use of and more global understanding of language arts processes, teachers also need to assess students' reading and writing performance. One method of assessing student papers that is efficient and enables students to understand their strengths and weaknesses is a scoring rubric. Through the use of a scoring sheet that identifies the qualities of an effective composition, the teacher may assess the qualities of a composition quickly and in a way that students accept as fair and objective.

There are many assessment procedures that teachers may use to evaluate students' language abilities. Effective systems communicate clearly to students that their work is valued and that they are part of the evaluation process. This encourages students to care about the quality of their work and to develop personal responsibility for acquiring language skills.

Conclusion

The language arts revolution discussed in this chapter is part of a century-long movement to encourage students to be lifelong learners and to acquire essential language arts skills. The movement for teacher and student empowerment has faced opposition from forces who wish to control and regulate teachers and students. In recent decades, nevertheless, considerable gains have been made in encouraging students and teachers to assume authority over what and how they will learn. Current innovations associated with forceful middle school curriculum have focused on learning subject matter in a holistic manner in the context of an integrated curriculum. The language arts are essential skills needed to communicate understandings and facilitate reflective thinking in all disciplines. The revolution toward increased cooperation between students and their peers and students and teachers exemplified by current language arts processes is a model that can be used by all teachers in all disciplines.

Discussion Questions

1. The language arts program described in this chapter differs radically from the methods used in the traditional junior high school. There is, for example, an increased emphasis on applying language arts skills through authentic learning experiences. Some would argue that this shift de-emphasizes traditional content such as punctuation and grammar skills. What would you present as evidence to either support or disagree with these critics? Write a letter to a critic presenting your views as to why you agree or disagree with the critic's views.

2. Approaches such as using writing process or literature circles requires a shift in content and approach from traditional language arts programs. Make a list of responsibilities for students and teachers when an integrated language arts program is instituted. In what ways are their responsibilities the same and different?

3. The language arts provide a catalyst for uniting the curriculum content of all subject areas. Some assert that the language arts should be integrated totally into the instructional program of other subjects. Others believe the language arts should stand alone and be taught as a separate subject. Choose one of these two positions and list reasons to support your views. Find a classmate with an alternate view and compare your lists. What is the most salient argument on both sides of the issue?

References

Ashton, P. T., & Webb, R. B. (1986). *Making a difference: Teachers' sense of efficacy and student achievement.* New York: Longman.

Block, C. C. (1997). *Teaching the language arts: Expanding thinking through student-centered instruction* (2d ed.). Boston: Allyn and Bacon.

Cambourne, B. (1984). *Language learning and literacy.* In A. Butler & J. Turnbill (Eds.), *Towards a reading-writing classroom.* Rozelle, NSW, Australia: Primary English Teaching Association.

Canady, R. L., & Rettig, M. D. (1995). The power of innovative scheduling. *Educational Leadership, 53*(3), 21–25.

Daniels, H. (1994). *Literature circles: Voices and choices in the student-centered classroom.* York, ME: Stenhouse.

Erb, T. O. (1992). What team organization can do for teachers. In J. H. Lounsbury (Ed.), *Connecting the curriculum through interdisciplinary instruction.* Columbus, OH: National Middle School Association.

Farnan, N., & Kelly, P. R. (1993). Response-based instruction at the middle school level: When student engagement is the goal. *Middle School Journal, 25*(1), 46–49.

Farr, R. (1996). Putting it all together: Solving the reading-writing puzzle. In R. D. Robinson, M. C. McKenna, & J. M. Wedman (Eds.), *Issues and Trends in Literacy Education.* Boston: Allyn and Bacon.

Feirsen, R. (1997). Creating a middle school culture of literacy. *Middle School Journal, 28*(3), 10–15.

Gatewood, T. E., Cline, G., Green, G., & Harris, S. E. (1992). Middle school interdisciplinary team organization and its relationship to teacher stress. *Research in Middle Level Education, 15*(2), 27–40.

Glatthorn, A. A. (1994). *Developing a quality curriculum.* Alexandria, VA: Association for Supervision and Curriculum Development.

Goodman, P. S. (1979). *Assessing organizational change: The Rushton quality of work experiment.* New York: Wiley.

Irvin, J. L. (1997a). *Reading and the middle school student: Strategies to enhance literacy* (2d ed.). Boston: Allyn and Bacon.

Irvin, J. L. (1997b). Using social proclivity to enhance literacy learning for young adolescents. *Childhood Education, 73*(5), 290–291.

Johnson, D. W., & Johnson, R. (1989). Social skills for successful group work. *Educational Leadership, 47*(4), 29–33.

Kane, C. M. (1994) *Prisoners of time research: What we know, what we need to know* (Report of the National Education Commission on Time and Learning). Washington, DC: Government Printing Office.

Lee, V. E., & Smith, J. B. (1993). Effects of school restructuring on achievement and engagement of middle-school students. *Sociology of Education, 66,* 164–187.

Lortie, D. (1976). *Schoolteacher: A sociological study.* Chicago: University of Chicago Press.

Lounsbury, J. H. (1991). *As I see it*. Columbus, OH: National Middle School Association.

Manning, L. M. (1993). *Developmentally appropriate middle level schools*. Wheaton, MD: Association for Childhood Education International.

Martin, T. (1993). Turning points revisited: How effective middle grades schools address developmental needs of young adolescent students. *Journal of Health Education, 24*(6), 24–27.

Miller, T. (1994). Improving the schoolwide language arts program: A priority for all middle school teachers. *Middle School Journal, 24,* 26–29.

Myers, J. W., & Hilliard, R. D. (1997). Holistic language learning at the middle level: Our last, best chance. *Childhood Education, 73*(5), 286–289.

National Association of Secondary School Principals (1989). *Middle level education's responsibility for intellectual development*. Reston, VA: Author.

National Middle School Association (1982). *This we believe*. Columbus, OH: Author.

Raphael, T., Goatley, V., McMahon, F., & Woodman, D. (1995). Promoting meaningful conversations in book clubs. In N. Roser & M. Martinez (Eds.), *Book talk and beyond* (pp. 66–79). Newark, DE: International Reading Association.

Routman, R. (1988). *Transitions: From literature to literacy*. Portsmouth, NH: Heinemann.

Ruddle, M. R. (1993). *Teaching content reading and writing*. Boston: Allyn and Bacon.

Ruddle, R. B., & Ruddle, M. R. (1995). *Teaching children to read and write: Becoming an influential teacher*. Boston: Allyn and Bacon.

Short, K., Harste, J., & Burke, C. (1996). *Creating classes for authors and inquirers* (2d ed.). Portsmouth, NH: Heinnemann.

Stiggins, R. J. (1997). *Student centered classroom assessment* (2d ed.). Upper Saddle River, NJ: Prentice-Hall.

Sutherland, Z. (1996). *Children and books* (9th ed.). New York: Addison-Wesley Longman.

Vars, G. F. (1991). Integrated curriculum in historical perspective. *Educational Leadership, 49*(2), 14–15.

Walley, C. W. (1989). Eight teachers' implementation of a literature based reading program: A qualitative study of change. Unpublished doctoral dissertation, Kent State University, Kent, OH.

Walley, C. W. (1991). A classroom of community. *Democracy and Education, 5*(2), 21–27.

Walley, C. W., & Walley, K. (1995). *Integrating literature in content areas*. Westminster, CA: Teacher Created Materials.

Warren, L. L., & Muth, K. D. (1995). Common planning time in middle grades schools and its impact on students and teachers. *Research in Middle Level Education, 18*(3), 41–58.

Wills, C. (1995). Voices of inquiry: Possibilities and perspectives. *Childhood Education, 71*(5), 261–265.

Whittin, D. J. (1994). Literature and mathematics in preschool and primary: The right connection. *Young Children, 49*(2), 4–11.

Chapter 10

Talent Development in the Middle School

JANE PIIRTO
GERI CASSONE
PAULA WILKES

Jane Piirto is Professor of Graduate Education, Director of Talent Development Education at Ashland University, Ashland, Ohio. She is the author of the Prentice-Hall textbook Talented Children and Adults: Their Development and Education, *as well as the nonfiction book* Understanding Those Who Create *(Gifted Psychology Press). A published poet and novelist, Piirto has authored five other literary books.*

Geri Cassone is Coordinator of Programs for the Gifted and Talented for the Strongsville, Ohio, schools. She has been a classroom teacher at the elementary school level and a coordinator of programs for the talented and gifted at the local and regional levels.

Paula Wilkes has been an educator in the Eugene, Oregon, school district for 20 years. She has taught at both the elementary and middle school levels, as well as at the university level as an assistant professor at the University of Oregon. She has presented workshops in the areas of the Hunter Model, peer coaching, cooperative learning, team building, multiple intelligences, and authentic assessment.

There is a "quiet crisis" in education, according to Secretary of Education Richard Riley (as cited in Ross, 1993). The crisis is quiet because the students are often quiet, nice kids, struggling to be good, not making waves, trying to teach themselves, to learn by themselves, to study for tests without the benefit of direct teaching matched to their abilities. These are our academically talented students. These students are silenced by a society and an education establishment that tell them that it is unfair, or somehow un-American, to want to learn at a faster rate than most of their peers. Their peers tell them that being interested in learning is odd, that they are geeks, nerds, bookworms, and the like.

The muzzle is also applied to the teachers of these students. They are told to "teach to the middle" or that "these kids will teach themselves" or, worse yet, that "the bright students learn a lot by teaching the other kids." For these teachers, some of whom have special training for teaching the talented, the restraints placed on them by administrative fiat and the expectations of colleagues are frustrating. They realize that talented students have the same rights to learn appropriate material, receive instructional attention, and have their intellectual needs met as do the other students "included" in the middle school classroom.

This chapter will explore issues related to methods currently used in middle schools to teach talented students, look at research about methods for grouping students in the middle school, and present two examples of middle school programming for academically talented students. The chapter concludes with a discussion of the "Pyramid of Talent Development" that may provide insight into appropriate planning for students in the middle grades.

The Middle School Revolution

The successful middle school revolution that has happened in many cities in the United States has numerous advocates and few detractors. When class size is reduced and when teachers have common planning time, much can happen that is developmentally appropriate for young adolescents. But what about the academically talented? Are their intellectual needs being met in the restructured middle school? Along with the excitement generated by the new structures and new ways of doing things the question remains: Are *all students'* needs being met?

Several studies have indicated that the goal of success for all students may give short shrift to the goal for "all" if the "all" includes academically talented students. Tomlinson (1994) said, "Gifted middle school learners are at special risk in the absence of appropriately challenging instruction" (p. 178). The conclusion that concrete learning is what middle school students need is problematic. Tomlinson noted that many academically talented middle school students are able to think at highly complex and abstract levels. When all the instruction is targeted for the concrete and the hands-on, these students may suffer the apathy and disengagement that are common for at-risk learners. Self-esteem is tied to accomplishment, and when accomplishment is easy or not struggled for, apathy can result.

Vars and Rakow (1993) advocated an integrative curriculum. Other terms that seem synonymous with *integrative* are *interdisciplinary, correlated, unified, fused, holistic,* and *core.* The purpose of such approaches to teaching content is to enable the students to make connections between knowledges common to the separate domains. This is often done through scheduling innovations such as block schedules or other ways of viewing school time and through manipulating sequence so that, for example, students in social studies read literature that is applicable to the topic being studied in social studies. Such integrative curriculum requires common planning time and deep subject matter knowledge on the part of the teachers, as well as a compatability of personality and philosophy. Teachers' "use of [a] judicious mix of heterogeneous and homogeneous groupings" allows students to have the experience of working with others of unlike ability and interest as well as the experience of working with intellectual peers.

However, Tomlinson (1994) said that the thematic approach common to middle school curricula falsely assumes that the academically talented learners will have their needs taken care of because higher-level thinking skills, creativity skills, and critical thinking skills will be folded into the thematic units. That all students need to do higher-level thinking is a given, but the question of pace and depth is still not answered; academically talented middle school students are fast learners who can master the knowledge (if that is, indeed, the goal of the school) in much less time than it takes most middle school students.

The following vignette gives a glimpse into a middle grades classroom in which the teacher, Mr. Barnes, is required to structure his classroom by the principle of differentiating curriculum according to ability. This sample illustrates Mr. Bryan's frustration about what and how to best teach all his middle school students.

A Vignette

> *I was visiting friends in a large U.S. city. Their eighth grade daughter, Mandy, so excitedly described her school that I asked whether I could visit it. I asked Mandy why she loved her school so much. "They care about us," she said. "There's kids from all races and backgrounds. I love the projects we do in the classes. We're all just excited about our school." I got permission to shadow her for a day. The Academic Middle School is based on the Coalition for Essential Schools principles. Mandy was in eighth grade, in a "house" of one hundred students and four teachers. The teachers had common planning time. The kids were multi-ethnic. It's an inner city school. There were nineteen to twenty-four students in the classes I observed. I observed Mandy's math class of nineteen students, with Mr. Bryan. At 8:50 he began with roll call. One of the girls asked whether she could go to the counseling office. He said, "If you leave the room, I'll have to put you on time track." It turns out that she and he have a conflict and the girl asks to leave class every day. On the board are written:*

Mini Extra-Credit
Due Wednesday/Thursday.
1. Place parentheses so as to make this equation true. 36/4 +5–2+2.3+12/3
   +1=6.
2. What is the ones digit in 7^{1000} ?

The algebra assignment was also written on the board.

p. 49 #31–36.
p. 52 #7–12, 29–32, 44–49.

Students were in six rows three or four deep, with the seven algebra stu-
dents, one-third of the class, in the back of the first three rows, in a circle. They
were talking among themselves and the noise was distracting. It seemed to me
that they could be moved farther back.

In the next few minutes, Mr. Bryan made statements such as these: "Correct
your own paper [to the group in front]. . . . Algebra students [to the group in
back]? I don't know if I can count on you doing that, but keep it down, will you?"

He called out answers. There were posters of problems up on the walls. "How
many cheeseburgers were sold? What percent of items sold were multicore burg-
ers? Which form closed boxes when folded? Give the volume and the surface area."

While the students were figuring out the problem, he came over to me.
"We're not allowed to teach algebra anymore."

"Why?" I asked.

"We don't have separate classes for academically talented students anymore.
It's against the rules. I'm certified in gifted and talented but I can't teach the ad-
vanced classes I used to teach."

There was a problem on the board. "While I was doing my own problem solv-
ing last night, playing with math, I ran into this problem. Who can solve it?"

10526315789472684 with a 2 at the end is always that # multiplied by 2.

More questions. A student asked, "Why do we need to do this?" He replied,
"Oh, philosophical questions, I don't know. I don't answer philosophical ques-
tions. . . . No calculators. Spread out."

He came to talk with me and said that the teachers have 2 hours of planning
per week: 1 for curriculum, 1 for at-risk students, on Mondays and Tuesdays
during electives. They don't consider academically talented students "at risk."

He told the students: "Write this fraction as a decimal: 3/4." He demon-
strated how. Then he said, "You try one. 1/4." He walked around giving encour-
agement. "Very good."

"Is $0.20 the same as $0.2?" he asked, and most of the students said yes.

They began a discussion of infinity. "How do you show infinity?" He asked
them by name: Geraldo. Jennifer. Dante. Jaime. Juan. Eric. Heather. Chris.

"Let me see your book with your name in it."

"May I sharpen my pencil?" Juan asked.

Mr. Bryan talked about repeating decimals. All this time the seven algebra students had been talking softly in the back of the room, not a part of the discussion of decimals and percents. Mr. Bryan then went to the kids working on algebra while the other students worked on page 104 in pairs. The algebra kids had questions about absolute value and the commutative property. There were five boys and two girls in the algebra group. They gathered around Mr. Bryan as he leaned over the back table and explained negative and positive numbers with a graph. He wrote –4/5 + (–3.8), and helped them work it out. One of the students asked, "Isn't the commutative property very similar to the associative property?" Mr. Bryan shook his head, then nodded his head, and said, "Yes." They are going to take a test on chapters 1 and 2 of the Algebra 1 book tomorrow. They have been teaching themselves algebra for 2 weeks, and last semester they had taught themselves pre-algebra, taking tests to move along in the book.

Then he turned to me, telling me that the next class will have even more kids ready for algebra—thirteen of twenty. "Is this any way to deal with the advanced students?" he asked. "I wouldn't do it at all if I hadn't been trained in gifted and talented education."

I asked him how much time he can spend with these advanced students. He said he spends 5 or 10 minutes total with them during a typical day. Later, over dinner, I asked Mandy whether he spent only this much time with the algebra students every day. She thought for a while (she was in the percents and decimals drill group), and said, "Yes. Sometimes he doesn't get a chance to work with them at all. He has to work with us to help us get the basic math so we can go to high school math."

I wondered how this was "essential" education; that is, what is "essential" is that the slower students get most of the time of the teacher and the faster students get less time and less instruction. As Mr. Bryan put it, "I'm not going to do another preparation for them. It's too much work." He used to coach Math Counts (a national competition) and have teams participate in math contests, but no more. The teachers prepare together for thematic and interdisciplinary education, and he can teach decimal points in his sleep. He would like to teach a class of advanced students together, but the organizational principle essential to the middle school model they had adopted did not allow for such grouping, as it was considered elitist at worst and unnecessary at best. Why should eighth graders even have algebra when high schools will teach it next year?

I wonder if the parents of the bright math students care that their children are teaching themselves, get to ask only one or two questions a day, and are chastised for being too loud when the group they are in gets interested in the topic and begins to fervently discuss the commutative property.

Tomlinson (1994) noted that there is "a pervasive uncertainty in the middle school movement regarding what constitutes appropriate curriculum for the middle school" (p. 179) and that this ambiguity bodes ill for all students. What to teach? How to teach it? What is the middle school curriculum? Mr. Bryan, the math teacher, planned in common with other members of his team and designed lessons that would fold mathematics into social science for sixth graders. For a thematic unit on oceanography he had made a series of number problems that included math facts about the ocean. Was this appropriate? Common thought would say yes. But if most of the students couldn't do percents, as was demonstrated in the math class for eighth graders, what good were the math facts when they couldn't understand them, when they didn't have the basic entry-level knowledge to appreciate the math facts in their oceanographic context? And what of the academically talented students, chomping at the bit to learn algebra in the eighth grade, for whom these percentages on the math facts sheet were appropriate in the sixth grade but for whom the instruction in the eighth grade was so watered down, that they had to teach themselves?

Tomlinson (1994) made several recommendations for middle schools about including instruction for their academically talented students:

1. Acknowledge that there are academically talented learners in the middle school, and note that they do have cognitive and affective differences.
2. Plan for the learning needs of these students; consider a coaching model.
3. Include flexible grouping; do not insist on heterogeneous grouping for all learning tasks.
4. Prepare the teachers to work with students in groups.
5. Define the curriculum that is suitable for these learners.
6. Utilize many learning strategies to encourage higher-level thinking in all students, but don't assume that because these are included that academically talented students' needs are taken care of.
7. Help teachers to plan for diverse needs of all students, including the academically talented.
8. Conduct staff development and encourage college courses in curriculum differentiation for academically talented learners.

The literature on the needs of the academically talented in the middle schools has focused on three main issues: (1) the appropriate use of cooperative learning groups (Coleman, Gallagher, & Howard, 1993; Coleman, Gallagher, & Nelson, 1993; Gallagher, Coleman, & Nelson, 1993; Joyce, 1991; Nelson, Gallagher, & Coleman, 1993; Robinson, 1990), (2) the differentiation of instruction for students who are able to think in highly abstract ways, and (3) the heterogeneous grouping that is deemed to be the best way to deal with the social development of middle school students.

Nelson, Gallagher, and Coleman (1993) conducted a survey of 420 educators, from the Cooperative Learning Network of ASCD, the International Association for the Study of Cooperative Learning, the National Association for Gifted Children, and the Association for the Gifted. With 314 responses, they arranged the responses thematically, differentiating between the opinions of those from the cooperative learning organizations and those from the organizations for the education of the gifted and talented. The results showed "a wide chasm between the two camps on the issue of heterogeneous and homogeneous grouping for cooperative learning" (p. 120). Most agreed that there should be more staff development about the needs and characteristics of gifted and talented students, as most teachers have only had 1 or 2 clock hours during their undergraduate training about this heterogeneous population of academically talented students.

Grouping and the American Middle School

A spate of literature (Oakes, 1985; Wells & Serna, 1996) has said that putting students into groups according to ability is discriminatory against minority youth, especially African Americans and Hispanics. This appeal to equity has led to a response that equality is not just treating everyone the same, but educating everyone according to their ability. The means for "detracking" have been (1) to encourage heterogeneous grouping and (2) to advocate cooperative learning. The technique of cooperative learning has permeated pedagogy in schools and has evolved to the point where students who don't like to work in groups are considered antisocial and not helpful. Many bright students have voiced the opinion that they don't like to do the work for the other students, yet they feel their own perfectionistic standards force them to do so, as they don't want to hand in work that is substandard. They fear speaking up and voicing this opinion because of disdain for their opinion from the teacher and from other students.

When the first author gave a group of academically talented high school freshmen the Myers-Briggs Type Indicator as a career planning strategy, many of the students turned out to be Extraverted (E). The stock interpretation for "E" students is to say that they prefer to work in groups, to gather energy from others, rather than from within, from oneself. To a person, the academically talented students said no, they hate to work in groups. When asked why, they said they hate to do the work for the others. When asked whether they like to work in groups of people who like to share the work equally and to discuss the problem at hand, they said, "Oh, yes. I like to work in those kind of groups. But in school I never get a chance."

Ability Grouping

Several types of ability grouping are available, as discussed in the following sections:

XYZ Grouping
XYZ grouping is done according to high, middle, and low ability based on test scores or other performance indicators. This is the grouping the de-tracking advocates don't like, as students often remain in the same group for years. Detroit had such a plan as early as 1919. Students had the same curricula and the same textbooks; the only differences were in pace of instruction and depth of enrichment. The top 20% in achievement were in the "X" classes, the next 60% were in the "Y"

classes, and the lowest 20% were in "Z" classes. A meta-analysis by Kulik and Kulik (1982) of fifty-one studies of the effectiveness of XYZ grouping showed that high-aptitude learners gained about 1/10 of a year with such grouping and curricula (Kulik, 1992a). Similar studies by Slavin (1987, 1991) showed no difference in the achievement gains among students in XYZ groups. Likewise, self-esteem of students in XYZ groups was studied by Kulik and Kulik (1984a, 1984b, 1987, 1990, 1991, 1997; Kulik, 1992a), and their studies showed that students in the lower group, the Z groups, had slightly higher self-esteem in such a configuration, but that students in the higher group, the X students, had slightly lower self-esteem.

Commenting on why the achievement and self-esteem effects were so small in XYZ groups, James Kulik (1992b) said that "curricular uniformity" was probably the main reason, for they were placements of "differential placement but not differential treatment." He said, "For example, children in the high group in a Grade 5 program may be ready for work at the sixth grade level; children in the middle group are ready for work at the fifth grade level; and children in the low group may need remedial help" (p. 4) but all had the same curricula.

Another name for XYZ grouping is "tracking." Critics such as Jeanie Oakes have called for elimination of all grouping—not only XYZ grouping—after studying the results of XYZ grouping on achievement. A call to "de-track America" has been raised by many educators. Kulik (1992b) said that "meta-analytic evidence suggests that this proposed reform could greatly damage American education. Teachers, counselors, administrators, and parents should be aware that student achievement would suffer with the total elimination of all school programs that group students by aptitude" (p. 6). He said that achievement results from schools replacing all XYZ classes with heterogeneous classes would show that students of higher aptitude would "fall slightly," while the level of achievement of the rest of the students would stay about the same. He cautioned: "If schools eliminated grouping programs in which all groups follow curricula adjusted to their ability, the damage would be greater, and it would be felt more broadly" (p. 6). It seems that Kulik's advice is being followed, and many districts are deciding to continue with honors classes, especially in academic subjects such as science, mathematics, social studies, and language arts, with all other students not in the honors classes grouped together for instruction. Qualification for honors classes is being broadened in many districts to include more criteria than aptitude or achievement test scores from tests given at very young ages. Such criteria often include self-nomination by students for honors classes.

Within-Class Grouping

A second type of ability grouping is *within-class* grouping, in which students in the same class are grouped for instruction according to their achievement. Common types of within class grouping are (1) mastery learning, (2) individualized instruction, and (3) regrouping by subject. In the most common form of within-class grouping, regrouping by subject, students are generally grouped into three or more levels, and they study material from different textbooks at different levels. Meta-analytic studies from the University of Michigan (Kulik & Kulik, 1984a, 1984b, 1987, 1990, 1992; Kulik, 1992a, 1992b) and from Johns Hopkins University (Slavin, 1987, 1991) found that this type of ability grouping had positive results, with gains for low-, middle-, and high-ability students averaging 1.2 to 1.5 years in a school year.

Cluster Grouping

A type of within-class grouping is cluster grouping. In this mode, several talented students are placed with a teacher who will treat them as talented and differentiate their instruction accordingly. Four to six talented students usually make up a cluster; with this size group the teacher is able to differentiate for their instruction and the workload is not horrendous. The advantage of this type of grouping is that it fits, philosophically, with the special educational practice of *inclusion*, while providing the students with a peer group. Teachers have found that cluster grouping helps the achievement of the other students as well. Cluster grouping should be used as a complement to pullout programming, and not as an end in itself.

Cross-Grade Grouping

Cross-grade grouping is another type of ability grouping. This was first tried in the Joplin Plan in Missouri in the 1950s. In this model, students in the fourth, fifth, and sixth grades were broken into nine groups reading from the second grade to the ninth grade level. Students went to reading class at the same hour, but to the level of instruction at which they were achieving. Other types of cross-grade grouping are (1) ability-grouped class assignments, (2) ability grouping for selected subjects, (3) nongraded plans, and (4) special classes (Mills & Durden, 1992). Meta-analysis showed that cross-grade grouping is an effective means of delivering instruction, and achievement gains similar to those of within-grade grouping were found. The key element, it seems, is that students study different curricula for different ability levels. Kulik and Kulik (1997), in discussing the complete removal of all ability grouping, warned:

> The damage would be truly profound if, in the name of de-tracking, schools eliminated enriched and accelerated classes for their brightest learners. The achievement level of such students would fall dramatically if they were required to move at the common pace. No one can be certain that there would be a way to repair the harm that would have been done. (p. 241)

The middle school movement has its strengths, but, as this discussion has pointed out, it also has possible weaknesses—or challenges, as we are so fond of saying in the field of education. Two school districts have addressed the dilemma of dealing with talented students at the middle school level in ways shown by the following case examples.

CASE EXAMPLE 1

Using Q-Sort Methodology to Define a School Program for the Talented

Geri Cassone

The District

This is a case study of the formation of a middle school program for the academically talented and gifted in a suburban district of 34,000 people. The school system serves approximately 5,000 students. There is one middle school serving about 1,200 students in grades 6 through 8.

The Program for the Academically Talented

Students are identified and placed in the Advanced Study Program based on the Rule for School Foundation Units in the State of Ohio, Rule 3301-51-15. Via this rule, which is somewhat outdated in its philosophy (having not been revised since 1984), eligibility criteria for talented students have been determined in the areas of (1) superior cognitive ability (or high IQ), (2) specific academic ability, (3) creative thinking ability, and (4) visual and/or performing arts ability.

The district has self-contained classrooms for students with superior cognitive ability (area 1) in grades three through six. Another part of the district's service to the academically talented is in the Advanced Study Program (ASP), which has a cluster-grouped classroom in first grade. This classroom is housed in an elementary school that serves as a magnet school for the other four elementaries in the district. The middle school recently shifted from the junior high school to a middle school orientation. A committee of teachers and administrators began to assess how this change in philosophy would impact the talented and gifted program.

Needs Assessment

Needs assessments were conducted with four populations: the teachers, the parents, the students, and the committee. Armstrong (1995) had proposed a Q-sort method based on research on recommended practices in gifted education (Shore et al., 1991). Their study was a meta-analysis of the research into the education of the gifted and talented, highlighting best practices. The committee decided to use the Armstrong Q-sort method (Armstrong, 1995a, 1995b) with *both the students and their parents* to get their perceptions as to how an ideal program for the gifted and talented would be structured in this district. (See Figure 10.1, which shows the Classroom Cues Adapt Form.)

**FIGURE 10.1   Armstrong Classroom Cues Adapt Form—
Ways I Think This Student Learns Best**

Source: Developed by Dorothy Armstrong, Grand Valley State University, Grand Rapids, MI ©1994.
Used with permission.

STUDENT'S NAME _____ DATE _____

GRADE _____ Boy   Girl (circle one)

PERSON COMPLETING THIS FORM _____

RELATIONSHIP TO STUDENT _____

Students like to learn in different ways. Sort the statements to show the ways that you
think this student prefers to learn. Your responses can be compared to those of the student
and the results can be used to plan appropriate learning experiences for the student.

You will need forty statement cards (made from the Summary Form), Summary Form, a
pen or pencil, and a desk or table at which to work.

1. Read the cards. Each card describes a way that one might like to learn.
2. Sort the cards into three piles:

>   Pile 1: YES: These are ways that I think this student would really like to learn.
>   Pile 2: MAYBE: These ways would be OK but not as appealing as those in the
>   "yes" pile.
>   Pile 3: NO: These are ways I think the student would rather not learn.

3. Record the number of your choices on the Summary Sheet. Look at the cards in your
   piles. Each card has a number. Put a Y (Yes) in the space after the number of each card
   in your YES pile. Put a N (No) after the number of each card in your NO pile. (You do
   not need to record the MAYBE pile.)

PRACTICE EXAMPLES:

__M__ 1. I should be expected to do high-quality work using real products as models.
__Y__ 2. I would like to learn a lot about fewer topics instead of learning a little about a lot
          of topics.
__N__ 3. I would like to do independent study with the guidance of the teacher.

Statement and Summary Form: Armstrong Classroom Cue Adapt Form

Note: These are to be made into Q-sort cards.

____ 1. I should be expected to do high-quality work.
____ 2. I would like to learn a lot about fewer topics instead of learning a little about a lot
         of topics.
____ 3. I would like to do independent studies with some guidance.
____ 4. I would like to learn how to be an independent learner.

Continued

**FIGURE 10.1   Armstrong Classroom Cues Adapt Form—
Ways I Think This Student Learns Best,** *Continued*

____   5. I would like to learn how to feel good about myself.

____   6. I would like to be in special classes or programs that are especially right for me.

____   7. I would like to understand what my special classes or programs are trying to teach me and why that is important.

____   8. My creative abilities should not be ignored/abused.

____   9. I would like to broaden my interests.

____ 10. I should not be forced to agree with others.

____ 11. I would like to be able to learn things in an earlier grade or at a younger age than I normally would.

____ 12. I would like to spend some of my time working with the rest of the class, but I would also like opportunities to work independently.

____ 13. It would be fine with me to work with other children who are not my age if we have similar interests and abilities.

____ 14. I would like to study some interesting things that are not already part of my regular classes.

____ 15. For at least some of the time, it is important to me to be in classes with students whose ability matches mine.

____ 16. I would like to study things that are of particular interest to me.

____ 17. I would like to work with people who really know a lot about the subjects they teach.

____ 18. I would like to be actively involved in learning; I like to be in classes where we do more than listen to the teacher.

____ 19. I would like to combine study in several subject areas at the same time.

____ 20. I would like to understand more about my feelings and opinions.

____ 21. I would like to learn about different careers.

____ 22. I would like to do more art.

____ 23. I would like to be asked to read things that make me think, not simple things that expect me just to give answers memorized from the book.

____ 24. I would like to learn with computers.

____ 25. I would like to learn more about what things might be like in the future.

____ 26. I would like to learn about famous people.

____ 27. I would like to learn in ways that take into account the ways I learn best.

____ 28. I would like to learn research skills.

____ 29. I would like to learn how to communicate more effectively.

____ 30. I would like to learn to think in both organized and creative ways.

____ 31. I would like to learn ways to work better with others.

____ 32. I would like to learn by going on field trips.

____ 33. I would like to learn how to plan better by learning how to set goals.

____ 34. I would like to learn about how I learn.

____ 35. I would like to learn by asking questions, doing experiments, and solving problems.

____ 36. I would like to learn how to find solutions to real problems.

____ 37. Teaching other children is a good way for me to learn.

____ 38. I would like to learn at my own rate, even if it is faster than the other students in the class.

____ 39. I would like to be taught skills that will help me so that my achievement matches my ability.

____ 40. I would like to decide whether or not I take part in a special project, class, or program.

Data Analysis

The survey results indicated that there were three major areas that must be included in the program for the academically and intellectually talented in the middle school: (1) strong academic focus, (2) high-quality expectations, and (3) a continuation of grouping by ability. The parent preferences from the Q-sort they completed showed (1) a strong desire for emphasis on academics and (2) a preference that their children be in classes with children of similar ability. Parents least preferred a program focus on (1) metacognition or (2) the affective domain. Student results from the Q-sort indicated that the students wanted to be active participants in their learning by focusing on (1) field trips and (2) areas of interest. Students, like parents, indicated that the program should (3) strongly focus on academics. Like the parents, students least preferred a program focus on (1) metacognition or (2) the affective domain.

The results of the teacher survey indicated a great difference between what they felt was most important and what the district had implemented.

Program Design

Based on the results, the committee suggested program features that included the following:

1. Providing a program with a strong academic focus.
2. Having high expectations for students, with an intervention assistance team to meet the needs of underachieving or nonperforming students.
3. Grouping by ability when the class size is too large to permit differentiating for the academically talented students.
4. Providing regular classroom teachers with adequate support services so that enrichment is available to able learners in the regular classroom. This led to the request for the hiring of an additional resource teacher.
5. Developing the most appropriate teaching strategies to maximize achievement.
6. Providing adequate staff development opportunities in providing for able learners.
7. Constructing an assessment guide for placement in classes and levels.

Based on administrative concerns and needs, the committee listed what the program must include.

1. The resource teacher must have Ohio certification in talented and gifted education. For counseling and coaching the team members must have the skills necessary in place or must be agreeable to obtain training.

2. The ASP teacher should have Ohio reading specialist certification. Other academic areas such as mathematics, social studies, and science would be added in the future.

3. The ASP teacher should be willing to take on a leadership role in the implementation of the newly adopted language arts curriculum and to serve as a resource for all teachers. An in-house language arts and reading specialist would aid and assist all teachers in the implementation process, which would include all students.

Contextual Framework of the Program

The committee recommended that the sixth grade would continue to include the option of the self-contained classroom, with enrichment in the regular classrooms for other academically talented students who did not meet IQ cutoff scores. At the end of sixth grade, all students who qualify for the Advanced Study Program in specific content areas would be identified. The top thirty students would be placed in the program. For students talented in language arts, the language arts block would focus on advanced literature and writing using units built around themes. Teams would focus on both student adjustment needs and on the development of interdisciplinary curriculum. The teacher hired for the enrichment position would aid in designing and weaving the themes into specific content areas for the team. This special new teacher would then be used as an intervention specialist to assist teachers in the regular classroom with academically talented students with needs in other academic areas.

Because the program development was data-driven, by both the Q-sort and the surveys, the parents of the academically talented students were receptive and supportive of the work of the committee, as were members of the community, teachers in the district, and administrators. The committee acted based on surveyed needs of the constituents. All stake-holding populations were part of the decision-making process and the program was designed in consonance with their input.

The Pyramid of Talent Development Model in the Middle School Setting

Educators have been trying to escape the tyranny of the IQ score since 1925, when Terman began his longitudinal study of high-IQ students in California. Gardner's (1983) designation of talents as "intelligences" and Sternberg's (1988) assertion that intelligence includes the practical, the creative, and the executive spoke to the hearts of many educators; their work was preceded by attempts to modify Guilford's model of the intellect for school purposes (Meeker, 1977). The first author of this chapter has worked for many years trying to minimize the influence of the IQ score in identification of the gifted and talented, as have many of her colleagues, using several models (e.g., the SOI model, the Taylor Talents Unlimited model, the Renzulli Triad model, etc.). New interpretations of the giftedness construct have recently arisen in models focusing on talent development and not on IQ level (Feldhusen, 1995; Piirto, 1994). The sketch of the human being and the developmental influences on that person is called the Piirto Pyramid of Talent Development.

The Piirto Pyramid of Talent Development

I. The Emotional Level

The four levels of the pyramid are the genes, personality attributes, minimum intellectual competencies, and specific domain talents (Figure 10.2).

Many studies have emphasized that successful creators in all domains have certain *personality attributes* in common. These make up the base of the model. These are the affective, or emotional intelligence aspects of what a person needs to succeed. These rest on the foundation of *genes*.

Among the personality attributes are *aggressiveness* (Simonton, 1984, 1992, 1994); *androgyny* (Barron, 1968; Csikszentmihalyi, Rathune, & Whalen, 1993; Piirto & Fraas, 1995); *creativity* (Piirto, 1992/1998; Renzulli, 1978; Tannenbaum, 1983); *imagination* (Piirto, 1992); *insight* (Davidson, 1992; Sternberg & Davidson, 1995); *intuition* (Myers & McCaulley, 1985); the presence of *overexcitabilities*, called OEs (Piechowski, 1979; Silverman, 1993); *passion for work in a domain* (Benbow, 1992; Bloom, 1985; Piirto, 1992); *perceptiveness* (Myers & McCaulley, 1985); *perfectionism* (Silverman, 1993); *persistence* (Renzulli, 1978); *resilience* (Jenkins-Friedman, 1992; Block & Kremen,1996); *risk taking* (MacKinnon, 1978; Torrance, 1987); *self-discipline* (Renzulli, 1978); *self-efficacy* (Sternberg & Lubart, 1991; Zimmerman, Bandura, & Martinez-Pons, 1992); *tolerance for ambiguity* (Barron, 1968, 1995); and *volition, or will* (Corno & Kanfer, 1993).

This list is by no means complete, but it indicates some of the work that has been done on the personalities of effective people. This work has converged to show that effective adults have achieved effectiveness by force of personality. Talented adults who achieve success possess many of these attributes. Winner (1996) in her synthesis of research has listed among the nine myths about giftedness the idea that IQ level should determine who should receive special programming; this idea should be put to rest as being inefficient, and personality factors should be looked at. Csikszentmihalyi, Rathune, and Whalen (1993) said such personality attributes make up the *autotelic personality,* in which "flow," or the ability to tap into optimal experiences, is accessible. These aspects of personality are present in some way in highly effective people. One could call these the foundation, and one could go further and say that these may be innate but they can also be developed and directly taught.

II. The Cognitive Level

The *cognitive* dimension in the form of an IQ score has been overemphasized. If there were no IQ tests, we would still be able to find and serve talented children, for the IQ test is often an abstract screen that obfuscates our efforts. The IQ was designated as a *minimum* criterion, with a certain level necessary for functioning in the world, but studies have repeatedly shown that having a high IQ is not

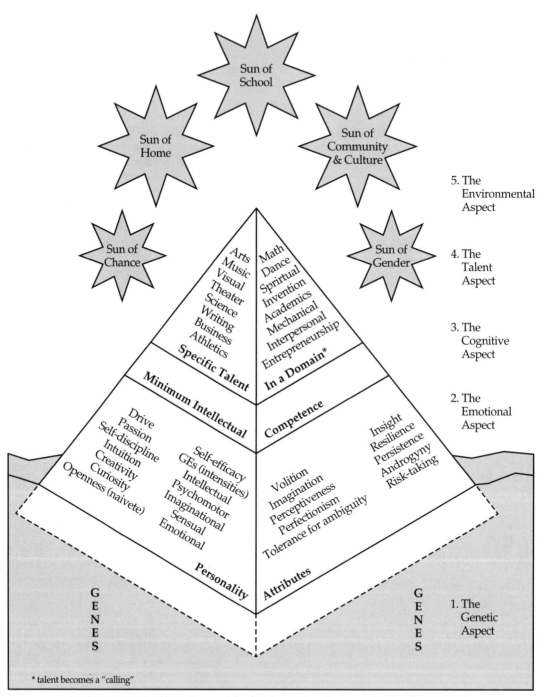

FIGURE 10.2 Piirto Pyramid of Talent Development. (Revised 2/98)

necessary for the realization of most talents (e.g., Baird, 1985). Rather, college graduation seems to be necessary (except for professional basketball players, actors, and entertainers), and most college graduates have above average IQs but not stratospheric ones (Simonton, 1995).

Talent in Domains

The *talent* itself—inborn, innate, mysterious—should be the focus. Each school has experts in most of the talent domains that students will enter. Talent is the tip of the pyramid. When a child can draw so well that he is designated the class artist or can throw a ball 85 miles an hour, when a student is accused of cheating on her short story assignment because it sounds so adult, talent is present. Most talents are recognized through certain *predictive behaviors*, for example, voracious reading for linguistically talented students and preferring to be class treasurer (not president) for mathematically talented students (Piirto, 1994). These talents are demonstrated within domains that are socially recognized and valued within the society.

Talent Multipotentiality: Feeling the "Thorn"

Although absolutely necessary, the presence of talent is not sufficient in itself. Many people have more than one talent and wonder what to do with them. What is the impetus, what is the reason, for one talent taking over and capturing the passion and commitment of the person who has the talent? A useful explanation comes from Socrates, who described the inspiration of the Muse (Plato, *Ion*; Piirto, 1992/1998), Carl Jung (1965) described the passion that engrosses, Csikszentmihalyi (1991) described the process of flow, and depth psychologist James Hillman (1996) described the presence of the *daimon* in creative lives. All these give clue to what talent a person will choose to develop.

Hillman (1996) described the difference between talent and giftedness in a way similar to Plato's and Jung's: "The talent is only a piece of the image; many are born with musical, mathematical, and mechanical talent, but only when the talent serves the fuller image and is carried by its character do we recognize exceptionality" (p. 251). Hillman's idea is similar to the notion of "vocation" or "call." I would call it inspiration or passion for the domain. Philosophers would call it "soul." Thus I have put an asterisk, or "thorn" on the pyramid to exemplify that talent is not enough for the realization of a life of commitment. Without going into the classical topics of Desire, Emotion, Art, Poetry, Beauty, Wisdom, or Soul (Adler, 1952), suffice it to say that the entire picture of talent development ensues when a person is pierced or bothered by a thorn, the *daimon*, that leads to commitment.

Feldman was close when he described the *crystallizing experience* (Feldman, 1982), but the thorn is more than crystallizing; it is fortifying. One of the definitions of "gift" comes from Old French for "poison," and this is what the talent that bothers may become to a person if the person doesn't pay attention to it. As well as a joy it is a burden. As well as a pleasure, it is a pain. However, the person who possesses the talent also must possess the will and fortitude to pursue the talent into whatever labyrinth it may lead. Teachers in the middle school are uniquely positioned to view the budding of the branch that will contain the thorn.

Environmental "Suns"

The four levels of the Piirto Pyramid could theoretically be called the individual person. In addition, everyone is influenced by five "suns." These suns can be likened to certain factors in the environment. Many teachers feel they are merely putting their finger into the dike because the students have so many outside-of-school influences that bear upon their school performance, and even upon whether or not the students can be taught. These have been called "suns." The three major suns refer to a child's being in a positive and nurturing *home* environment, and in a *community and culture* that conveys values compatible with the educational institution and that provides support for the home and the school. The *school* is a key factor, especially for those children whose other "suns" may have clouds in front of them. Other, smaller suns are the influence of *gender* and what *chance* can provide. The presence or absence of all or several of these makes the difference between whether a talent is developed or atrophies.

Unfortunately, it could be said that when a student emerges into adulthood with his or her talent nurtured and developed, it is a miracle, because there are so many influences that encroach on talent development. We all know or remember people with outstanding talent who did not or were not able to use or develop that talent because of circumstances such as represented by these "suns." For example, a student whose home life contains trauma such as divorce or poverty may be so involved in that trauma that the talent cannot be emphasized. The school's role becomes to recognize the talent and to encourage lessons, mentors, or special experiences that the parents would otherwise have provided had their situation been better. The "suns" that shine on the pyramid may be hidden by clouds, and in that case, the *school* plays a key role in the child's environment.

As another example, in a racist society the genes that produce one's race are acted upon environmentally; a person of a certain race may be treated differently in different environments. The *school* and the *community and culture* are important in developing or enhancing this genetic inheritance. Retired general Colin Powell has said that he entered the army because he saw the military as the only place in a racist society where he would be treated fairly, where his genetic African American inheritance would not be discriminated against, where he could develop his talents fully.

I have elsewhere explicated my ideas about the influences on talent and talent development with more detail (Piirto, 1992/1998, 1994, 1995a, 1995b; Piirto & Fraas, 1995). This sketch was developed with a view that students, teachers, and parents should find it understandable and usable, while it should also be research-based and powerful, simple, and elegant. Perhaps the situation of students' not making use of their talents can be helped by teaching them directly about the factors that lead to optimum development conditions; when we do not do things *to* children ("Surprise, surprise—you're gifted and talented because we got the results of that IQ test! Now sit back and we'll put you into a program"), but instead work *with* students, empowering them to work with themselves. Perhaps the model discussed here can help.

Case Example 2

Using the Pyramid of Talent Development in the Middle School

Paula Wilkes

During the past 5 years, I have been trying new strategies that have increased the effort and quality of my students' work. I have taught them to use mind-mapping, multiple intelligences, portfolios, self-assessment rubrics, and project-based learning. I do a lot of consulting and speaking to other teachers, and I have also used these strategies with them. However, the real breakthrough came to me in January, 1995, when a colleague who knew I was interested in Howard Gardner's multiple intelligence theory and the misuse of IQ as intelligence told me of Jane Piirto's Pyramid of Talent Development and gave me an article that had been published in Europe (Piirto, 1995).

After reading Piirto's explanation of the pyramid, which had been written as part of a textbook called *Talented Children and Adults: Their Development and Education* (1994), I knew that with a little modification and work I could make it a model for my classroom, a full-inclusion classroom of thirty-four fourth and fifth graders. The class included five students on special education IEPs (two with behavior plans) and twelve identified talented and gifted students, so it would be a challenge to find any model that would have meaning for such a diverse group of students. I used the Piirto Pyramid model because *all* students need to develop the aspects of their personality that lead to classroom success, not only the academically talented. The academically talented students would also benefit from the individualization the model intends.

The only change I made to the model, so that 9- and 10-year olds could understand, was to relate the top third to the seven multiple intelligences, which they already knew. Thus, I linked talent in writing to linguistic intelligence; talent in mathematics and science to logical-mathematical and spatial intelligence; athletic talent to bodily-kinesthetic intelligence; acting talent to bodily-kinesthetic, linguistic, and the personal intelligences, and so on. Piirto has linked these in her book *Understanding Those Who Create* (1992) as well as in the textbook, and I felt using multiple intelligences clarified the top of the pyramid for the students. At the bottom of the pyramid I deleted personality attributes that the students might not understand, such as androgyny, which Piirto said means flexibility and lack of rigidness in sex role stereotyping (personal communication, April 1996). I chose key words that the students could relate to such as *self-discipline, drive, persistence, passion, resilience, leadership,* and *imagination.* Each student was given a copy of the pyramid. The "suns" were colored as I gave concrete examples, and the students put their copy under the "self smart" section (i.e., intrapersonal and interpersonal intelligences) of their portfolios.

During the 1995–96 school year, I taught twenty-eight fifth graders, twelve of whom I had had the previous year and who were familiar with the pyramid. I decided to start off the first day with an overview of the Pyramid of Talent Development. It was wonderful to have students who were able to give "kid examples" of the meaning the pyramid held for them. Two students built a 3-D poster of the pyramid, and it became a year-long bulletin board. When students or I found articles in magazines or newspapers that typified an aspect of the pyramid, we would discuss it and add it to our growing collection.

For example, we found articles about a motivational speaker who, because of his personality attributes and the shining sun of his adoptive mother, was able to overcome great hardship. We talked about a local high school senior who was among forty students nationwide in the Westinghouse Science Talent Search. In an article in our local paper, this high school student said that she didn't consider herself that much brighter than anyone else. She said that she worked hard and loved to do it. That's what makes the most difference. She felt that perhaps it's not a matter of innate ability as much as knowing what you love to do. We talked about her personality attributes and the fact that the suns of home and school had been shining on her by providing her with challenging learning experiences.

We also read articles about a teenager trying to escape three generations of poverty by being the first member of her family to attend college. We read about, and later met, a 15-year-old tuba player whose innate talent and self-discipline had won him a prestigious scholarship to a music academy. We also talked about a dyslexic college student whose hard work earned him an international mathematics award. It seemed as though nearly every week we were able to find examples about how the personality attributes of individuals and/or the suns that shone on them had made a significant difference in helping them realize their talents.

The pyramid made its way into Back to School Curriculum Nights, parent conferences, and newsletters to families. It became an important framework for the way I taught and the way students worked. At the end of major projects the students were asked to assess their effort, their persistence, and/or the quality of their work. By the end of the year, most of the students had realized that they were in control of the amount they learned and the projects that demonstrated that learning. For students who did not have the sun of home shining down on them, I made an effort to get them to reach out to others when they needed assistance rather than using that cloud as an excuse.

Not only were students aware of the progress they had made, but so were many of the parents. "Carolyn" was a student who had felt that she wasn't "smart," and her mother had spoken with the school psychologist several times the previous year about her negative self-image. Carolyn was really taken with the idea of the pyramid and discussed examples with me. During fall term, she and her classmates were asked to read an historical novel, of which six of the sixteen chapters needed to be illustrated and summarized. Carolyn made an outstanding illustration and summary for all sixteen chapters! She realized that she was in charge of the base of the pyramid, and there was no stopping her. In May, she entered her portfolio in a county-wide competition and earned a medal.

"Maggie" was the only student I've ever had who had gifted abilities in all seven intelligences. She took the SAT in the Johns Hopkins Center for Talented Youth Talent Search program and scored "high honors" in both the verbal and mathematical categories. At a district track meet, she won the 100-yard dash, and she was an outstanding soccer and basketball player. Her musical skills included not only singing and playing the piano and recorder, but she was also able to put a poem to music. Perhaps her greatest talents were in the personal intelligences. She was quite reflective about her work and her relationships, and she was chosen as a peer conflict manager. This was a student whose personality attributes headed her for success while keeping her relatively free of stress. She displayed great emotional intelligence (Goleman, 1995). I came to realize that directly teaching about personality attributes and encouraging students to develop these attributes was what Goleman had been talking about in his recent book, which fit right in with the pyramid and the multiple intelligences focus I had been using.

"Simon" was a boy who had experienced the loss of two significant male relationships due to divorce, and he appeared to lack self-esteem in most areas of his academic life. During his fifth grade year, his first project was of very poor quality, so I asked him to redo the assignment. Rather than doing it on his own, he was rescued by his mother, who did most of the work. When he presented it to his peers, they asked who had done the drawing, and he said his mom had. There wasn't a real sense of ownership. I sat down with Simon and talked with him about how it would be his personality attributes that would determine whether he would realize his talents. At the end of last school year, after a year and a half of focusing on what the pyramid was showing, Simon submitted a wonderful portfolio of learning. He told his classmates in a final class meeting that he had learned how important it was to work hard and produce quality work, and that he was proud of himself for the effort he was now putting into his learning.

Are every one of my students realizing their talents? Definitely not! But the pyramid gave us a good place to focus our attention. At the end of the year I gave my students a blank pyramid and asked them to color the suns that were shining on them, to identify the talents they possess, and to list personality attributes they were "currently using" in one column and those they were "still learning about" in another. Although all the students had made progress toward becoming independent learners, the three students I continued to worry about had listed "drive" and "self-discipline" as areas still needing to be developed. Perhaps their middle school teachers will see the applications of the Pyramid of Talent Development.

In *Emotional Intelligence* (1995), Goleman cites several psychologists who suggest that being able to get into "flow" while doing work is the difference between students who do well in school and those who do not. It is not a matter of IQ or other measure of "intelligence," but of being challenged by and getting satisfaction from the work we do. I believe that understanding the Pyramid of Talent Development gave my students the impetus to work harder, and the result of that effort was a sense of accomplishment and a willingness to continue to strive to be the best that they can be. The Pyramid of Talent Development, with its strong visual presentation and ideas that can be understood by parents and students alike, is a powerful tool that should be shared with students.

Summary

In summary, this chapter has focused on three main points: (1) that the middle school concept as currently implemented often shortchanges the needs of academically talented students, (2) that current research can be utilized in designing optimal middle school programs that meet the needs of talented students, and (3) that the Pyramid of Talent Development can serve as a framework for meeting the needs of all youth in an inclusionary setting.

Discussion Questions

1. Look at the Pyramid of Talent Development and discuss your own middle school experience and how your talents were helped or harmed by the experience.
2. Discuss the concept of ability grouping as it relates to meeting the academic needs of high-ability students in the middle school.
3. Debate the arguments for ability grouping in the middle school.
4. Debate the arguments against ability grouping in the middle school.
5. How can we develop a person's personality attributes, internal motivation, and desire to learn?

References

Adler, M. (1952). *The great ideas: A syntopticon of great books of the western world.* Chicago: The Encyclopedia Britanica.

Armstrong, D. (1995a). *ADAPT: Armstrong Diagnostic and Prescriptive Technique for accommodating both group and individual differences among gifted and talented students in the classroom.* Grand Valley State University, Grand Rapids, MI: Author.

Armstrong, D. (1995b). *Gifted students' preferred programming practices: A followup study.* Paper presented at National Association for Gifted

Children conference, Tampa, FL, November.

Baird, L. (1985). Do grades and tests predict adult accomplishment? *Research in Higher Education, 23*(1), 3–85.

Barron, F. (1968). *Creativity and personal freedom.* New York: Van Nostrand.

Barron, F. (1995). *No rootless flower: An ecology of creativity.* Cresskill, NJ: Hampton Press.

Benbow, C. P. (1992). Mathematical talent: Its nature and consequences. In N. Colangelo, S. G. Assouline, & D. L. Ambroson (Eds.), *Talent development: Proceedings from the 1991 Henry B.*

and Jocelyn Wallace National Research Symposium on Talent Development (pp. 95–123). Unionville, NY: Trillium Press.

Block, J., & Kremen, A. M. (1996). IQ and ego resiliency. *Journal of Personality and Social Psychology, 70*(2), 346–361.

Bloom, B. (Ed.) (1985). *Developing talent in young people.* New York: Ballantine.

Coleman, M., Gallagher, J., & Howard, J. (1993). *Middle school site visit report: Five schools in profile.* Chapel Hill, NC: Gifted Education Policy Studies Program, University of North Carolina at Chapel Hill.

Coleman, M., Gallagher, J., & Nelson, S. (1993). *Cooperative learning and gifted students: Report on five case studies.* Chapel Hill, NC: Gifted Education Policy Studies Program, University of North Carolina at Chapel Hill.

Corno, L., & Kanfer, R. (1993). The role of volition in learning and performance. In L. Darling-Hammond (Ed.), *Review of research in education* (vol. 19) (pp. 301–342). Washington, DC: American Educational Research Association.

Csikszentmihalyi, M. (1991). *Flow: The psychology of optimal experience.* New York:

Csikszentmihalyi, M., Rathune, K., & Whalen, S. (1993). *Talented teenagers: The roots of success and failure.* New York: Cambridge University Press.

Davidson, J. E. (1992). Insights about giftedness: The role of problem solving abilities. In N. Colangelo, S. G. Assouline, & D. L. Ambroson (Eds.), *Talent development: Proceedings from the 1991 Henry B. and Jocelyn Wallace National Research Symposium on Talent Development* (pp. 125–142). Unionville, NY: Trillium Press.

Epstein, J., & MacIver, D. (1990). *Education in the middle grades: National practices and trends.* Columbus, OH: National Middle Schools Association.

Feldhusen, J. (1995). Talent development versus gifted education. *Educational Forum, 59*(4,) 346–349.

Gallagher, J., Coleman, M., & Nelson, S. (1993). *Cooperative learning as perceived by educators of gifted students and proponents of cooperative education.* Chapel Hill: Gifted Education Policy Studies Program, University of North Carolina at Chapel Hill.

Gardner, H. (1983). *Frames of mind.* New York: Basic Books.

George, P. (1988). Tracking and ability grouping. *Middle School Journal, 20*(1), 21–28.

Goleman, D. (1995). *Emotional intelligence.* New York: Bantam.

Hillman, J. (1996). *The soul's code.* New York: Random House.

Jenkins-Friedman, R. (1992). Zorba's conundrum: Evaluative aspect of self-concept in talented individuals. *Quest, 3*(1), 1–7.

Joyce, B. (1991). Common misconceptions about cooperative learning and gifted students. *Educational Leadership, 48*(5), 72–74.

Jung, C. (1965). *Memories, dreams, and reflections.* New York: Vintage.

Kulik, J. A. (1985, August). Effects of inter-class ability grouping on achievement and self-esteem. Paper presented at the 93rd annual convention of the American Psychological Association, Los Angeles.

Kulik, J. A. (1992a). Ability grouping and gifted students. In N. Colangelo, S. G. Assouline, & D. L. Ambroson (Eds.), *Talent development: Proceedings from the 1991 Henry B. and Jocelyn Wallace National Research Symposium on Talent Development* (pp. 261–266). Unionville, NY: Trillium Press.

Kulik, J. A. (1992b). An analysis of the research on ability grouping: Historical and contemporary perspectives. *Research-based decision making series.* University of Connecticut: National Research Center on the Gifted and Talented.

Kulik, J. A., & Kulik, C.-L. C. (1982). Effects of ability grouping on secondary school students: A meta-analysis of evaluation findings. *American Educational Research Journal, 19,* 415–428.

Kulik, J. A., & Kulik, C.-L. C. (1984a). Effects of accelerated instruction on students. *Review of Educational Research, 54,* 409–425.

Kulik, J. A., & Kulik, C.-L.C. (1984b). Synthesis of research of effects of accelerated instruction. *Educational Leadership, 42,* 84–89.

Kulik, J. A., & Kulik, C.-L.C. (1987). Effects of ability grouping on student achievement. *Equity and Excellence, 23,* 22–30.

Kulik, J. A., & Kulik, C.-L. C. (1990). Ability grouping and gifted students. In N. Colangelo & G. A. Davis (Eds.), *Handbook of Gifted Education* (pp. 178–196). Boston: Allyn and Bacon.

Kulik, J. A., & Kulik, C.-L. C. (1991). Ability grouping and gifted students. In N. Colangelo & G. A. Davis (Eds.), *Handbook of gifted education* (pp. 178–196). Needham Heights, MA: Allyn and Bacon.

Kulik, J. A., & Kulik, C.-L.C. (1997). Ability grouping. In N. Colangelo & G. A. Davis (Eds.), *Handbook of gifted education* (2d Ed.) (pp. 230–242). Boston: Allyn and Bacon.

MacKinnon, D. W. (1975). IPAR's contribution to the conceptualization and study of creativity. In I. A. Taylor & J. W. Getzels (Eds.), *Perspectives in creativity* (pp. 60–89). Chicago: Aldine.

MacKinnon, D. (1978). *In search of human effectiveness.* Buffalo, NY: Bearly.

Meeker, M. (1977). *The structure of intellect.* Columbus, OH: Merrill.

Mills, C., & Durden, W. (1992). Cooperative learning and ability grouping: An issue of choice. *Gifted Child Quarterly, 36*(1), 11–16.

Myers, I. B., & McCaulley, M. H. (1985). *Manual: A guide to the development and use of the Myers-Briggs Type Indicator.* Palo Alto, CA: Consulting Psychologists Press.

Nelson, S., Gallagher, J., & Coleman, M.R. (1993). Cooperative learning from two different perspectives. *Roeper Review, 16,* 117–121.

Oakes, J. (1985). *Keeping track: How schools structure inequality.* New Haven, CT: Yale University Press.

Piechowski, M. M. (1979). Developmental potential. In N. Colangelo & R. T. Zaffrann (Eds.), *New voices in counseling the gifted* (pp. 25–57). Dubuque, IA: Kendall/Hunt.

Piirto, J. (1992/1998). *Understanding those who create.* Tempe, AZ: Gifted Psychology Press.

Piirto, J. (1994). *Talented children and adults: Their development and education.* New York: Macmillan.

Piirto, J. (1995a). Deeper and broader: The Pyramid of Talent Development in the context of the giftedness construct. In M. W. Katzko and F. J. Mönks (Eds.), *Nurturing talent: Individual needs and social ability* (pp. 10–20). Proceedings

of the Fourth Conference of the European Council for High Ability. The Netherlands: Van Gorcum, Assen.

Piirto, J. (1995b). Deeper and broader: The Pyramid of Talent Development in the context of the giftedness construct. *Educational Forum, 59,* 364–369.

Piirto, J., & Fraas, J. (1995). Androgyny in the personalities of talented adolescents. *Journal for Secondary Gifted Education, 1,* 93–102.

Plato. *Ion.* Chicago: Great Books Foundation.

Renzulli, J. (1978). What makes giftedness? Re-examining a definition. *Phi Delta Kappan, 60,* 180–184, 261.

Robinson, A. (1990). Cooperation or exploitation? The argument against cooperative learning for talented students. *Journal for the Education of the Gifted, 14,* 9–27.

Ross, P. (1993). *National excellence: A case for developing America's talent.* Washington, DC: U.S. Department of Education.

Shore, B. M., Cornell, D. G., Robinson, A., & Ward, V. S. (1991). *Recommended practices in gifted education.* New York: Teachers College Press.

Sicola, P. (1990). Where do gifted students fit? An examination of middle school philosophy as it relates to ability grouping and the gifted learner. *Journal for the Education of the Gifted, 14,* 37–49.

Silverman, L. K. (Ed.) (1993). *Counseling the gifted and talented.* Denver, CO: Love.

Simonton, D. K. (1984). *Genius, creativity, and leadership: Historiometric inquiries.* Cambridge, MA: Harvard University Press.

Simonton, D. K. (1988). *Scientific genius.* New York: Harvard University Press.

Simonton, D. K. (1992). The child parents the adult: On getting genius from giftedness. In N. Colangelo, S. G. Assouline, & D. L. Ambroson (Eds.), *Talent development: Proceedings from 1991 Henry and Jocelyn Wallace National Research Symposium on Talent Development* (pp. 278–297). Unionville, NY: Trillium Press.

Simonton, D. K. (1994). *Greatness: Who makes history and why.* New York: Guilford.

Slavin, R. (1987). Ability grouping and student achievement in elementary schools: A best-evidence synthesis. *Review of Educational Research, 57,* 293–336.

Slavin, R. (1990). Ability grouping, cooperative learning, and the gifted. *Journal for the Education of the Gifted, 14*, 3–8.

Slavin, R. (1991). Synthesis of research on cooperative learning. *Educational Leadership, 47*(4), 3.

Sternberg, R. J. (1988). *The triarchic mind: A new theory of human intelligence.* New York: Viking.

Sternberg, R., & Davidson, J. (Eds.) (1995). *The nature of insight.* Cambridge, MA: MIT Press.

Sternberg, R., & Lubart, T. I. (1991). An investment theory of creativity and its development. *Human Development, 34*, 1–31.

Tannenbaum, A. (1983). *Gifted children.* New York: Macmillan.

Taylor, C. W. (1969). The highest talent potentials of man. *Gifted Child Quarterly, 13*, 9–20.

Tomlinson, C. A. (1992). Gifted education and the middle school movement: Two voices on teaching the academically talented. *Journal for the Education of the Gifted, 15*, 206–238.

Tomlinson, C. A. (1994). Gifted learners: The boomerang kids of middle school? *Roeper Review, 16*(3), 177–182.

Tomlinson, C. A. (1995). Deciding to differentiate instruction in middle school: One school's journey. *Gifted Child Quarterly, 39*(2), 77–87.

Torrance, E. P. (1987). Teaching for creativity. In S. Isaksen (Ed.), *Frontiers of creativity research: Beyond the basics* (pp. 190–215). Buffalo, NY: Bearly Ltd.

Vars, G. F., & Rakow, S. R. (1993). Making connections: Integrative curriculum and the gifted student. *Roeper Review, 16*(1), 48–53.

Wells, A. S., & Serna, I. (1996). The politics of culture: Understanding local political resistance to detracking in racially mixed schools. *Harvard Educational Review, 66*(1), 93–118.

Winner, E. (1996). *Gifted children.* New York: Basic Books.

Zimmerman, B. J., Bandura, A., & Martinez-Pons, M. (1992). Self-motivation for academic attainment: The role of self-efficacy beliefs and personal goal setting. *American Educational Research Journal, 29*(3), 663–676.

Chapter 11

With Art at the Heart of Writing

JANICE GALLAGHER

Janice Gallagher is Gifted Education Coordinator for Euclid City Schools in Euclid, Ohio. She has taught English at the middle school and high school levels, where she worked extensively to integrate art into the school curriculum.

If writing teachers answer the question "What do middle school students need?" they will also answer a familiar question centering on how to get middle school students to write. Recently participants in an art and writing academy gave me the answer. A visiting art critic presented slides of Lauren Greenfield's award-winning book *Fast Forward*, a photo journal look at teens living in the glitter capital of the world, Los Angeles, California. After showing the students seventy-seven slides of teens doing various activities at home, at school, and in the community, the art critic asked the students how these teens were similar to them. I was amazed at the answers. Overwhelmingly the students from mid-western Ohio responded that while the teens in Greenfield's work had more money, better clothes, and a totally different set of values, they were all searching for the same things: acceptance, self-respect, and love.

My 25 years in public education confirmed what these young people revealed: Middle school students do need acceptance, self-respect, and love. From my own research involving adults who describe themselves as lifelong writers, the message also rang true. Adults in my study credited positive reinforcement from significant people, primarily teachers, as the major factor in their development as a writer. Encouragement from teachers fulfilled their need for acceptance and self-respect.

One of the participants in my study was Barb Slater, an 83-year-old freelance writer. She admitted that she'd kept the essay she'd written about a sunset in the sixth grade because her teacher had read it in front of the entire class. Similarly, Terry Barrett, author and art critic, remembered a priest who nurtured him on his way to becoming a writer by complimenting him for writing "beautiful" sentences. Praise and encouragement, however, usually come after students have written something.

Few teachers would disagree with teacher and author Mem Fox, who writes that students must "ache with caring" about their writing. She relates a story about surveying her freshman college students about things they wrote in their pre-college days. Few could remember any particular writings; they had just fulfilled a teacher's assignment and then forgotten about it.

Most English and language arts teachers want more from their students than meaningless writing. If the assignment opens a path to the student's heart, heartfelt writing is the reward. Researchers and theorists have suggested many ways to guide students to that inward path, and most agree that common story starters or writing prompts fail in that regard. For writing to be meaningful, topics must be student-generated.

Rico's *Writing the Natural Way* (1983) was the first book in which I encountered clustering as a prewriting exercise. Clustering, Rico suggests, is a "magic key for getting in touch with these secret reserves of imaginative power" (p. 28). It begins with students writing a topic in the center of the paper and drawing a circle around it. They draw lines from the circle to possible connecting ideas. The clustering is always completed within a minute or two, with the nucleus word serving as the stimulus for recording all associations that spring into the mind. After students complete the clustering, they use the web to write their stories from it. Thus they have overcome the major stumbling block, that first step, finding a topic.

Other authors advocate ways of helping students find topics for writing. Lucy McCormack Calkins, for example, suggests that observation is the first step in topic finding. She maintains that students, even as young as second grade, should keep journals. In their journals they record daily observations of the world in which they live. At the end of the week or so, students leaf through what they've written to find a topic to "gather around." Her example was the young girl who selected to write about a litter of kittens she'd found under her back porch. Her "gathering" amounted to writing down all that she knew about cats and any cat connections. The student had generated the topic and had gathered all the data she needed to write about kittens.

In *A Book of One's Own* (1990), Paul Johnson used the metaphor of a door to describe entrance into the imagination:

> *Some doors into the imagination open easily, and some do not. But most are penetrable, providing the appropriate stimulation is applied. The rusty door— This kind of door, by far the most common, does not yield easily. It is fastened by misuse and needs constant oiling of hinges. It is typified by children being given ideas for a story, none of which are taken up and fed inwardly. So much care must be taken here for crafted means of entry are needed. To scrape away*

too rigorously ("Now I want us to think out all the furnishing inside the underground castle. John, you tell us all about the pictures on the walls, and Mary, you tell us all about the things on the mantelpiece . . .") *can damage the door itself, making entry even harder. Children can so easily be frightened by not being able to "think of something," to be terrorized into non-participation, by insistence. Most destructive of all is the attempt to destroy the door with a hammer blow* ("What an unimaginative lot you all are. Now come on, Peter, surely you can think of something!") *So much depends upon the rapport between teacher and taught. Children must feel at ease. . . . (p. 15)*

Students have many doors that, when opened, will lead to successful writing. One door might be marked memory; another might be marked models; another logic. For me, art was at the center of making the creative writing chemistry work. Using art as a prewriting activity makes it possible for children to "fly through the keyhole, and so reach inside themselves" (Johnson, 1990, p. 16).

Johnson used a door as a metaphor for getting inside the writer. My experience confirms that the best writing comes from within. In 19 years of teaching reading and writing to middle school students, the best strategy was the Creative Hook. The Creative Hook permits creativity that "springs from deep inside you, flowing outward to help us handle new experiences, and, most of all, to help us express our individuality" (Marks-Tarlow, 1996, p. ix). The Creative Hook sets students in the right direction by meeting some of the needs particular to this age group.

The Creative Hook involves students in writing from art they have created. It is important to say that the art may not necessarily be "great" art, and it is not meant to be. The art is meant to open the path that leads students to discover things they know, but they don't know they know. Creating the art is a springboard for the writing; it also helps the students shed the shell of self-consciousness and self-absorption and gives them freedom to cast aside concerns about appearances and fitting in.

The Creative Hook is a magical, exciting, and challenging way to teach creative writing. It allows students to tap the power of both the creative brain and the logical brain by beginning the writing process with an art start. As students create a main character or a setting for a story, their minds begin to create a mental draft of what they will write. Later this image takes shape as the works are written on paper.

The hands are a magic connection between the logical brain and creative brain. Once the students have created the main character of the story with their hands, they know the character. They can imagine relationships that their main character might have with other characters, both friends and adversaries. Adventures in which their main character might be involved seem plausible and real.

Another important advantage of the Creative Hook is that it provides an immediate experience from which to write. "All real learning is experiential," wrote Johnson (1993, p. 3). The Creative Hook allows the writer to create an experience that connects the inner and the outer worlds. Once this connection is made, the writer can draw from internal wells of data. Writing becomes a personal and enjoyable activity instead of a chore of shaping words into a predetermined and intensely impersonal scheme.

Just like the prewriting exercises described by other authors and educators, the Creative Hook helps students generate information and gather data about a topic before they begin to compose their stories. The art that the students create is nonthreatening and fun, which makes the writing also fun. It is important that students learn that writing can be fun. "Writing for fun is not just for fun—it's for the long-term, conspicuous development of the craft itself. Within the fun of writing there is also power" (Fox, 1993, p. 18).

Creative Hook Writing Ideas

Creative ideas for connecting art activities with creative writing opportunities are described in the following subsections. Each demonstrates how students use the power of the creative inner self to help guide them in creating unusual and highly individual compositions.

Writing from Food Coloring Trails

Writing from food coloring trails draws on the childhood experience. Using drinking straws and dots of food coloring placed on white paper, students blow the food coloring and "chase" it in winding trails across the paper. Standing at their desks, they laugh and chat as they blow the food coloring across the paper. Sometimes they give advice to one another, or they announce discoveries. "Hey, look at this!" said one of the males in my class. "If you put your straw right in the center of the drop, and you blow really quick and hard, you get a kind of starburst—like a fireworks or an explosion."

"Yeah," answered another, "and if you turn your paper you can really make zig-zaggy trails—reminds me of legs on a daddy long legs."

When they've finished, they examine the shapes and the negative shapes, as if finding shapes in clouds. One of my students looked at her straw-blown trails and remarked, "Hey! I have two women who are wearing fancy hats to a dressy party. They are arguing with each other because one is saying that she has a better hat than the other. The other one is saying, 'No! Mine is better!'"

"Write that story," I whispered to my student. She had all she needed; she had the setting, the characters, and the plot. She even had the dialogue, and all of it came from a simple little prewriting art activity.

"See this?" said another student, "It's a man running, and it's like he's running for his life—not in a race or anything, but like time is running out and he's running and running."

"Write it," I whispered. "You've got your character. You've got your plot. Time is running out. What will happen to him? Will he beat the clock? Will he get to do all the things he wanted to do with his life? Will he accomplish his dreams? As you write, you will find the answers to those questions."

Creating the artwork connected the students to internal knowledge. The student who saw the hats knew something about the passion for fashion. She also knew something about competition among women. The young man who saw a man running knew something about mortality and the limitations of human beings. When I looked at their food coloring trails, I could see the images that they pointed out to me. If I had been given the images without the interpretations; however, I am certain that I would have found something entirely different. Responses to the art, just like responses to literature, are deeply rooted in personal experience. Individuals draw upon internal knowledge based on personal experience to interpret the meaning in the world around them.

To complete this project, students wrote a story based on their food coloring trails. The artwork became the cover for the story, and I displayed the stories around the classroom. Each class enjoyed examining the work of the other classes to see if they could discover the mystery of the trails and guess the subject for the story. Few traditional writing assignments have produced the level of enthusiasm as this one. In addition to creating writing of which they could be proud, students satisfied their needs for self-respect and acceptance as they encouraged each other with suggestions and praise. When I recall this Creative Hook, I remember the laughter and the fun we had as we stood at our desks blowing food color trails across white paper.

Food coloring and straws are cheap. There is very little cleanup involved in the project and it is virtually fail-proof. The biggest risk for teachers comes in the mini lesson needed to demonstrate the process. Teachers must model how to create the trails, and they must model how to find the images. In addition, teachers should share the story they would write based on the images they discover. "Nobody writes alone," writes Donald Graves. Nancie Atwell, too, advocates modeling writing for students as the most important thing teachers can do because students will imitate word usage and sentence structure.

Paper Clip Writing

Another Creative Hook begins with distributing a single object to the students. The assignment is to incorporate the object into a drawing. The purpose of the activity is the writing that will follow the art. It can be a poem, a story, a letter, or an essay. The rules change slightly, depending upon the object that students incorporate into a drawing.

For the paper clip writing, for example, students can bend the clip into any shape, but they are not permitted to break it. This rule is mostly for the safety of the students, but limitations also help the students by reducing possible things to do with the paper clip. Students can share several bottles of white glue to fix the paper clip to the paper. This means they will be able to practice their manners by saying, "Please pass me the glue." It also means that they will be permitted to stand up and walk to a person who has the glue. The students can share boxes of colored markers, too, which reinforces the use of manners and encourages "quiet confusion" when students respectfully interact with each other.

Amy shaped the paper clip into a circle. She incorporated the circle of wire as a part of the mouthpiece of a trumpet. Then she wrote a story about a young boy who wanted a trumpet for Christmas. Amy drew upon her own knowledge of playing a musical instrument in the band. She knew what it was like to practice; she knew the desire to have your own musical instrument. Writing the story validated her need for music and a musical instrument.

Todd bent his paper clip to form part of a sledding ramp. He wrote a story called "Timmy and a Day at the Sledding Slope." Todd loved the winter, and snow time meant play time for him. He had deep experience in sledding and ice skating and tobogganing. He had no trouble writing about the preparations Timmy made, the clothes he wore, or the thrill he felt as he raced down the snowy slope. These were all part of his bank of experience.

Alissa straightened her paper clip into a straight piece of wire that became the braces in a story about Laura and a trip to the orthodontist. Of course, Alissa wore braces. When she read her story to the class, she was able to share through the voice of her main character what it felt like to have braces, especially the contradiction between wanting them and hating them. She was able to share the embarrassment the braces caused her main character and the pain she suffered from the taunting and teasing of peers and adults. We all learned a lesson from Alissa's story, and Alissa felt a wave of concern as her classmates listened compassionately to her story.

Tim bent the paper clip into a shape that formed the hump of a camel. Instead of a story about a camel, Tim wrote a humorous poem.

Camels
Camels are the mammals of the desert
They trample and rample
Just the same, people
Never hunt them for a sample

The class had recently read "The Most Dangerous Game," so they laughed at Tim's poem. Then, when someone mentioned that the game room of General Zaroff contained no camel heads on the wall, they revisited the idea of big game hunting and tried to imagine why anyone would hunt a camel. One class member changed the direction of the discussion of Tim's poem by pointing out the word "rample." The class agreed that it probably was not a real word, but in our classroom, it became standard usage. Every now and then I would hear someone say, "Why'd you have to come over here and rample on my paper?" or "Be careful with my project! Don't rample it." Tim gained tremendous self-respect by inventing a word that his classmates adopted.

It is difficult to imagine any writing prompt that would deliver more variety or more enthusiastic student participation students than paper clip writing. The students were connected in their use of the paper clip, but their individual responses were so personal and so varied that they were pleased and interested in sharing stories with each other.

Red Foil Hearts

A paper clip is not the only object that can be used as a prewriting art start. Red foil hearts can also be part of the Creative Hook bag of tricks. The best time to purchase red foil heart stickers is after Valentine's Day, when they are drastically reduced. The stickers will keep for the following February, just when students need a jump start. Using red foil hearts is a writing exercise that is especially fun for middle school students, who are not quite certain about abandoning all of their elementary school traditions.

For this assignment each student receives one red foil heart and a piece of white paper. The students must incorporate the red foil heart into a drawing that will serve as an inspiration for writing, but the rule is to push beyond being "cute" or "obvious." Pictures of a person giving another person a valentine, a tree with a heart carved in it, or a teddy bear with a red foil heart on his chest would qualify as cute or obvious. The heart must be something other than a heart in the drawing. Another rule is that students can cut or tear the red foil heart, but they have to use all parts of the heart in the picture. As in the paper clip writing, students share magic markers. Their artistic and literary compositions begin to take shape.

Andrea used the heart as a sun and used markers to create a colorful sunset between purple mountains on a blue sea. Based on the drawing, she wrote a vivid piece of descriptive writing, her best writing of the year. Creating the picture made it easier for her to describe the beauty of the mountains and the sky.

Brian separated the heart into two half-circles and a square. The half-circles formed the ears of a mouse and the square became its nose. Brian wrote a story about "Mortiver the Mouse," a fantasy about a mouse living secretly with a family.

The heart formed the lips on Reyanne's gold and yellow fish. Her story was about a beautiful but vain goldfish that learned an important lesson about appreciating the beauty around it and keeping a positive attitude.

Jeff tore the red foil heart in half and drew a door opened to the dark night. The two halves of the red foil heart became shining red eyes of a wild creature.

Laura drew a skier with a heart-shaped ski hat and created a story about George, a courageous skier in the Swiss Alps. Although Laura had not been to the Swiss Alps, she drew on her personal experience of family vacations skiing in Colorado to write her story.

As the examples illustrate, every student had something interesting to write about. Creating the art helped to create the story or the poem, and the varied projects were entertaining to share. Often the artwork even helped the student connect with some understanding deep inside to write the story. For example, Reyanne was struggling with some ethical issues about the importance of making good decisions.

Great Pretzel Writing

Pretzels can go into the Creative Hook bag of tricks along with the paper clips and the red foil hearts. To begin the "great pretzel writing," tell the students that they are about to receive two objects to integrate into a picture. Assure them that they can do anything they choose with the two objects, except one thing. When they demand to know the one exception, tell them, "You'll know the answer to that question when I give you the two objects."

Next, give each student two small pretzel knots. As soon as the pretzels are placed on their desks, they will know the one thing they cannot do—eat them. The students can break the pretzels, but they have to try to use all of the parts. The directions are similar to those for using the other objects described previously.

Jay, who had been a reluctant seventh grade writer all year, created a mouse-like creature with sunglasses and big pretzel ears. Then Jay wrote about his adventures with a strange creature called a wooby from the land of Woobaca. The wooby and Jay became friends, but the wooby had to return to his own land. The story ended with Jay waiting and waiting for his return.

Jerry broke the pretzels into pieces to create an elephant. He drew a baby elephant beside the pretzel one. Her story was about the relationship between a mother elephant and her baby.

 Wendy used one pretzel turned upside down for the nose of a dog and broke the other pretzel in half to make the dog's eyes. She then wrote about a dog named Scrappy and the family he lived with.

Joe wrote about a stingerfly that was a cross between a butterfly and a bumblebee: "It flies like a butterfly and it stings like a bumblebee. It is one of the best pet security systems around. If a thief breaks into your house, he thinks he sees your honest-looking butterfly."

Just as with the food color trails and the red foil hearts, students generate original and exciting topics for their stories. If asked, the students would tell you that they never even thought about such things as a stingerfly or a wooby before they entered into creating the art. The experience of producing the art facilitates the writing.

This use of art is different from the way most students combine art and writing. Generally students write first and then illustrate the story or poem afterward. The traditional process makes creating the art a secondary activity, just something to embellish the written word. Teachers take advantage of students' interest in art by telling them ". . . And when you finish writing your story, you can illustrate it."

The Creative Hook reverses the process. I was surprised at a children's literature conference when I heard children's author and illustrator Gail Haley describe her artistic process. It bore remarkable similarities to the Creative Hook. She told the audience that she actually created the character of her story first as a doll. She lived with the character, posing it on her desk, setting it on her window sill, and having it climb her plants for weeks before she began to write. Seeing the character in such settings filled her mind with possibilities for a story.

Enthralled with the idea that a professional writer was using art as inspiration for her writing, I returned to my seventh grade English class with a new vision. The school where I taught had just developed a land lab. The principal encouraged other teachers besides the science department to make use of the lab, so I decided to have my students identify wildflowers and trees that grew in the land lab and make brochures for other classes to use.

Before they entered the land lab, however, they created earth spirits to take with them. The earth spirits were made of pieces of old nylon stockings and polyester fiber fill. I had never made soft sculpture before, but I'd seen dolls that others had created, and I thought the seventh graders and I could learn how to do it. I bought a large pack of needles, a spool of brown thread, and some small beads for eyes. I practiced making one at home, and I thought I was ready to teach the students how to make the dolls.

I was wrong about teaching them. They taught me. I began explaining how to make the dolls, and before I knew it, one student came up with a better way to make the nose, and other students took over the class to show how to make fingers or the mouth or how to sew on the hair. We had so much fun learning together. The students brought felt and bits of fabric from home so that they could dress their earth spirits. When we went into the land lab to identify the flora, we took the earth spirits with us. Like Gail Haley, we posed them on tree branches, on rocks, and under leaves. When the students returned, they had an abundance of ideas for writing their stories. They included the names of plants and trees they had identified in the land lab. They mentioned insects they had noticed along the path from the school to the land lab, and they included the silvery minnows they observed in the stream. On the covers of their books they attached their earth spirits.

A teacher knows in many different ways when a project is successful. My favorite way of measuring the success of a project is by the number of samples I have in my file. If I have few student samples, I know that the children wanted to take their projects home. Except for my own, I have no student earth spirit samples.

Different Intelligences for Creativity

The discussion of the Creative Hook and how it meets the needs of middle school children has been filtered through lenses created by students. Students listed acceptance, self-respect, and love as the common needs of teenagers. In examining the writing instruction I've done with middle school children, I have held it up to the standard of meeting the needs identified by the students themselves. There is, however, another lens to use in reflecting upon the success of writing that has art at the heart of it.

Howard Gardner (1982, 1983, 1991, 1993) has done extensive research with Project Zero to arrive at the identification of eight separate intelligences: visual/spatial, interpersonal, intrapersonal, logical/mathematical, verbal/linguistic, musical/rhythmic, bodily/kinesthetic, and environmentalist. None of the Creative Hooks was designed specifically to address multiple intelligences. Examining them through the multiple intelligence lens, however, reveals that every one includes more than two of the eight intelligences. Allowing the students to stand at their desks to create the food coloring trails and move around the room to retrieve markers or glue nurtures the children whose strength lies in bodily/kinesthetic. Sharing markers, glue, and food coloring; helping each other learn how to create a soft sculpture doll; and sharing personal writing all involve intrapersonal intelligence. Interpersonal intelligence is addressed during the students' introspection and reflection as they create both the art and the writing. Visual/spatial intelligence is employed in the completion of every drawing.

The strength of art at the heart of writing relies on the fact that "each of us possesses at least eight entirely different ways to understand the world and to express ourselves. Each intelligence has its own means and modes of expression. Each represents an area of expertise with a specific body of knowledge in any domain (Marks-Tarlow, 1996, p. ix). Each Creative Hook embraces more than two intelligences, relying on the combination to stimulate self-expression. "Creativity thrives in the soil where two or more Intelligences mix. Here, individuals can shuttle back and forth between different symbol systems, media, and modes of self-expression as best suits their personal, social and cultural idiosyncrasies" (Marks-Tarlow, 1996, p. x).

Teachers' shelves are filled with books on writing. Many are familiar with George Hillock's (1986) meta-analysis of writing instruction, which decries frontal presentations by teachers and lauds building a community of learners. Teachers own Regie Routman's (1988, 1991) books on writing in the elementary grades, and they know the importance of writing and publishing. Middle school teachers are familiar with Nancie Atwell (1987) and her work on writing workshops and the importance of engaging students in discourse about their writing. Many teachers are familiar with the researcher Donald Graves (1983) and his methods of modeling writing for children. They have read Donald Murray (1987, 1989, 1990). They are familiar with Janet Emig's 1971 research on protocol analysis and Mina Shaughnessy's (1977) error analysis. New works such as Tom Newkirk's *Critical Thinking and Writing* (1989) support teachers who want to understand more about writing instruction. All of these works focus on assisting teachers to guide students in becoming lifelong writers. None mentions using art as a way to open the door to the imagination and the pure joy of creation.

Marks-Tarlow (1996) writes:

Many of us are caught in a work ethic that associates productivity with suffering, work with being serious, and play with idleness. Yet history tells us that some of the most brilliant discoveries have occurred when people were not trying, by playing or just fooling around. Gunpowder, the telescope, and the Mobius strip were invented as toys. At least one aeronautic design emerged from spontaneous play with paper airplanes, and plenty of the most creative business environments include recreational facilities to relax and energize their employees. (p. 13)

Art at the heart of writing is creative and fun, and middle school students need both as a means of self-expression and a way of building self-respect.

Johnson (1993) confirms my own findings, but he takes them a step further when he states that just as there is no integration of art into the theory and practice of teaching writing, there is no integration of writing into the theory and practice of teaching art. He writes:

> *A great deal has been written about children's literacy development, from research into the sociology of reading to children at home to "let's-make-writing-fun" type books. Equally, art educators have produced a welter of books, from studies into the psychology of children's drawing to manuals on art techniques. What has been markedly missing in both literacy and visual camps are publications that discuss the relationship between the two. (p. 17)*

English teachers want their students to "ache with caring," as Mem Fox (1993) puts it. Creating art opens the door to the imagination and fosters involvement with the writing that fosters that caring ache. The Creative Hook helps students experience the power and the joy of writing.

By the time students reach the middle school, many of them believe that they cannot create good art. Somehow they have forgotten the childhood joy of watching something appear as they make marks on the paper. The Creative Hook is a connection to that first image making. The art activities are nonthreatening, and most students experience delight and success in their involvement. One of my students wrote, "Creating the bird is what prompted my writing. The bird and her problems came to life as she emerged on the paper. Her name and the solution to her problems became clear as I looked at her." From remarks like these, I know the rich rewards of using art at the heart of writing. Middle school students report that they miss the fun in learning that they remember from elementary days. Integrating art as a prewriting activity returns a little fun back to the work. "The Greeks understood the close relationship between learning and having fun; their word for education, *paidia,* was almost identical to the word for play, *paidia*" (Marks-Tarlow, 1996, p. 13).

The Creative Hook opens the door to the imagination, inspires creativity, and fosters pride. Whether looking through the lens of middle school students or the lens of the theorist, art at the heart of writing meets the needs of middle school students. I must confess that in my experience of teaching writing, art at the heart of writing meets the needs of even younger students and adults as well.

Discussion Questions

1. The Creative Hook opens the mind to new possibilities and encourages students to write creatively. How could this same approach be used to encourage factual writing in subjects such as history or science?

2. Some would say that the methods described in this chapter are too "juvenile" for today's adolescents, yet they appear to work. Why do you believe these ideas seem to be so readily accepted by middle school students?

3. Currently teachers appear to be seeking creative ideas such as the approaches described in this chapter. However, other forces are seeking to make teachers responsible for content that can be assessed through standardized tests. How does the integration of art and the language arts encourage or discourage the acquisition of language skills?

References

Atwell, N. (1987). *In the middle: Writing, reading, and learning with adolescents.* Portsmouth, NH: Heinemann.

Calkins, L. (1986). *The art of teaching writing.* Portsmouth, NH: Heinemann.

Calkins, L. (1991). *Living between the lines.* Portsmouth, NH: Heinemann.

Dyson, A. (Ed.) (1994). *The need for story.* Urbana, Il.: National Council of Teachers of English.

Foster, H. M. (1993). *Crossing over: Whole language for secondary English teachers.* Fort Worth, TX: Harcourt Brace.

Fox, M. (1993). *Radical reflections.* San Diego, CA. Harcourt Brace.

Gallagher, J. (1994). Developing lifelong writers. Unpublished doctoral dissertation, Kent State University, Kent, Ohio.

Gardner, H. (1982). *Art mind and brain: A cognitive approach to creativity.* New York: Basic Books.

Gardner, H. (1983). *Frames of mind: The theory of multiple intelligences.* New York: Basic Books.

Gardner, H. (1991). *Unschooled mind.* New York: Harpers Collins.

Gardner, H. (1993). *Multiple intelligences: The theory in practice.* New York: Basic Books.

Gardner, H. (1993). *Creating minds.* New York: Basic Books.

Graves, D. (1983). *Writing: Teachers and children at work.* Portsmouth, NH: Heinemann.

Hillocks, G. (1986). *Research on written composition.* Urbana, IL: ERIC Clearinghouse on Reading and Communication Skills, and the National Conference on Research in English.

Johnson, P. (1990). *A book of one's own: Developing literacy through making books.* Portsmouth, NH: Heinemann.

Johnson, P. (1993). *Literacy through the book arts.* Portsmouth, NH: Heinemann.

Marks-Tarlow, G. (1996). *Creativity inside out: Learning through multiple intelligences.* Menlo Park, CA: Addison-Wesley.

Melton, D. (1985). *Written and illustrated by. . . .* Kansas City, MO: Landmark Editions.

Murray, D. M. (1968). *A writer teaches writing: A practical method of teaching composition.* Boston: Houghton Mifflin.

Murray, D. M. (1987). *Write to learn.* New York: Holt, Rinehart & Winston.

Murray, D. M. (1989). *Expecting the unexpected.* Portsmouth, NH: Heinemann.

Murray, D. M. (1990). *Shoptalk.* Portsmouth, NH: Heinemann.

Newkirk, T. (1985). *Breaking ground.* Portsmouth, NH: Heinemann.

Newkirk, T. (1989). *Critical thinking and writing.* Urbana, IL: National Council of Teachers of English.

Newkirk, T., & Atwell, N. (1988). *Understanding writing.* Portsmouth, NH: Heinemann.

Peters, H. F. (1960). *Rainer Maria Rilke: Masks and the man.* Seattle: University of Washington Press.

Routman, R. (1988). *Transitions: From literature to literacy.* Portsmouth, NH: Heinemann.

Routman, R. (1991). *Invitations: Changing as teachers and learners.* Portsmouth, NH: Heinemann.

Schon, D. (1988). Coaching reflective thinking. In P. P. Grenmett & G. L. Erickson (Eds.), *Reflection in teacher education* (pp. 21–22). New York: Teachers College Press.

Shaughnessy, M. P. (1977). *Errors and expectations.* New York: Oxford University Press.

Chapter 12

Social Studies in the Middle Grades: The Story of an Emerging Team

RUTH H. HORNER

> *Ruth Horner earned an undergraduate degree in political science from the University of Nevada, Las Vegas in 1982 and credentials for teaching the learning-handicapped from California State University, Long Beach. She is presently in her seventh year of teaching seventh grade world history.*

Our middle school's experience with teaming began on a modest scale. We launched our first year with a two-subject core of a teacher for social studies and another for language arts. Our initial attempt with seventh and eighth graders was marginally successful, but for the second year a major improvement was made by arranging our teams to include four members. Each person represented a content area: social studies, language arts, science, or math.

The California Department of Education strongly endorses teaming. For example, in 1987, they published *Caught in the Middle*, which had some strong words about the value of teaming:

> *The use of teaching teams in a core curriculum instructional block represents a significant staffing option. . . . The team concept also allows students to experience the combined skills and knowledge of two or more teachers, including the potential for a dynamic, synergistic instructional effect. (p. 94)*

Other schools had been using this approach for several years, but teaming was new to us. We quickly recognized the value of working together. Teachers taught in their area of expertise and students benefited from the connections that teachers forged between each other and between themselves and their students.

Nevertheless, we recognized that any restructuring or meaningful change is a difficult task. It takes time to plan and adjust to new procedures. Credit for our first year success goes to the professionalism of our staff, despite some minor rumblings and grumblings. We successfully set up our teams and went about the business of determining what a team does.

Discipline

We made it through the first year of teaming with some difficulty for ourselves and for our students. The students, for example, had never experienced being members of a team, and they suddenly found themselves part of a foreign organizational structure. They were initially unsure what to think about it. As the year progressed, signs appeared that the teaming concept was proving beneficial for our students. They began to accept common rules in each of the core classes. Problem students were also identified quickly by all team members, which enabled the team to effectively address behavior problems. Eventually the students appreciated the benefits of consistent academic and behavioral expectations.

Effective discipline policies did not occur accidentally. We realized that any worthwhile instructional idea is meaningless without effective classroom management. This required a strong and consistent discipline policy. Our first task was to develop a set of universal rules. Our team discovered that we had many common rules already in place; there were also areas in which our views differed. Developing a consensus on rules provided a useful training exercise for our later efforts at curriculum planning. We began by reviewing all the rules that were held in common. This provided a foundation that helped build team spirit. Next we listed our individual rules and discussed why we thought they were necessary and valuable. The discussion helped us understand one another and appreciate our capacity to develop solutions to problems. Based on our discussion, we developed a tentative list of discipline expectations. The team reviewed this list, and if a team member strongly objected to a rule, it was struck from the list. Agreement on the rules was essential for their consistent enforcement by all team members. In the end the process helped us understand our discipline policy and enabled us to implement the rules fairly and uniformly within our team. In addition, we learned to work together and to appreciate the unique strengths of each team member.

As time passed, we reviewed our rules as team members changed and the demographics of our students evolved. For example, groups of students have caused revisions to the rules regarding put-downs. Our initial list had a section on put downs, but racial and ethnic slurs were not included. Unfortunately, this emerged as a bothersome issue, and now the policy is very specific about racial intolerance. When we review the rules with students at the beginning of the year, we are specific on this issue, and racial slurs are no longer a problem.

The overall effect of the consistent discipline policy is clear expectations for students, and teachers are prepared to address issues as they arise. We use a system of rewards and consequences that is easily understood and implemented due to our productive planning discussions. With discipline clearly under control, our school is relatively tranquil, as much as a middle school can be, and our team can focus on teaching the subjects we enjoy. The opportunity to plan together made it possible for us to create the unity that is appreciated by students and parents.

Planning

As a social studies teacher, I found the transition to teaming personally difficult. The pressure to cover over 1,200 years of history and adjust to the demands of working with three other teachers was taxing. The curriculum and teaming problems were increased by the lack of a common planning time. We had to devote afterschool time to planning units and activities.

About midway through the first year the school acquired a new principal who was familiar with the teaming concept. He immediately arranged the schedule to allow for a common planning time twice a week. This permitted us to create curriculum, discuss students, or meet with parents. The revised scheduling arrangement turned out to be the saving grace for teaming at our school.

Parents quickly became enthusiastic supporters of the team concept. In particular, they enjoyed communicating with a team of teachers with a unified focus rather than four individual teachers with varying rules, instructional approaches, and opinions. They observed immediate benefits for themselves and for their children. The positive attitude of parents was a welcome source of support for the teaching teams.

How to Teach and Team at the Same Time

Working with adolescents on a daily basis requires knowledge and appreciation for how they think, act, and socialize. Atwell (1987) asserts that effective teachers appreciate the adolescent's unique qualities.

> *We won't get the best from our junior high students until we stop blaming adolescents for their adolescent behavior and begin to invite their distinctive brand of junior high best. . . . Confusion, bravado, restlessness, a preoccupation with peers, and the questioning of authority are not manifestations of poor attitude; they are hallmarks of this particular time of life. (p. 25)*

Social studies presents the challenge of teaching a subject matter that is not always taught with a great deal of energy or enthusiasm in the elementary grades.

Students frequently dislike history, and the teacher's ability to make it interesting is vital to the subject's acceptance by students.

While teaching social studies is challenging, it can be done effectively. One avenue to success is to capitalize on the adolescent's often overlooked desire to learn. Atwell (1987) asserts, "Classrooms provide active, lively learning environments where students are challenged, excited, and motivated to push toward successively higher levels of personal academic achievement" (p. 53). Her comments underscore that the universal tenets of good teaching apply equally well to middle school students. Atwell points out, for example, that adolescents love to work together. Their desire for social interaction can be used to foster learning in the social studies classroom.

Cooperative learning groups are effective if the group is given specific tasks and each student has a job to do. They also enjoy evaluating their group's performance if they are given a scoring rubric. Many teachers, however, feel frustrated when a cooperative learning group fails to function effectively. Working in groups is a skill that not all students have learned; they must be taught the rules of group work. These skills are taught more effectively when the students experience group work in several classes within the team. The consistent application of cooperative learning rules and procedures reaps benefits as the year progresses, and students easily take on increasingly more complex tasks. Group work of all kinds, nevertheless, can be overdone. Students also need a chance to work individually on independent assignments. A balance between group and individual tasks adds variety to the school week and provides an opportunity for students to learn important lessons about responsibility and individual initiative.

A balance in the types of activities assigned to students is also important. My assignments include something for my visual, kinesthetic, and auditory learners. Often visual learners like to read about a subject and then prepare a written project like a diary or book of poetry. Others like to draw and enjoy showing off their talents. Kinesthetic learners seem to be fond of models or dioramas. Auditory learners might enjoy interviewing someone and preparing a tape of the conversation. Thus, each student can learn the required material in a way that capitalizes on the student's interests and abilities.

Projects are an important part of the middle school curriculum. Atwell (1987) talks about their importance:

> In each core curriculum subject the most important instructional objectives at each grade level shall be taught, in part, through student projects. Projects shall be designed to enable students to apply skills and to use facts, ideas, concepts, and generalizations in addressing issues and problems related to central themes of a subject. (p. 44)

After a few months the students are accustomed to the project format and begin to transplant ideas they learned in other classes into new applications. They also begin to understand valuable research skills at a more rapid pace than if a lone teacher taught the procedures in isolation. Caution, however, should be taken to avoid making projects too much of a routine. Anything can be overdone, including projects. Teams should be careful to schedule breathing space between projects to avoid having projects lose their power to motivate student enthusiasm. Scheduling a continuous stream of projects is bound to produce sloppy work, burned out students, and critical parents.

There is a natural pressure that teachers feel to cover everything in the curriculum and avoid skipping any piece of information. This attention to every curriculum detail is not always possible or even recommended. Less is frequently more. By spending more time on smaller chunks of content, students will learn at a deeper level than if they move quickly over an unreasonable amount of material. Projects help to avoid this cursory approach to curriculum. For example, by assigning an historical novel project, students focus on a specific historical time, personality, or empire. They learn more about this specific subject than through the country-a-week approach. The best part is that they teach their peers about their topic when they make their project presentations. In this way, everyone is both a student and a teacher.

The link between social studies and literature is a valuable way to strengthen the social studies program. Stories have power over people, particularly middle school students with their active imaginations. In the traditional curriculum, language arts class was where students heard stories and read tales of long ago. In history class, students read dry summaries of who was king and when and what empire he conquered. With the advent of teaming the history teacher and the language arts teacher have an opportunity to create a powerful historical and literary curriculum.

Literature helps capture the imagination of students more than almost anything else in the classroom. It reveals in a dynamic way how people long ago thought, acted, and felt. Literature provides a level of intimacy between the reader and people in the past that appeals to the adolescent's curiosity about others. Middle school students are interested in understanding people, and if the person just happens to be someone their own age, so much the better. In recent years the increased number of novels and nonfiction works geared toward adolescents that focus on historical subjects is gratifying. There are high-quality books for any subject and reading ability that enhance students' interest in historical events.

In addition to quality reading materials, technology provides a rich instructional resource. Computer programs are being created that focus on history and geography. These programs motivate even the most reluctant learner. In addition, the Internet offers a world of information to every classroom. The World Wide Web enables students to access authorities and bodies of information from around the world. Lombard (1996) describes using a novel about a young girl immigrating to Switzerland as part of his social studies class. Based on this novel, the class explored the immigration rights of children in Switzerland compared to immigrants coming to the United States. Using the World Wide Web, the students located a copy of the Swiss Constitution under the heading "Constitutions of the World." The contents of the Swiss document were compared to the rights outlined in the U.S. Constitution. This one project taught the students how to use technology to obtain information, involved them in literature, and enhanced their reasoning abilities. In addition to the computer, technology includes items such as camcorders and video discs.

As our team began to work together more, we noticed that our curriculum overlapped in many areas. In particular, the social studies and the language arts have a natural connection. By working together, the social studies and language arts teachers strengthen one another's efforts. When students see the same material covered in multiple classes, they have an improved chance to remember what is being taught. In addition, the two teachers can cover the material efficiently. The transitions from one subject to another are made easily because the students are already familiar with the material. Teachers can quickly move into new information when it continues what was covered in a previous class.

Subjects such as math and science are more difficult to coordinate in an interdisciplinary curriculum. Nevertheless, when teachers meet to plan and discuss the content of the four curriculum areas, natural connections begin to surface. For example, the mathematics teacher may cover tessellations when the social studies class is studying an Islamic unit. At the same time the science class may discuss the contributions of early scientists from the Middle East and Africa.

Most of the time it is unnecessary to recreate a whole curriculum. Natural pairings begin to occur. It makes sense to study oceanography, for example, when studying the Age of Exploration in world history. Thus, scheduling curriculum meetings as a team is the first step toward interdisciplinary instruction. There are times when each discipline has specific content that must be addressed independent of the other subjects. It is unnecessary for all subject areas to work in an integrated manner every day. Students can make the desired connections when only two or three of the team teachers are working on the same theme. Many teams experience difficulties when they try too hard to connect disparate curriculum areas just for the sake of creating an appearance of cohesiveness.

In the third year of our teaming, our school decided to create one interdisciplinary unit that would last for 2 weeks and include all four content areas. As a staff, we decided the theme would be ecology. The way we planned this unit provides some insights into effective team planning. We began by designing activities that were simple to accomplish in a manageable amount of time. When longer blocks of time were required for an activity, we used our flexible scheduling to make a few longer class periods. If a longer period of time is needed to meet with the class or if the class needs to visit the public library, the team's schedule can be reapportioned to permit classes to still meet. This flexibility also helps classes to participate in field trips and outside-of-school events. Often teachers see these as frustrating intrusions into the standard school curriculum. To adolescents, however, they may be the most important part of the school program. Middle grades students are highly motivated by social interaction with peers, so these activities also create a powerful motivation for students to adhere to discipline rules.

Collegiality

Much has been written about the isolation experienced by teachers. Lortie (1976), for example, described teachers as people who lead lives of loneliness, much like prisoners in a cell. They are commonly placed in a room with a group of students period after period. Their only contact with adults occurs before and after school or during hectic lunch periods. Some enjoy the independence associated with this solitary professional life, but most teachers quickly appreciate the opportunity to discuss professional concerns with peers. It is easy to assume that other teachers are more successful with difficult students or that others' instructional strategies are always effective. On the other hand, when team members share ideas and concerns, they discover that problems and concerns are also being experienced by teammates.

Together they support one another and develop effective ways of teaching and addressing difficult students. Teams provide a built-in network and support system for teachers. A frequent comment for teachers new to a team is "I don't know what I'd do without the team to support me." It only takes one challenging group of students to pass through a team to develop teachers' enthusiasm for teaming.

There is a downside to teaming. There are days when the expectation of one more meeting is unwelcome. There are many meetings associated with school restructuring and working closely with other teachers. One caution for school administrators and teachers is to avoid unnecessary intrusions into team meeting times. It is easy to have meeting times usurped by school business and district-level issues. This is a time to raise the red flag and assert the necessity of keeping team meeting times solely for team concerns.

At the end of the second year of teaming, our school joined a partnership called Middle Link Network, a consortium of a dozen middle schools involved in restructuring. Just as with teachers, schools can feel isolated without a means of communicating with other schools in similar situations. The schools in the link shared issues such as scheduling, course electives, school uniforms, and curriculum content. For many teachers the opportunity to discuss curriculum with other teachers is a welcome source of professional support. The partnership gave social studies teachers an opportunity to discuss curriculum and instructional ideas with others who were using the same textbooks and resource materials and perhaps had similar students.

The partnership provided additional opportunities for staff development. Meetings were arranged to discuss topics such as writing across the curriculum or constructivist principles applied to the middle grades. In-service presentations were provided for each subject area and grade level. These presentations offered a chance to invigorate the curriculum with new instructional ideas.

Previous to teams, we also had in-service sessions related to restructuring and teaming. As we continued in the restructuring process, staff development opportunities were continued that focused on subjects such as interdisciplinary instruction and shared decision making. A good team, like a good student, is always in the process of learning something new. By participating in staff development activities, we were continuing to grow professionally and modeling to others that learning is a lifelong challenge.

Conclusions

Teaching social studies to middle school students is a rewarding, if demanding, job. Teaching as part of a team makes this effort more rewarding for most teachers than trying to balance curriculum demands, discipline problems, and professional growth without peer support. When the same standards, rules, and consequences are applied across a team of teachers, each person is freed to spend less time and energy on discipline. The energy formerly devoted to behavior problems is reallocated into instructional considerations.

Teaming has become popular with students and parents for a variety of reasons. Parents like the increased communication they have with the school. They also like the idea that the teachers know their students academically and emotionally. They feel the teachers are able to know their students well and to address each child's individual needs.

Students also appreciate the close contact with teachers. To illustrate, each June the students write a letter telling what they liked and disliked about the past year. Several students wrote about how much they enjoyed being part of a team. One letter in particular stands out. A good student who never seemed particularly attached to the team idea wrote about how much he enjoyed being part of a team. He wrote, "The teachers seemed to really understand us better than most people." He definitely felt the impact of the team approach.

Linking groups of professionals appears to help teachers feel more professional and to be invigorated about teaching. The connections between areas of the curriculum creates a web of ideas that is dynamic as opposed to the static nature of isolated subject areas. Whenever teachers come together in a group to discuss teaching, their combined ideas will be different from anything they would have created by themselves.

These connections may be particularly valuable for the social studies teacher. So much of what is taught in math, language arts, and science parallels what is taught in the social studies classroom. By making the connections between subjects, each area is viewed as a piece of the entire body of human knowledge. Students begin to see how all events and ideas are presented in a unified context. This association enables them to accept the qualities of all subject areas and helps them be successful students.

While there are negative aspects of teaming, such as seemingly endless meetings, the benefits make the effort worthwhile. Remembering the benefits, such as being able to teach rather than being a discipline warden or the day a reluctant student was excited when he began working on a projection map, helps overcome fatigue from frequent meetings. Teaming works, and interdisciplinary instruction and teams are a powerful tool for the middle school teacher.

Discussion Questions

1. How does team teaching benefit the social studies teacher? In what ways do these benefits parallel the advantages for students?
2. What are the drawbacks of teaming for the social studies teacher?
3. This chapter described 3 years of implementing the team approach. Identify the phases this team passed through as they developed as a team.

References

Atwell, N. (1987). *In the middle*. Portsmouth, NH: Boynton/Cook.

California State Department of Education (1987). *Caught in the middle: Educational reform for young adolescents in California's public schools*. Sacramento, CA: Author.

Lombard, R. H. (1996). Using tradebooks to teach middle level social studies. *Social Education, 60*(4), 223–226.

Lortie, D. (1976). *Schoolteacher: A sociological study*. Chicago: University of Chicago Press.

Chapter 13

Integrating Technology into the Middle Grades

THOMAS GILLIOTTI

Thomas Gilliotti is presently the Middle School Computer Coordinator for the Euclid City Schools, Euclid, Ohio. He has taught both English and industrial arts. His primary focus is interdisciplinary teaming and technology in the middle school, and he has organized and taught courses in technology on all grade levels.

A major difference exists between using technology and actually integrating technology into the middle school. This chapter focuses on how technology augments existing school curriculum. The methods used to encourage integration of technology are discussed only tangentially. The initial section of this chapter discusses several elements essential for integrating technology into the middle school. The second portion provides specific examples of how technology is currently being used in the classroom.

Planning

An integral part of applying technology is the planning stage. There should be an organized approach developed by the school district to use technology (Kinnaman, 1991). Ideally, the plan represents each level of education to ensure a continuum of experiences for the student. Some districts have a technology committee consisting of a senior administrator, a technology director, and coordinators who represent all grade levels. Lockard, Abrams, and Many (1990) state, "To work toward a goal of curriculum integration, a carefully developed plan is important for many reasons. . . . A district plan commands support at the building level and signals commitment. We favor something that provides a framework without excessive specificity" (p. 363). Using a committee that includes all levels ensures broad-based support for technological innovation and facilitates coordination across all grades and buildings within the district.

Funding

Included in this plan should be a method of funding. Ideally, a percentage of the budget is dedicated to purchasing technology and related materials such as software, tapes, laser discs, and CD-ROMs. Sometimes districts have to be creative to obtain necessary funds. Hill (1993) provides an example of how one district obtained funding for technology:

> *The superintendent of Lake Charles, Louisiana schools, Charles Oakley, went to the school board and proposed a four and one-half percent local sales tax to help cover any budget cuts and subsidize the cost of instructional materials . . . mostly technology. None of the money was used for salaries or non-curricular purposes. . . . The tax passed with 68 percent of the vote. At the end of the four-year period the superintendent would let the public be the judge of how the money was spent. Public trust is a must if a program like this is to survive. (p. 27)*

Partnerships between school districts and local businesses can be an effective way to purchase needed technology; however, this type of funding is fluid and tends to change as the economy shifts. A more controversial method is to enter into a contractual agreement with a private enterprise that produces a daily current events program, including commercial advertising that is part of the technology agreement. One such venture is Whittle Communications. In return for contracting this service, the district receives a television mounted to the wall in each middle school and high school classroom. Whittle also furnishes a cable distribution system connected from a satellite dish to a centrally located videocassette recorder linked to the classrooms. The principal of each building maintains the right of censorship over these broadcasts. In exchange for these services the school district shows the 12-minute daily broadcasts to all sixth through twelfth grade students. The controversy arises because 2 minutes of commercials are included in each broadcast. Some people have strong feelings about encroachment of commercial enterprises into the school. The second part of this chapter will show how inclusion of this equipment can be incorporated into the school plan.

School Development

In the past, staff development frequently consisted of an in-service day, when large groups of teachers, either district-wide or site staffs, listened to a speaker followed by short breakout sessions. Other times a computer lab was filled with thirty teachers, two to a computer, who learned a computer program in a 2-hour afterschool or Saturday session. Many times the training sessions frustrated teachers and reaffirmed their fears of technology. The teachers were introduced to ideas and materials but were unable to transfer their cursory knowledge into classroom practice. Lockard, Abrams, and Many (1993) observe:

> *Of immediate importance is support for those teachers ready to implement computers. Staff development cannot mean the same thing for everyone. There may be small groups in need of training to use a common software product, perhaps a word processor or data base. There may be enthusiastic teachers with minimal basic knowledge. . . . The areas in which to offer development activities are those identified by the user. . . . Institute days with one speaker are not the answer. (p. 364)*

A more successful approach to staff development is a customized system in which a wide variety of development activities is delivered to smaller groups, focusing on specific teachers' software needs. Small groups of teachers are accommodated during work hours because their schedules are customized without disrupting the entire district. Another possibility is to rotate substitute teachers over a specific time period. As a result, teachers receive training that can be directly applied to their subject areas (Kinnaman, 1993).

Another trend in staff development is to place a computer in each teacher's room. When they have ready access to computers, the teachers spend more time with individual students, feel professionally empowered, and spend less time with clerical work and more time on lesson preparation (McCarthy, 1989). To help teachers develop computer competence, they must be encouraged to take equipment home on weekends, holidays, and summer breaks.

Teachers also need support during the school day. Teachers have many responsibilities, and it is difficult for them to take the time to learn about technology. In addition, sometimes teachers benefit from a person who coordinates the technology efforts in a school or district. This person, a computer coordinator, is a helpful aid in effective computer use as well as a knowledgeable advisor for selecting appropriate software (Kepner, 1989). The responsibility of effectively integrating technology into the curriculum is enormous. Someone has to make decisions as well as possess knowledge of equipment and software to help teachers with problems or to give advice. The question of how or at what level coordinators are assigned is a district-level decision.

The last suggestion for improved implementation of technology through staff development is to encourage school districts to require knowledge and skills in the use of technology when hiring additional staff (Lockard, Abrams, & Many, 1990). In this way, new employees invigorate existing staff and institute a technologically savvy faculty.

Computer Placement

There are four patterns for computer distribution in a school. The decision of computer placement should come from the school's development plan on how to integrate computers into the curriculum.

One computer in the classroom has many potential applications, such as creating tests, posters, or an electronic grade book. Combined with a projection panel, it can also be an impressive demonstration device. In addition, there are many curriculum applications; however, most of these take additional preparation time.

Putting several computers on carts and having these mobile units scheduled for special lessons also makes computers available at a cost-efficient price. With this method, teachers serve small groups or use computers with individual students, providing a related activity is planned for the other students in class.

Computer laboratories, where an entire class works with one or two students per computer, offer the most student–computer exposure time, but teachers or coordinators must schedule in advance and may be unable to schedule the desired dates. Positive and negative factors are involved in all computer placement patterns; Table 13.1 compares these patterns.

The fourth application is not shown in the table. It is a media center for students and staff. This center contains computer stations with peripheral devices such as scanners, modems, CD-ROMs, and laser disc players. The center may also include an interactive video station and video editing equipment.

All four computer placement applications should be offered in the middle school. As schools move from an industrial model of education to an information age model, students need as much experience with technology as possible. A recent report prepared by Braun (1992) stated:

> *Learning environments should include access to a wide range of technology and to the entire world of information. They should offer opportunities for creativity, critical thinking, information access and manipulation, communication, and multisensory stimulation. In early times a person worked a single job for a lifetime; now a worker may have two, three, even five substantially different jobs during a 40-year career. (p. 1)*

When educators talk about implementing technology, the topic quickly turns to computers. There are, however, new technology applications that ei-

TABLE 13.1   Characteristics of Three Possible Computer Patterns

Factors	Fixed Lap	Mobile	Individual Classroom
Usage	Individual or group	Individual or group	Individual unless with video projection
	Requires scheduling, decreasing flexibility	Requires scheduling, decreasing flexibility	Readily available
	Curriculum integration if routinely accessible	May encourage integration	Encourages integration
	Tool, tutor, learner roles	Same potential as a lab with enough computers	Mostly tutor for enrichment and remediation
	Can include specialized hardware and interfacing		
Personnel	Should have staff (own or LRC)	Personnel to transport	No new personnel
	May require and justify computer specialist who lacks content expertise for students sent there	Draws primarily on content expertise	Draws primarily on content expertise
	Teachers need software skills	Requires teacher training	Requires teacher training
Cost	Based on number of systems	Number of systems, and items such as carts	Could involve any number of machines
	Potential economy from networking	Movement may increase repair costs	May require most copies of software
	Highest security	Moderate security	Least security
Common Site Level	High school or middle school	Any	Elementary school

Source: Lockard, 1990.

ther work with the computer or do not involve the computer at all. Novelli (1993) notes:

> As more and more middle schools include integrating technology among their efforts at reform, more and more teachers are relying on computers, camcorders, telecommunication hookups and other high tech equipment to meet the challenges of teaching in the middle grades. The benefits of using technology at this level are undeniable. Middle school students are comfortable with computers, camcorders, VCR's and the like. They are also motivated by their use. The hands-on active learning encouraged by technology also meets the needs of restless adolescents. (p. 28)

Interdisciplinary Teaming

Key characteristics of the middle school are interdisciplinary teams of teachers sharing groups of students, a common planning time, and adjacent room space. The most often cited advantages of interdisciplinary teaming include instructional flexibility, more coordination of learning skills, better student–teacher relationships, and improved discipline (Lake, 1989). Interrelationships of the major subject areas also can be maximized through interdisciplinary teaming. When teams work out behavioral and operational policies, students benefit from the resulting consistency. George and Stevenson (1988) believe that interdisciplinary teaming helps every child succeed in specific ways, and even small achievements are recognized.

Using computers to bridge the gap between subject areas in interdisciplinary teaming allows for teacher flexibility. Johnson (as cited in Gursky et al., 1991) states:

> *The interdisciplinary approach [to teaching] supports the use of technology since teachers aren't confined by the traditional school day. If teachers want to use technology to do something, they don't have to be limited to a forty minute period. (p. 29)*
>
> *In another example, the middle schools in Calcasiu Parish, Louisiana found, . . . that for the middle grades, technology is a natural. We use an interdisciplinary approach which gives us the power to tie the teachers' teams together via technology resources—computers, video discs, and CD-ROM units. Using cooperative learning, our students are no longer bound by the four walls of the classroom; they can connect with the real world and concentrate on real problem solving. There is no limit to the learning possibilities using technology. (p. 27)*

Technological Possibilities

Word Processing

Recent research indicates a need for word processing in our schools and society. Tone and Winchester (1988) assert, "The computer is a technology that will almost certainly become more and more accessible in the lives of students including young writers" (p. 2). They add: "Many of these students will be writing regularly using computers. Whatever the limits of the experience they get using computers, it can be a valuable one" (p. 3).

Bangert-Drowns (1989) published a response to critics' charges that word processing may have a detrimental effect on writing. He compared word-processed documents to handwritten documents in five categories: (1) number of revisions, (2) composition length, (3) students' attitudes toward learning, (4) basic writing skills, and (5) overall quality of written documents.

In the area of revision, little difference was proven; however, in all the studies, the revisions of the word-processed works were impossible to measure accurately because many of them take place before a printed copy is made.

The category of composition length showed that word processed documents were significantly longer. In addition, for 75% of the groups studied, students using word processing expressed more favorable attitudes toward writing than those who wrote in longhand. The word processing groups also improved over the handwritten groups in basic writing skills such as spelling, punctuation, and grammar. Finally, in fifteen studies, judges gave holistic ratings to compositions produced by both groups, and thirteen found the word-processed documents superior. Bangert-Drowns (1989) concludes, "In spite of the various pitfalls that plagued these studies, word processing still proves to be a beneficial addition to writing instruction" (p. 4).

A study produced by Owston, Murphy, and Wideman (1990) measured the effects of word processing on writing for eighth grade students. During the school year, each of four classes had specific handwritten and word processing assignments. All of the students had access to computers and at least a year and a half of experience using them. Results of the study revealed:

> When the writing produced by students under these two conditions was compared, we found that the computer written work was significantly better in overall quality and better on the competency and mechanical subscale of the Scale for the Evaluation of Narrative Writing. Students also produced significantly longer pieces of writing on the computer and they reported very positive attitudes toward computer-based writing and editing. (p. 26)

At our school, word processing is part of the seventh and eighth grade English curriculum. With the help of each interdisciplinary team's English teacher the computer coordinator teaches a five-lesson unit using the word processing feature of *ClarisWorks* during the first quarter. Upon completion of the unit, teachers reserve the computer lab for students to complete word processing assignments. Because the lab is staffed by a paraprofessional, teachers may send half of a class to the lab while keeping the other half in the regular classroom for small-group activities. When the first group is finished word processing, the groups switch.

The following example illustrates how one seventh grade team applied the learned word processing skills taught in the English class to other core subjects. While teaching symbolism, the reading teacher asked students to write an original fable using the word processor. Later in the year, students read a "classic" and the book report was also processed. In the social studies class the students used the word processor to write an essay for the local Martin Luther King, Jr. essay contest. The science teacher used a computer program called *Geology Search,* and students word-processed a report in conjunction with the program and used graphing skills learned in math class. In the spring the culminating activity for word processing involved the English and social studies teachers. They required a word-processed research paper on Ohio history. The English teacher emphasized the mechanical aspects of a research paper, while the social studies teacher emphasized historical accuracy and proving a thesis statement.

The teachers appreciated the neatness, quality, and lack of errors in the word-processed work compared to previous written assignments. Originally these teachers were concerned about the loss of class time spent in the computer lab. At the conclusion of the assignments, they decided that the time was worthwhile.

Desktop Publishing

For the middle school, desktop publishing programs are valuable tools. Programs like *The Writing Center* are user-friendly and produce high-quality documents. More sophisticated programs such as *PageMaker* are mastered with a little more effort and also produce high-quality documents. The most obvious application in the middle school is the school newspaper. The student staff may produce a first-rate publication with a computer, a quality printer, and access to a photocopier. In districts in which interdisciplinary teaming is employed, each team may publish its own newsletters for parent/teacher conferences and other occasions. Also, desktop publishing is an excellent, easy-to-use aid for communicating departmental information within the school district.

In addition, desktop publishing incorporates other technologies. For example, documents can be imported into the desktop program from other word processors. Emblems, drawings, letterheads, and documents are easily scanned and saved for insertion into a publication. An exciting technological development in recent years is the video still camera. This camera is simple to use and enhances the quality of desktop publishing. The pictures are saved to either a small reusable floppy disc or photo-CD. The pictures are displayed on any monitor or television or transferred to videotape for editing or later viewing. These photographs can also be saved as a computer file and placed as needed in a desktop publishing document. Students have the capability of taking a picture for a class report, inserting a picture in the report, and printing it within 15 minutes after taking the picture.

Teacher Utilities

Aside from word processing and desktop publishing, new computer programs are being developed that reduce the teacher's workload. There are programs that create seating charts, grade books, tests, and worksheets such as word searches, word links, crossword puzzles, and word bingo. They add to teacher efficiency by saving time, thus allowing more attention to students.

Technology also assists teachers in communicating with parents. For example, some school districts have installed computer calling systems. Teachers or teams of teachers have an extension number where daily or weekly assignments are recorded so parents can call at their convenience. Messages can also be left for the teacher.

Most grade book programs have a built-in progress report feature that provides a detailed progress report on groups of students, individual students, or all students. There are benefits to using these reports. For example, they take a minimum of time to prepare, and they can be given as often as desired. Sometimes teachers are so busy focusing on students having difficulty that the successful student goes unrewarded. With the computer programs, reports can be given to good students as well as struggling students.

In Hendershot, Nevada, student–teacher conferences are videotaped and sent home to parents. The taped sessions are approximately 15 minutes in length and are sent home quarterly. It is difficult to videotape students each quarter, but each student can be taped at least once per year. Novelli (1993) reports:

> *Copies of all videos go home for parents to view and keep. Teachers make follow-up phone calls in cases of problem solving conferences. Parents are thrilled with the videos . . . even when a conference covers a problem, we find they're glad to know what's going on. (p. 30)*

Teachers using portfolio assessment to record student progress over time know how much paper can be generated for just one student. Annette Hamilton, a sixth grade teacher at Mary Hogan Middle School in Middlebury, Vermont, is a multimedia teacher when it comes to using technology. Novelli (1993) explains how she uses a Macintosh computer with the *Grady Profile Assessment* program in conjunction with a set of *Hyper Card* stacks, *Video Spigot Board*, video camera, scanner, and *Quick Time:*

> *Each student has a set of cards on the computer for collecting, organizing, and presenting portfolio information. Some cards, for example, allow a student to show actual work samples (by recording sound, scanning works on paper, and videotaping performances). Options on the cards let both the student and teacher assess the work. (p. 31)*

As teachers become proficient and comfortable in using these kinds of applications, there is a likelihood that technology applications in the classroom will follow naturally.

Telecommunications

A computer, telephone, and modem can provide access to information throughout the world. There are many applications for both the student and the teacher. One such application is C2ME, a problem-solving bulletin board service offered by the Cleveland City Public Schools in conjunction with Cuyahoga Community College. This bulletin board service offers mathematics word problems to any school that is interested. Each week, one problem per day is offered at four levels of difficulty. Students enter their answers to check their accuracy.

Janis Coffman, a Decatur, Illinois, geography teacher, makes her curriculum meaningful by using a modem and the AT&T Learning Network. Novelli (1993) explains how she uses the network:

> The network is a curriculum-based computer network that joins classrooms electronically. The Learning Network offers seven options—from programs that study community problems to those that address global issues. Coffman's kids chose Places and Perspectives to explore history, culture, government, and geography of different places around the world. (p. 28)

This network allows students to telecommunicate with other classes in other countries. Before going on line, classes exchange "Welcome Packets" with other participating classes. The packets humanize the computer experience by providing tangible objects from the sender's life such as photos and objects of personal interest.

Video and Multimedia

Earlier in this chapter it was suggested that contracting with a company like Whittle Communications provides a color television wired to a central location for every classroom. In 1988, our district entered into an agreement with Whittle. Once the color televisions were installed, video recorders were purchased and mounted with each television unit. Each morning, selected students come to school early to direct, produce, and videotape the announcements that are broadcast to the entire school. In addition, students produce skits promoting school events. At other times the television service provides instructional support for interdisciplinary teams. They can show tapes, for example, that are related to course content. During one unit on survival the team showed the movie *The Call of the Wild* to bring closure to the series of lessons. The students were able to view the movie in their own classrooms instead of in the auditorium.

Earlier in this chapter, examples of classroom multimedia applications were presented. The term *multimedia* describes items such as computers, hard drives, video players (disc and/or cassette), televisions, printers, scanners, video cameras, digitizers (audio and/or video), speakers, CD-ROMs, sound sources, keyboards, telephones, and modems. "With multimedia, teachers create exciting and effective learning environments where students are active participants rather than passive recipients of information" (Bruder, 1991, p. 22).

Bruder (1991) cites the use of multimedia in the university classroom:

> In classrooms using multimedia, learning becomes an active process where the student uses the technology to communicate his understanding of a subject to those around him. Often, as a result, classroom structures change. Seats set in rows start to form clusters where teams can work. Teachers may adjust methods to become navigators, no longer feeding information to students for storage and regurgitation on tests. And students are expected to take information in, process

it, and put back something of themselves that says yes, they understand what it was they've been exposed to. (p. 23)

The use of multimedia enhances both the holistic approach to teaching and cooperative learning in the middle school.

Cooperative Learning

For the creative teacher, technology is a valuable tool. The possibilities of curriculum-related multimedia projects are only limited by the available equipment and the teacher's imagination. Even word processing can become a collaborative activity. One method was discussed earlier that used telecommunications with other schools. Another method might be a computer lab where a teacher from an interdisciplinary team assigns each student a specific computer to use. The first student of the day receives a topic for a story and starts writing. The next student assigned to the computer reads the work done by the previous student and continues the story until all the classes have provided input and the story is completed. In addition, software companies have software for computers that are networked and will allow four or five students at separate computers to edit a single document at the same time.

Most teachers are familiar with the program *Oregon Trail*. The developers of this program created a cooperative version of this program, *Wagon Train 1848*. This program allows networked computers to be assigned to groups. These grouped computers become wagon trains. The students choose a wagon master and share in the decision making as the wagon train travels the Oregon Trail.

Subject Area Applications

Many subject-related technology applications have been discussed in this chapter. There are many additional applications. Teachers must seek out software they are comfortable using and that fits into their curriculum. The district's building or system technology coordinator can be a valuable resource by providing sources for purchasing software and help with problem solving, simulations, drill and practice, word processing, keyboarding, system design, and programming.

Conclusion

As teachers integrate technology into their classrooms, the curriculum will begin to evolve, and the teacher's role will change to one that is more like a facilitator. Bruder (1991) quotes Fred D'Ignazio, president of Multimedia Classrooms, Inc., who says, "Teachers have to realize that they can assume a new role that is both better for them and for the student. It will be a role that passes control, along with trust, onto the kids, who can then participate to their fullest potential by creating multimedia representations of knowledge" (p. 26).

Discussion Questions

1. It is generally accepted that many middle school students are more comfortable using technology than are their veteran teachers. What strategies do you believe may be effective in helping these experienced teachers accept and use technology as an instructional aid?
2. Technology is perhaps the most rapidly changing aspect of education. In this chapter, various methods for training teachers and improving technology skills were discussed. What do you see as the advantages and disadvantages of large-group training versus professional development for individual teachers or small groups of teachers?
3. Technology is an expensive portion of the school budget. Many schools struggle to implement even the simplest technological advances, while others constantly add the newest technological innovations. This disparity between districts has the potential to aggravate the existing socioeconomic differences between groups in our society. Should this disparity be addressed? If so, what should be done to alleviate it?

References

Bangert-Drowns, R. L (1989). *Research on word processing and writing instruction*. San Francisco: American Educational Research Association.

Braun, L. (1992). *Vision: TEST (Technology enriched schools of tomorrow)*. Eugene, OR: International Society for Technology in Education.

Bruder, I. (1991). Multimedia: How it changes the way we teach and learn. *Electronic Learning, 11*(1), 22–26.

George, P. S., & Stevenson, C. (1988). *Highly effective interdisciplinary teams: Perceptions of exemplary middle school principals*. Gainesville: University of Florida.

Gursky, D., Koepke, M., Ladestro, L., Meade, J., Schuls, E., Williams, S., & Wolcott, L. (1991). Teaching with technology. *Teacher Magazine, 2*(4), 29–57.

Hill, M. (1993). Technology and the new middle school. *Electronic Learning, 12*(5), 20–27.

Kepner, H. S., Jr. (1989). *Computers in the classroom*.

Washington, DC: National Education Association.

Kinnaman, D. (1991). Strategic planning for a new generation of American schools. *Technology and learning, 12*(1), 20–30.

Kinnaman, D. (1993). Making professional development pay off. *School and College, 10*(2), 11–14.

Lake, S. (1989). *The rationale for the middle level school* (Practitioner's Monograph no. 9). Sacramento, CA: California League of Middle Schools.

Lockard, J., Abrams, P., & Many, W. (1990). *Microcomputers for educators*. New York: Harper Collins.

McCarthy, R. (1989). A computer on every teacher's desk. *Electronic Learning, 12*(7), 10–14.

Novelli, J. (1993). Middle school challenges: Technology solution. *Middle Years, 12*(3), 28–32.

Owston, R. D., Murphy, S., & Wideman, H. H.

(1990). *On and off computer writing of eighth grade students experienced in word processing.* New York, Ontario: York University Centre for the Study of Computers in Education.

Tone, B., & Winchester, D. (1988). *Computer assist-* *ed writing instruction.* Bloomington, IN: ERIC Clearing House on Reading Communication Skills. (ERIC Documentation Reproduction Service No. Ed 293 130)

Chapter 14

Parent Involvement

LINDA CAUGHEY
SUSAN WYNN

Linda Caughey and Susan Wynn worked together for 13 years in middle level education. They were instrumental in creating parent involvement in their school along with staff-student recognition and a positive school climate. They have both been active in the Ohio Middle School Association and the National Middle School Association for 10 years.

Our changing world of increased communication, theories of education, and diverse family structures encourages the parent involvement movement. Even though this topic is not as technical as most aspects of education, parent participation is becoming a critical issue. Far from the family structure of yesteryear with the father as the sole source of income and the mother as the homemaker, we now see the complex family structure of single parents, broken families, and combined families. Due to the fast pace of living, the changes in the family nucleus, and outside distractions, it is becoming increasingly important that the parents and schools become partners for the sake of academic, moral, and social education of our future—our children.

Evolution of Parent Involvement

Parent involvement in schools is not a new idea. Numerous surveys and research in the last half of the twentieth century have endorsed the idea of education of children as the joint responsibility of educators, parents, and communities. This movement began as a token inclusion of parents and has snowballed into wide spread involvement of parents in our school.

In the late 1960s and early 1970s, parent advisory councils emerged as a way for parents to become involved in the education of their children. These parent committees were considered to be consultative and frequently were a token attempt to include parents to comment on school activities.

The Effective Schools Research movement of the 1970s originally discounted parent involvement as one of the factors critical to school effectiveness. Edmunds (1979), an influential effective schools researcher, initially discounted parent involvement because it would reduce the school's responsibility to educate all children. Edmunds's focus was to restrict the research and practical application of those factors to what the schools could control.

However, the importance of parent involvement continued to be debated as the Effective Schools Research expanded. As a result of the practical applications of the research, parents were included in the projects associated with effective schools. This was done mainly to ensure the support of all constituents of the educational process. Once again, parents were involved, but their authority and influence were limited.

In the decade of the 1980s, the government became openly involved with educational goals to improve current practice. In 1986, the U.S. Department of Education published *What Works* as a report on research and practical knowledge to be used to improve schools and better educate children. Numerous references and research findings cited in this publication substantiated the importance of parent involvement in education. The research cited listed three main topics: home, classroom, and school. In each of these areas, parents are a crucial catalyst in ensuring the academic success of their children. Research findings state that "Parents are their children's first, and most influential, teachers. What parent do to help their children learn is more important to academic success than how well-off the family is" (*What Works*, 1986, p. 7). Furthermore, it is cited that "Parental involvement helps children learn more effectively" (*U.S. DOE*, 1986, p. 19). Finally, all constituents of education, that is, administrators, teachers, students, parents, and community, should concur on the goals, curriculum, and climate of the school.

Changes in society, family structure, and increased pressures on adolescents in the 1990s emphasized the need for continuing parent involvement from the elementary grades into the middle grades. Although 10- to 15-year-olds outwardly desire freedom and socialization, adult direction and parental involvement are still needed to help them make choices leading them to become lifelong learners and responsible adults. An abridged version of *Turning Points: Preparing American Youth for the 21st Century*, a report prepared by the Carnegie Council on Adolescent Development's Task Force on Education of Young Adolescents (1990), cites the importance of continuing parent involvement into the middle grades.

Consequently, the thrust toward educators, parents, and the community coming together to benefit and educate our youth has become a focal point. The most recent and prominent publication, *America 2000: An Education Strategy*, was adopted by the president of the United States and the state governors in 1990. The emphasis is to place the responsibility on state and local governments and communities rather than creating another federal program. The goals stated in this publication have become the guidelines for education in the 1990s. They strongly stipulate that our children are the joint responsibility of the educators and communities. *America 2000* encourages communities to adopt the six national education goals and set a community strategy to attain them. Specifically, greater parental involvement is urged through the joint efforts of parents and educators to encourage children to study more, learn more, and strive to meet high academic standards (*America 2000*, 1991, p. 33).

Why Involve Parents

In the days of the one-room schoolhouse the main emphasis was on the "three R's"—reading, writing, and arithmetic. Although academic achievement remains the primary focus of education, the realization that we must be concerned with the "whole" child has also come to the fore. To ensure academic success, we must address the emotional, social, and physical needs of our adolescents.

With increased pressures, disintegrating moral values, and the temptations present in our rapidly changing world, our children need a unified adult effort to make a lasting impact on their character and desire to achieve. Schools cannot provide guidance and reinforcement for students throughout their daily lives when the children are outside the scope of the classroom and school environment. Only in conjunction with parents and communities can educators hope to make a permanent impression on adolescents.

Successful Academic Achievement

The foremost consideration of education should, of course, be academics. Parental interest and support encourage students to strive to excel academically. If parents stress the importance of academic success, students will likewise place more credibility in this aspect of their education. If parents place more value on activities outside the school, such as hobbies, television, and so on, these will become the focal point for the students. This is substantiated by almost all research, publications, and studies conducted on the topic of academic achievement. There is no acknowledged research that indicates negative factors related to parent involvement. "Involving parents in education significantly improves student achievement" (NCCE, 1987).

Active involvement demonstrates to students the parents' willingness to invest time and effort in their education. Although adolescents outwardly protest this association, it increases feelings of security and a sense of well-being for the child. Accordingly, all students benefit from parent involvement; however, the children whose parents are actually involved show significantly higher gains.

Therefore, the goal should be to involve as many parents as possible to attain the highest levels of achievement.

There is a greater challenge today for enabling children to reach higher standards of learning than ever before. It is stated in the Goals 2000: Educate America Act as one of its eight education improvement goals: "Encourage parents and all family members to become more involved in children's education."

Our world today often appears segmented. Many parents and educators still cling to the theory that families nurture children and the schools educate them. They appear to fear crossing boundaries to build a true partnership between school and home. The truth is that schools and families must try to change. It is proven that students with the highest levels of achievement are those whose families support their education.

Increased Communications

Communication is a critical issue in every aspect of our lives, including education. Through parent involvement and communication the educators and the school can promote increased awareness and understanding with both parents and the entire community. Involving parents can help erase the mystery and fear of the unknown that so often become stumbling blocks to creating a positive school climate. Parents who are uninformed often are unsupportive of school efforts. By sharing as much information as possible, as often as possible, educators construct a foundation of confidence for the programs, curricula, and themselves and build an educational partnership with parents.

All too often, when elementary students move into secondary or middle level education, parents are unaware of what role they should assume. There are no simple parenting handbooks or guidelines that offer step-by-step instructions. Even the most active elementary school parents become timid, waiting for a sign or indication of their current place in the educational process of their child. The majority of parents, especially with a first child, can only relate back to their own experience and the fact that parents were not involved at this level. That is why it is important that educators take the initiative to extend the invitation and establish a working partnership with parents at the earliest opportunity.

When parents are involved, conversations with their children progress from the vague references to the school and staff members to a more productive and personalized level. As parents become familiar with the school, they demonstrate a more caring attitude about it. No longer are teachers just a science teacher, math teacher, or art teacher; they evolve to become Mr. Smith, Miss Jones, or Mrs. Clark.

In addition to creating a partnership with educators and improving communication with their children, parents can develop a support group among themselves for each other. Through parent groups, committees, and programs a support network can be established to assist parents with basic issues of parenting adolescents. Without the contact of other parents the only sources of information about social and moral issues may be the students themselves. Parents can support other parents about decisions pertaining to drinking, drugs, hairstyle and fashion, curfews, television and movie viewing, and on-line exposure, to list just a few concerns. In this way, individual parents can feel more confident that they are not too permissive or too strict, rather than relying on a "hit and miss" system of discipline.

This partnership with parents has its rewards for educators too. An informed, involved, and supportive parent is the school's best public relations tool. The citizenry expects administrators and teachers to profess excellence, especially at voting time. But when parents are supportive of the school in passing conversation, at a social gathering, or at civic meetings, they have a lasting impact on the community. The parents are a part of the community and therefore are considered more trustworthy than teachers with a vested interest in furthering school issues.

Enhanced Curriculum

Parents can be an endless source for curriculum augmentation. For example, resources and information about countless vocations and avocations are easily accessible through the parents and family members of students. Furthermore, parents can be used to arrange visits to the workplace and give students experiences in the world of employment.

Historical events being studied can be brought to life through the first-hand accounts of parents or grandparents who lived during that time. Even though history is recorded in our textbooks or on film strips, what better way to make a lasting and personal impact than through an interview or speaker? Eyewitness testimony about the trauma, fear, or anxiety of an historical event is more memorable to students than the statistics presented in history books.

All too often an inspired project or program may be "left on the drawing board" because of lack of materials. Parents might make the difference in bringing these to fruition by locating or donating necessary items.

Alleviation of Budget Problems

Few schools can boast a financial situation that provides everything necessary to give students a "top notch" education. Few teachers assert that they have everything in their classroom to present their subject the way they would like. However, some relief can be realized by enlisting the aid of parents.

Volunteer parents can alleviate some budget problems. For example, parents can perform some of the daily clerical duties. This enables teachers to spend more time on educational efforts. Clerical work, tutoring, monitoring, taking attendance, doing library or office aide duties, audio-visual or classroom assisting are all important to the educational process but can be done by parents with minimal training.

Other more technical duties can also be undertaken by parents. Medical testing for hearing and scoliosis are now a part of the school's responsibility. Although the testing must be conducted by a medical person, parents can assist in organizing and recording the testing procedure. In this area as well as others, there are restrictions and confidentiality factors that must be observed; however, volunteer assistance should be considered to alleviate personnel constraints of these time-consuming processes.

Developing a Parent Involvement Plan

Before launching into the practical application of a parent involvement master program, there are some factors that should be considered. If some parent programs are in place, they should be scrutinized to verify that the goals originally sought are being attained.

Parent partnerships should be developed to address the geographical location of the school and community. Rural, urban, and suburban communities may have differing opportunities for parent involvement. Although parent participation is a common denominator, the procedures for implementing a successful program will most certainly be as varied as the communities themselves.

Parent populations also differ widely. Usually parent careers are diversified between business and industry. However, some communities have developed as a result of a specific factory or industry that employs the majority of citizens. This information can be helpful in constructing the parent partnership. The business–school connection may establish a working relationship with the employer that benefits the school and also aids the business community.

One approach to developing a successful parent program is to research former programs that have failed and the reasons for their failure. The degree of success may depend on the effort spent in rectifying former mistakes and developing solutions to past problems. Some of the programs in place may be salvaged; some may be succeeding, providing a nucleus for expanding parent participation. Also, keep in mind that constant review and revision should be a part of any strategic plan. As time progresses, needs, participants, and goals often change. Therefore, constant attention must be given to review, revision, and improvement to continue a quality program.

Part of this attention is to set clear expectations for what parents can do. Priorities should address crucial areas needed for parent involvement and/or communication. A few things done well are better than several things done badly. It is better to implement a few key components of a parent involvement program than to haphazardly implement a range of ineffective ideas.

Be prepared to recruit volunteers. So often, when a notice is published or a blanket invitation is extended, parents are too timid to volunteer. They don't know if they "belong" or are unsure of what they may be "getting themselves into." Draft both staff members and parents to participate in developing these programs. Choose parents wisely or ask for volunteers to ensure recruiting supporters dedicated to attaining the parent involvement and partnership desired. Also, incorporate diversified participation; avoid limiting the committee membership to one or two groups of "friends." Otherwise, many parents will feel unrepresented and unwelcome. Ultimately the alienated parents will work against school goals.

As in any other partnership, it may be helpful to formulate a list of expectations. Whenever an agreement or partnership is established, a fundamental understanding assists in creating mutual respect and a sense of mission for everyone involved in the project. Parents and educators will realize that both factions have an important role in the partnership and a vested interest in fulfilling their responsibilities in the educational life of the students.

Practical Applications

Creation of a personalized parent involvement program differs from school to school. Many factors influence the needs and solutions. A program utilized effectively in one school may need to be revised, simplified, or expanded to be successful in another school. Even though the actual programs may be applied in a variety of ways, the premise and goals remain the same—get the parents involved!

Orientation

Becoming familiar with a school and its procedures is a way for parents to feel a part of the school. A school-wide orientation is a common activity to introduce students to their daily schedule, teachers, administrators, classroom and building rules, expectations, and the facility. Often this activity is limited to the entrance-grade-level class and newly enrolled students. However, some schools find a yearly orientation beneficial to all students. The facility and basic rules remain the same each year, but the individual classes and teachers will vary. Orientation usually occurs during the days immediately preceding the opening of the new school year or, for entry-level classes, the preceding spring. This is an ideal opportunity to introduce parents to school expectations, faculty members, discipline policies, and curriculum. A common orientation program begins with an assembly at which the principal addresses students and parents. This may include a welcome, an introduction to school philosophy, and distribution of a handbook for the upcoming year. After this opening, parents accompany students through a shortened daily schedule to visit each classroom, meet the teacher, receive basic rules, and hear a subject overview. To complete the activity, a social time for parents, students, and staff may be arranged with a simple dessert potluck and/or beverages in the lunchroom. This allows time for a more casual exchange among all factions of the partnership-building process.

An alternative for students and parents who have heard the orientation is to host a "Meet the Teacher" night or an open house. Families familiar with the basics of the school will still like to meet teachers and visit the classes their children will take during the school year. This activity should be held as soon as arrangements can be made following the opening of the new school year, to answer questions from parents and students, inform parents of class requirements and policies, and set a positive tone.

Parent/Teacher Conferences

Grade cards are traditionally the primary system for sharing student academic progress. Although this is the most efficient method for reporting the overall status of individual students to parents, a series of numbers or letters leaves many problems unsolved and parent questions unanswered. Parent/teacher conferences can assist parents, teachers, and students in improving the student's academic achievement. The format for these meetings between parent and teachers can be as varied as the schools that develop them. Parent/teacher conferences vary from arranged appointments to address problems of an individual student to a complicated schedule that encompasses an entire day or two while the student population is excused from attending classes.

Schools often establish a policy for parent/teacher conferences. Due to pupil/teacher ratio and the limited time available, some require that only parents of students at risk be contacted. Others incorporate all parents into some form of conference at least once a year. And still others have dispensed with the organized schedule of conferences but encourage teachers to contact parents of students who are struggling in a specific subject. When considering the value of including all parents in a successful partnership program, the most beneficial program is to confer with all parents.

Parent/teacher conferences are an important tool in communicating to parents the problems of individual students and improving student performance before a situation is beyond control. In the past these meetings were often simply a process of the parent being contacted for an appointment, the teacher reporting the basic facts, and the parent returning home to confront the student about the problem. However, much progress has been accomplished in this area. Guidelines have been developed to assist parents and teachers in participating in fruitful conferences. The criteria include preparation activities, information that can be collected in advance of the meeting, reasons and goals for parent/teacher meetings, suggested questions that parents should ask, and possibly overall results that may be expected. Often each school publishes its own pamphlet developed by a parent/teacher committee or uses published material from educational and governmental agencies to address productive conferencing.

Parent Advisory Councils

Parents should be included as collaborators in the educational process. At least, a representative faction should be elected, appointed, or asked to volunteer to participate with teachers, administrators, superintendents, board of education members, and possibly even students themselves in advising on school decisions. These councils or committees, for example, may participate in periodic meetings with teachers and principals to discuss discipline problems or activities. The advisory councils may be for a specific site or be expanded to make contributions to district-wide decisions affecting curriculum, school policies, and financial budgeting.

Some schools use the leadership of an existing parent group such as the parent/teacher organization, while others prefer to create a separate council. Whichever procedure suits the individual school system, it is important to formulate a purpose and function for the committee so that all participants will understand their role. It is easy for advisory committee members to assume they are the ultimate decision-making body. The members must all understand the limitations of their advisory powers.

Another consideration is to keep the climate of the meetings positive. A good rule of thumb is "If you bring a problem to the group, be prepared with a suggestion or a solution." In this way the participants will be inclined to focus on problem solving and productive discussion. It is easy for an advisory committee to reduce its agenda to a list of complaints about school procedures, teachers, or administrators. This is unproductive for all parties as it leads to suspicion by teachers about the role of the committee and fosters a negative school climate.

Parent Volunteer Programs

Volunteering is one of the fastest-growing aspects of parent involvement. These programs may range from individual teachers recruiting room parents and chaperones for field trips to a detailed format designed by a combined committee of parents, teachers, and administrators that is usually directed by a parent volunteer and the school principal.

Volunteers provide a solution to many common problems in the era of expanding enrollment and shrinking budgets. With some encouragement and minimal training, volunteers serve as room parents, chaperones, one-on-one tutors, classroom assistants, clerical assistants, club advisors, assistant coaches, receptionists, fund raisers, hall monitors, lunchroom supervisors, bus monitors, and library and office aides. When volunteers perform these daily tasks, teachers and other school staff people have more time to devote to educational duties.

Once again, important ingredients in the success of a volunteer program are thoughtful organization, an open invitation to all parents to participate, and clear instruction as to the position and responsibilities of the volunteers. In most school situations, volunteers must understand that their role is a supportive one and the teacher or school personnel are in charge. A volunteer who observes or experiences a problem should be instructed to report to the school supervisor. As volunteers, their assistance is valued, but they lack authority to implement disciplinary policy, for example.

Parent Programs

Increasing pressures and temptations of gang membership, drug and alcohol abuse, and sexual experimentation create a climate in which educators must work with parents to guide and protect adolescents. It is difficult for parents to acquire the information, statistics, and knowledge necessary to deal effectively with these societal threats. It therefore falls on the school to educate parents about existing problems, the steps being taken at school, and how parents can participate in helping children make effective decisions.

Special parent gatherings are the perfect opportunity to give parents a chance to gain support from other parents on a multitude of decisions regarding curfews, outside activities, television and movie viewing, attire, and friendships. The importance of these decisions will be directly reflected in the daily discipline and the atmosphere of the school. The more parents understand key issues influencing the daily life of adolescents, the more likely they will be to support policies and disciplinary procedures established by school authorities.

Also, meetings allow parents to gain detailed information concerning issues such as standardized testing, proficiency tests, curriculum changes, and scheduling. Parents need to understand the procedures, results, and repercussions so that they can effectively help the adolescent prepare and deal with the results of items such as standardized test score results.

Informal Involvement

In structured activities like parent programs, many benefits for students, parents, and educators are realized. However, much can be gained in an informal setting when everyone can casually chat about whatever topic surfaces. Under this premise some schools are inviting parents to attend a breakfast, lunch, or tea with an administrator, guidance counselor, or group of teachers. This occasion allows both parents and educators to talk spontaneously about concerns, school programs, activities, and school issues without the pressures and formality of a meeting or speaking out in a group.

The optimal plan is to rotate the schedule to include different times of the day to give all parents an opportunity to participate and to invite every parent at some point during the school year. However, time and resources frequently limit this luxury. The goal should be to offer the chance for parents to attend and perhaps assist in making scheduling arrangements.

Another consideration is, of course, the financial aspect of providing refreshments. The options might be to research the possibilities of available funds from the principal's fund or student council, or to approach the parent organization for assistance. At any rate, refreshments are not the primary concern, as much as are the benefits gained by all participants.

Additional Parent Involvement Components

The programs discussed and outlined thus far require a great deal of organization and effort. Even though these programs are important, there are numerous avenues that encourage participation, and communication helps achieve parent involvement goals.

Practically every school publishes some form of periodic newsletter as a source of public information. These are issued weekly, monthly, or by grading period. The U.S. Postal Service or the more common, but not as reliable, student delivery method is used for distribution to parents. Contents of the school newsletter usually include recent successes of individuals, clubs, or teams; current events or programs occurring in the school; and announcements of upcoming dates. The news in these publications is the main attraction for parents, but measures could be taken to specifically address parents in several ways. In each publication an article should be devoted to helpful hints or suggestions for parents to use at home. Some possible topics are: homework guidelines, upcoming television programs or movies that may benefit the student or relate to study topics in school, availability of materials and resources for parents' use on various issues affecting adolescents, or perhaps assistance in dealing with a specific concern affecting the school or community at a particular time (such as a violent incident that has occurred recently). A response tear-off might be included to give parents a chance to ask questions, request a conference, or to make comments and recommendations. This is an avenue many parents may prefer rather than approaching a teacher or principal in person. Always encourage positive feedback as well as negative.

A library for parents is a positive step toward establishing a good rapport with parents. There are an unlimited number of publications, videos, handbooks, and pamphlets that address every aspect of educating, parenting, and coping with adolescents and the problems and pressures facing them today. Teachers should also be encouraged to become familiar with the resources available to develop personal knowledge of the information to recommend to parents as the need arises.

Homework hotlines and answering machines are another service schools are using to improve communications with families. Although these are simply recorded messages, parents realize that this is an effort on the part of the educators to serve them and the students. In this way, assignments can be monitored by parents for absent or forgetful students, messages can be left for teachers during afterschool hours, and absences can be reported by parents who are working during the school day. This venture may involve some costs, but it is worthwhile for students, parents, and educators.

Although the programs and services are intended to inform and include parents, some apprehension or hesitation may remain for parents. One solution is to create a Parent Advocate position or committee. The Parent Advocate serves as a liaison or representative for parents to the school. The title of this position in itself may reassure parents that they have a representative to help them deal with a problem at school, answer questions they might otherwise hesitate to ask, or accompany them to conferences that may be uncomfortable or complicated. Once again, the creation of this position may be decided by the budget limitations of the school; however, some advocacy assignment might be incorporated into an existing position.

One of the most common obstacles of parent involvement is child care. More often than not, adolescents have younger siblings who need care and supervision while their parents are gone. Many parents cannot procure caregivers for the time they might spend at programs, committee meetings, or events. If arrangements can be made for middle school students to be available at the school during parent involvement, the increase in attendance will undoubtedly increase. Of course, adult supervision is recommended, especially if the numbers are great. But one adult with several adolescents can manage a surprising number of younger children and solve the babysitting problem.

Rewards and Awards

The greatest rewards of a successful partnership for both educators and parents are improved student achievement, positive school climate, and the satisfaction of guiding adolescents along the path to responsible and productive adulthood. However, everyone enjoys and appreciates an occasional pat on the back. Therefore, some thought should be given to recognition of parents who give their time and resources to make the parent–school partnership a success.

A simple thank-you note composed and signed by the students is rewarding for all parties. This impresses upon the adolescents the importance of social amenities and encourages them to give some thought to the time and effort their parents are contributing to them. In addition, parents realize that their efforts are appreciated by their children and their teachers. These notes should be encouraged by administrators, teachers, advisors, and coaches for any help given throughout the school year. If the task appears to be overwhelming, the students and teachers can be even more thankful for the numerous donations of time and materials being made for their benefit.

In addition, it is customary at the conclusion of the school year to issue awards for various student accomplishments such as honor roll, extracurricular activities, and sports. This is an ideal opportunity to recognize the contributions of parents. At the beginning of the year, educators should be asked to keep a list of all parents who make contributions to their class, to be submitted at a later date. An economical certificate designed on a school computer and printed on stock paper is a small price to pay for the satisfaction and sense of accomplishment it bestows on the recipient. These awards can be distributed through the mail or the student delivery system, included in the student awards assembly, or bestowed at a specific function such as an appreciation tea or potluck.

Conclusion

The strategies included in this chapter are intended to serve as a foundation for building successful, individualized partnerships between parents and educators. The spectrum of parent involvement is as unlimited as the creativity and ingenuity of the developers. Furthermore, the concept of a parent–educator partnership goes beyond mom, dad, and the teacher. In consideration of today's diversified family structure, grandparents, aunts, uncles, caretakers, noncustodial parents, stepparents, and community citizens without children currently attending school should be included in the invitation to participate. Likewise, educators should be considered as all persons associated with the school—board of education members, superintendents, administrators, teachers, and classified staff.

A unified effort of the school, family, and community will have a positive and rewarding effect on adolescents. During this period of confusing and complex transition from childhood to adulthood the influence of a stable connection between home and school may well be the deciding factor between failure and success of the transescent, not just academically but socially and morally.

Every educational publication, research report, or conference includes some type of reference to the importance of parent–school partnerships or parent involvement. Educators are notorious for the pride they exhibit in the programs they have developed and their willingness to share with others. Everyone should use what has previously been done, revise and expand it to fit their needs, and then contribute to others in the future.

On a classroom wall in a middle school in rural Ohio, amidst an assortment of class reports, posters, and student recognition displays, hangs a sign that proclaims, "They don't care how much you know until they know how much you care"—a simple (anonymous) statement that, when given some thought, is the perfect motto for educators and for all people. Planning and executing a parent involvement program is an excellent way to demonstrate a caring attitude and concern for the whole child. Parents and educators together are responsible for cultivating and developing our greatest future resource—*our children!*

Discussion Questions

1. This chapter strongly endorses the active involvement of parents in the middle school. If you were to establish such a program, what limitations do you believe should be placed on the responsibilities assumed by volunteers?
2. Enlisting quality volunteers is vital to the success of a parent involvement progam. Prepare a letter that will be sent to parents and community members requesting their participation in a new volunteer program. You should address the purpose of the program, possible duties, and that this program is beneficial to the students.
3. Although school-wide parent involvement is important, define ways the individual teacher might include parents in the classroom.

References

Alliance for Curriculum Reform (1995). *Handbook of research on improving student achievement.* Arlington, VA: Educational Research Service.

America 2000: An education strategy (1991). Washington, DC: U.S. Department of Education.

Bluestein, J., & Collins, L. (1989). *Parents in a pressure cooker: A guide to responsible and loving parent/child relationships.* Rosemont, NJ: Modern Learning Press.

Canter, L., & Canter, M. (1991). *Parents on your*

side: *A comprehensive parent involvement program for teachers.* Santa Monica, CA: Lee Canter and Associates.

Carnegie Council on Adolescent Development's Task Force on Education of Young Adolescents (1995). *Turning points: Preparing American youth for the 21st century* (abridged). Washington, DC: Author.

Childs, D. B. (1991). Changing the school environment to increase parent involvement. *National Association of Secondary School Principals, 75*(535), 84–88.

Edmunds, R. (1979). Effective schools for the urban poor. *Educational Leadership, 32,* 15–27.

Epstein, J. L. (1987). Parent involvement: What research says to administrators. *Education and Urban Society, 19*(2), 119–136.

Fruchter, N., Galletta, A., & White, J. L. (1992). *A new direction in parent involvement.* Washington, DC: Academy for Educational Development.

Henderson, A. T., Marburger, C. L., & Ooms, T. (1986). *Beyond the bake sale: An educator's guide to working with parents.* Columbia, MD: National Committee for Citizens in Education.

Holliday, A. E. (1987). Public relations/communications and student achievement: What is the connection? *Journal of Educational Public Relations, 10*(1), 4–7.

Howell, R. L. (1991). Parent advisory committees link school and community. *National Association of Secondary School Principals, 75*(532), 117–118.

Johnston, H. J. (1990). *The new American family and the school.* Columbus, OH: National Middle School Association.

Melaville, A. I., Blank, M. J., & Asayesh, G. (1993). *Together we can: A guide for crafting a profamily system of education and human services.* Washington, DC: U.S. Department of Education/U.S.Department of Health and Human Services.

Meyer, R. J. (1995). One parent's dilemma: Colliding assumptions between home and school. *Current Issues in Middle Level Education, 4*(2), 42–59.

Myers, J. W. (1985). *Involving parents in middle level education.* Columbus, OH: National Middle School Association.

Myers, J., & Monson, L. (1992). *Involving families.* Columbus, OH: National Middle School Association.

National Committee for Citizens in Education (NCCE). (1987). Editorial Comment. *Journal of Educational Public Relations, 10*(1), 8.

National Education Goals Panel (1995). *The national education goals report: Building a nation of learners.* Washington, DC: Author.

National Middle School Association (1995). *This we believe: Developmentally responsive middle level schools.* Columbus, OH: Author.

U.S. Department of Education (DOE). (1994). *Strong families, strong schools: Building community partnerships for learning: A research base for family involvement in learning.* Washington, DC: Author.

U.S. Department of Education (DOE). (1995). *Employers, families, and education: Promoting family involvement in learning.* A report by the Families and Work Institute commissioned for the Family Involvement Partnership for Learning. Washington, DC: Author.

U.S. Department of Education (DOE). (1986). *What works: Research about teaching and learning.* Washington, DC: Author.

Wanat, C. L. (1994). Effect of family structure on parental involvement: Perspectives of principals and traditional, dual-income, and single parents. *Journal of School Leadership, 4,* 631–648.

Wheeler, P. (1992). Promoting parent involvement in secondary schools. *National Association of Secondary School Principals, 76*(546), 28–35.

Chapter *15*

Wuz Up?

JANICE GALLAGHER

Janice Gallagher is Gifted Education Coordinator for Euclid City Schools, Euclid, Ohio. She has taught English at the middle school and high school levels, where she worked extensively to integrate art into the school curriculum.

In the beginning, (some believe) God (or something) created man. Then, He created middle school. Sometimes I wonder why, but none-the-less, it's here. And I still have to go. I still don't understand why.
—*KRISTIN (age 13)*

My interest in adolescent students' views about middle school began innocently enough. I was visiting my friend, Mike, during the Christmas season. His seventh grade son walked into the living room and I said, "Hi, Greg. How do you like the middle school?"

"It's so boring," he answered.

I felt the hair on the back of my neck bristle. I'd taught seventh and eighth grade English for 20 years. Nothing bothers me quite as much as a remark like "It's boring." I pushed my ire aside and asked Greg, "What makes it so boring?"

"You know last year all my teacher said was, 'You have to work hard to learn this because you will be expected to know it when you get to middle school.' We worked so hard, and I really felt as though I were prepared for middle school. Then I got there and all we've done is stuff we did in sixth grade. I'm not learning anything new. It's boring."

That conversation started the wheels in my head turning. Of course, I wondered at the accuracy of Greg's statements. I also began to wonder what different responses I would get if I asked the same question of other middle school students. Would middle school students in a suburban school have a different view from Greg, who lived in a small college town?

Gathering the Data

Informally I talked with teachers at Glenridge, the middle school that Greg attended. My husband is a teacher in Greg's school district, so meeting and talking with teachers is a normal part of our lives. Over coffee or at school functions I asked about the structure of the middle school and configuration of the district. I learned that there were seven elementary schools in the town; each was a neighborhood school containing grades K–6. Students from all over town came to one middle school for seventh and eighth grades, with 350 students in each grade.

The intent of my inquiry was to explore how middle school students viewed their experiences. I wanted good informants, but I did not want to hand-select the students, as I was concerned that "selection" would taint the findings. My desire was to obtain letters from a cross-section of students to sift through and analyze for commonalities and differences.

I wrote a letter to three seventh grade English teachers and three eighth grade English teachers inviting them to have their students write me a letter explaining what life was like for middle school students. Because I knew the teachers would want to connect the letter to their curriculum, I gave them a month to return student letters to me. Each teacher had a classload of approximately 125 students. If all the teachers honored my request, I would have more than 700 letters to read. I received 147 student letters from two teachers, and, after I'd begun writing this paper, I received another 50 letters.

At the same time, I wrote to six English teachers in Lakeview, a middle school near a large city, asking them to have students write to me about life in their middle school. If all teachers honored my requests, I would have more than 700 additional letters to read. Three teachers had their students write letters. I received 342 letters from seventh and eighth graders in the Lakeview School District. An additional 70 letters arrived later, and I was able to include them in this report.

The configuration of the Lakeview School District was similar to Glenridge's. There were four neighborhood schools housing grades K–4, one science magnet school with grades K–6, one 5/6 building, one middle school, and one high school. The middle school population was divided into three teams in the seventh grade and three teams in the eighth grade. Two of the three teams contained honors classes.

I began my quest believing there would be a difference between the views of students from a small-town middle school and what students from a larger suburban district felt about their experience. I thought the major thrust of my inquiry would be a comparison of the differences between the two educational environments. I was astounded that what the suburban students disliked about the middle school were the same things that the small-town students disliked. It was impossible to make a distinction between the two. I present their views, therefore, as if all were gathered from the same school district, and I do little comparing of the differences between the middle school experience for suburban students and small-town students.

Because I had given the teachers specific questions for the students to consider as they wrote their letters, classifying their responses was an easy task. I looked for five major issues:

1. What did the students like about middle school?
2. What did they dislike about middle school?
3. How was middle school different from their elementary experience, and what did they miss about elementary school?
4. How did they feel about the teaming approach? (This was a new structure for all of the students, whether they were enrolled in Glenridge or Lakeview.)
5. I also looked for any extraneous remarks that provided insight into the world of the middle school student.

Because I wanted to represent important common concerns of the middle school students, I used direct quotations from the letters to represent common views. I also consciously selected an equal number of males and females and an equal number of white and black students. I used only the first names of the students. While every letter contained valuable quotations, it was not possible to include them all. If you read quotations from two students named Mike, you can be certain that two different students with the same first name authored those comments.

I began with the opinion of one single student in my head. If I had any expectations, it would be that other students would describe the middle school experience as "boring." That was not the case. I read only three other letters that described middle school in this way. While others may have been dissatisfied, few of them used the word "boring" to describe their school.

It is difficult to determine how much influence the teachers had over what their students wrote. One teacher at Lakeview, for example, made the letter an integral part of her curriculum. She distributed an assignment sheet that clearly outlined what students were expected to do. Letters from her class were composed on plain white paper and were complete with heading, inside address, salutation, body, and closing (some of which were signed and then printed beneath the signature). In an entirely different approach, another teacher sent me letters that were informal and written on notebook paper. The focus of these letters was to answer the questions I posed, and students paid little attention to form or mechanics. I could tell that one teacher had given the assignment as an opportunity for extra credit, because I could see the points she'd awarded (from 1–10) in the upper right-hand corner of the letters.

I sent a letter of thanks to the classes who wrote to me. After sharing my letter with her students, one teacher confided in me, "You know my students were not too keen about writing the letter to you. I told them to be honest in what they had to say. They would get a homework grade from me, but I would not read the letters they wrote to you. They grumbled, but they did it. Then when I read them the letter you wrote to them, suddenly they became so interested. They said, 'Is she really going to come talk to us? Can I write to her again? I have more to tell her!'"

Reading the letters gave me an enjoyable glimpse into adolescent life. The students took the assignment seriously, really wanting to express their feelings about the middle school. Some letters were composed in a conversational tone, and I could hear the student's voice in the writing. I want to share some of them with you just so you will get the flavor of what I read.

Lydia wrote:

Hey! Wuz up? My name is Lydia Nicole Jazemin. I'm 13 years old about to be 14 years old on April 8. I'm a eighth grader at Lakeview Middle School. I have good grades in some classes except for math, that's the worst subject for me. I'm a athlete running track this spring to help my teammates. The reason why I joined track is because I can run, and I just want the other girls on my team to win races, and tournaments against other schools.

Kellie wrote:

My name is Kellie, I'm 14, and I'm in the eighth grade at Lakeview Middle School. I have been attending Lakeview Schools since the third grade. My hobbies include, horseback riding, playing the violin, playing the keyboard, collecting animal figurines and collecting anything Disney.

I heard that you're writing a book about the positives and the negatives about middle school, and that you would like some input from students that are presently in middle school. Here's what I have to say about the subject.

Near the end of sixth grade, I started getting very nervous about seventh grade. It would mean a new school (such a big school), all new teachers, switching classes, a whole new experience, much different than what I had been used to. Also, I had heard a lot of rumors, about the school in general. Fights, people bothering you, I really started getting scared.

I left home that first day of seventh grade, very apprehensive. Once I got there however, all my fears vanished. It wasn't so bad after all. Everyone was very helpful, and besides, I was in the same boat as the other three or four hundred other seventh graders. The teachers were all great too. They knew how scared all us kids were, and they did their best to make us feel welcome.

I was touched with the way Kellie expressed her fears and her courage, so typical of adolescent feelings and thoughts. This is a wonderful letter that risks revealing her innermost emotions. What is even more poignant is that Kellie is totally blind.

Jay wrote:

My name is Jay, and I'm a seventh grade honor student at Lakeview. To   answer some of your questions, I give you the following responses. Yes, middle school is very much different from elementary school. When you were younger the teachers were pretty nice and understanding about stuff. Now, they're pretty harsh— like "Tough luck, man."

Kristin's letter was full of life and originality. She wrote:

Welcome to the middle school experience. I wish you the best of luck and honor your courage. Relax and take in as much as possible. Use caution, not all scenes are lovely. In the beginning, (some believe) God (or something) created man. Then, He created middle school. Sometimes I wonder why, but none-the-less, it's here. And I still have to go. I still don't understand why.

I found this definition of middle school in Nicholas's letter: "In response to your letter, I think middle school is like beginning to walk for babies. It is very different from elementary and much more confusing." Mike offered another definition: "Middle school is a lot different from elementary school. Elementary school is all about the basics and having fun. Middle school gets more serious, and having fun isn't really an option."

What I enjoyed most were letters like Arek's, in which the student tried to share something with me before answering the questions I posed. He wrote, "Hi. Let me introduce myself. My name is Arek. I like to play sports, play the piano, draw, and play video games. I am a nice person and also, I like to write."

The "Goodness" of the Middle School

Changing Classes

Many students mentioned a positive attribute of the middle school was the environment, especially changing classes. Alison wrote: "Middle and elementary school have a lot of differences. A few are that in middle school we switch classes; it's very cool because it makes the day go by faster." Laurel wrote: "In middle school we switch classes and have more different teachers each period so it makes it more interesting. When you're switching classes, you can see all your friends in the hallway and this includes the ones on different teams." Nate wrote: "I like the fact that students have different teachers each day. It lets you see what teachers you like and which you don't." Shawntee put it like this:

My opinion on middle school is that it is a lot different from elementary school. I like middle school much better. The very best thing I like about middle school is that we change periods. We get to talk to our friends between classes, instead of sitting in one class all day.

The Physical Plant

Students liked other physical differences about the middle school.

Julia wrote: "Middle school is very different from elementary school. The halls are wider, the drinking fountains are higher, and the school is larger." Mike wrote, "The fun things about middle school are that we have different languages to take in eighth grade." Jason wrote: "Middle school has a lot more to offer than elementary does. There are a lot more teachers and students, so you can make more friends. Middle school offers school sports and many other programs." Nathan wrote: "Our school is really set up with things. For example, we have two gyms and a pool." About the pool, Lindsey wrote:

> The most greatest thing that a third grader could think of was that Lakeview had a pool!
> I guess what a child in middle school would think of as being such a big deal, older kids find as nothing at all. But coming from a school with no playground, no swings, this was a dream come true!

In describing his school and his middle school experience, Brian wrote, "I also like that we have some things that other schools might not have—like a swimming pool, two gyms, and a large auditorium."

Importance of Sports

I was surprised at the number of students, both males and females, who mentioned sports activities as a real plus in the middle school experience. Mike's letter contained the strongest support for sports: "My bright spot of the day is sports. Sports help me get good grades. No sports—then I'd probably get all F's." Ronald wrote, "I am a young black male and I enjoy football, basketball, soccer, gymnastics and karate." Rahman wrote, "The fun thing in middle school is playing basketball during recreation time." Mary said, "My name is Mary and I am 13. I go to Lakeview Middle School. I enjoy mostly sports, particularly soccer, diving and gymnastics." Brian said, "The best parts of the school day are lunch and after school sports."

Freedom

Middle school students are aware of the increased freedom they have at the middle school. Angela wrote: "I feel more in control of my life. I feel I have more freedom." Bonnie wrote, "The fun thing in the middle school is the amount of freedom you are given." Jayson said, "The difference between elementary school and Lakeview Middle School is that they don't act childish towards you and you feel like you get more freedom than in elementary school."

"In middle school," wrote Julia, "we get more freedom. We no longer need to stand in single file lines or anything."

Briana mentioned trust as a part of the freedom: ". . . middle school is better because you have more trust, and you can do more and different things." Bethany also spoke of trust when she wrote about having lockers in the middle school:

One of the things in middle school is that you are trusted to not have your stuff in a classroom. You can join different clubs and sports teams. We are trusted with walking to our next class without having to walk in lines with our teachers. We are trusted with sitting by our friends at lunch and in our classes.

Responsibility

Closely tied to freedom in the letters was responsibility. "I have much more responsibility," Tina wrote, "such as getting to class on time, getting long term assignments turned in and having all the materials you need in your locker to get right away."

Jason said, "The funnest thing about middle school is that your parents trust you more because you can do more things with your friends. Since you are older, you can be trusted."

Amber said, "Middle school is very different from elementary school. First of all, you are expected to do more homework in less time. You are also expected to be more responsible for getting your homework done and to get to your classes on time."

Melissa talked about the difference in responsibility between elementary and middle school:

You have more responsibilities then elementary because when you would turn it in (homework) in late, you must turn it in late. Now you turn it in late, and it's at least fifty percent off. In some classes you get your work maybe 3 weeks ahead of time, and it's up to you to keep up with it.

Jim wrote, "I like middle school better than elementary because I think the kids are more mature now than when they were little."

Jennifer wrote, "Middle school is very different from elementary school. You're treated more like an adult in middle school. You are very independent when you're in middle school. Everyone depends on you to remember all of your supplies and where you have to go."

Kiara wrote, "It's fun. You get to finally be up here with the big kids."

Friends

Both Glenridge and Lakeview brought students together from across the city to one middle school. The larger school and the challenge of making friends from outside the neighborhood were common topics in the letters I read. It became obvious early in my reading of the letters that having friends is a compelling part of the middle school experience. Almost every letter mentioned the importance of friends in one way or another. What the students wrote about friends will be explained later in the "goodness" section, as well as in the "badness" section.

Some students found the middle school a positive environment for nurturing new friendships. Vicki wrote, "The thing that I look forward to coming to school is that everyone is my friend, and I love to see my friends in school or out." Alison said, "In middle school, people also have more friends and get to know more people in your grade/team." Eddy wrote, "Coming to Lakeview was sort of a rebirth in my life. Through elementary school I had very little friends. And with the team learning style at Lakeview, it is much easier to make friends."

Teaming in the Middle School

Students had much to say about the goodness of teaming. The most important factor of teaming was that if students were absent from school, they could call just one friend and get all their assignments. Pedro wrote, "Teaming has made many changes for me. It is much easier to get assignments from friends because they have the same teachers as I do. I am now able to work in groups without having to argue."

Doug wrote, "I like the idea of teaming. It puts less stress on us, because they will not give us four tests in one day, and you sort of get closer to your teachers." Tony wrote, "The teaming that we have in Glenridge has really helped my grades because in 7th grade they didn't have this yet and I wasn't doing very well." Adelia wrote, "Being on a team is good because if you forget what your assignment is, you can call the people who are on our team." Hans wrote: "The changes that teaming has made for me is that your teachers can all help on homework or on tests. I think the teachers care more when we have teams." John wrote, "The team teaching has made my classes more like elementary school. . . ." Matthew stated, "The best thing about having teams is that there are more people that have the same teachers so more students can help each other."

The "Badness" of the Middle School

Lakeview Middle Schools instituted the teaming approach 8 years before I began my study. For Glenridge, however, the team approach was in its first year. The eighth graders who wrote to me from Glenridge knew both climates, the climate of the junior high school and the climate of the middle school. New to teaming or knowing nothing but teaming made no difference in the objections of students when it came to being separated from friends.

"I don't like teaming," Bob wrote, "because my friends aren't in the same team as me and I don't get to see them very often. The best time of the day for me is lunch because I eat lunch with people from other teams." Heather wrote, "The new teams are all right but if your friends aren't on your team then you normally only see your friends at lunch or in the halls." Adam wrote this about what he would change in the middle school: "I would also add the chance to spend time with my friends from my elementary school. I would also have friends in one or all of my classes."

Sean expressed a very strong opinion about teaming: "Teaming has been a waste of time. I think it has made a difference for teacher preparation for classes, but it has almost killed some friendships that I've had for years." Natalie stated it this way: "The teams have separated Glenridge into pieces. Now there is not a good chance that you will get to eat lunch with your friends or have the same classes." "I really don't care for the team idea," Mike wrote," because you're stuck together with the same group of kids."

Elizabeth complained, "Teaming is not a very good change. You see the same people in all of your classes! And, I don't think it really benefits us any way from regular teaching last year." Allison leveled these charges about teaming: ". . . the people who invented it, don't have to live it. Maybe if I hadn't had a non-teaming seventh grade, I would feel differently."

Jackie wrote:

> *Teaming has made many changes also. Because of teaming I am not able to see some of my friends all day. The only time I can see friends on other teams is in between classes. Also from teaming I have to stay in the same parts of the build-ing all day.*

Kelly made a general statement about teaming: "On the issue of teaming, I suppose the intent of the idea was good, but I have found that there are many things I preferred better last year." Dave's opinion was stronger: "Teaming is the worst thing that could be done! Don't try that at school. It may be harmful to students' health."

What really amazed me about the letters from Glenridge was the number of students who perceived teaming as an organizing vehicle imposed upon them for the convenience of the teachers. Kristi, for example, wrote, "I know that it's easier on the teachers, but I don't like it." Jacob wrote, "The teaming was a great idea for the teachers. It's probably easy for the teachers to get all of their grades to-gether at once." Krystle wrote, "Teaming has made no changes for me, but I think for the teachers it has made it easier to get together and talk about students and their weaknesses in school work and how they could improve." Meagan's com-ment about teachers and teaming was a complaint of sorts: "Now that we have this teaming, it seems like I can't just please one teacher; it's got to be all of them." Matthew eloquently stated his position like this:

> *The teaming aspect of middle school has many strengths and weaknesses. Being exposed to a non-team school last year at Glenridge and a teamed school this year allows me to weigh the pros and the cons. The best thing about teaming is that the teachers can save lots of time by coordinating schedules that won't con-flict with each other.*

The overwhelming majority of students said that what they missed most from elementary days was recess. They missed the opportunity to run freely with their friends. "I miss having recess and all the time playing on the swings and monkey bars," wrote Tiffany. Chanita wrote, "There are a lot of things I miss about elementary. I miss the outside and being with all my friends." Jennifer said, "What I miss the most would be recess outside. I love the outdoors (and it beats sitting in the gym for 20 minutes)." Geoffrey wrote, "The recesses were the best thing that I can remember about elementary school." Rene wrote, "Another disadvantage is we don't get to go outside at recess after lunch. We have to stay in the building all day. Also there are very few windows. So we never get to see the outside that often." Sam wrote, "We don't ever get to breathe fresh air."

Personal Relationships with Teachers

I was unprepared for the vast number of students who said they missed their elementary teachers. John wrote, "I sure do miss elementary days, but I miss nice teachers more." Sandy wrote, "The things I miss from elementary are recess and the relationships with teachers. In elementary the teachers know you more. And there's a more personal relationship and I miss that." Adam stated, "In elementary the teachers knew you better and your parents were involved more than in middle school." Christopher wrote, "One thing I miss about elementary school is the student/teacher relationship. You don't spend as much time with your teachers, so you don't know them as well." Brandon said, "The thing I miss from elementary school is the teachers. They really helped me out through the school year. They let me know when I was slipping in class." Stephanie wrote, "I do miss the fact that I got more attention in elementary school. However, this is to be expected because each middle school teacher has at least 100 students." Shondor had a slightly different view: "What I miss from elementary school are the parties we used to have with our teachers. Middle school, with all the switching, we don't have enough time to have a party with one teacher, and that's kind of bad."

Amy said, "As I said before, I went to a relatively small elementary school and people there were especially close. The principal, nurse and secretaries all knew the kids, unlike Lakeview. I feel that my elementary school cared more about me as a person." Jason echoed a similar view: "If I could go back to elementary school, I would. You may ask why would I want to do a thing like that? Because in my opinion, the food in the school was better and the teachers gave you enough attention if you needed it."

Chris wrote:

> *The thing that I miss from elementary school is the fun. All it is today is study, study, study. Back then, everything was made fun. My elementary teacher did everything she could do to make it fun. You know what? Sometimes I wish I was a kid again.*

Many students made positive remarks about their middle school teachers or classes. When they did say something positive, almost always there was an explanation attached to it. For example, George wrote: "The bright spot of my day is eighth period and Miss B, because she understands us the most. She makes learning more fun and interesting." Geoff wrote, "Science is the best class of the day for me. In science we do experiments." Justin said, "Science is so fun that I long for it all day. I love the science experiments." Rachel also stated that she liked science class best. "My favorite part of the day has got to be science," she wrote "because science is the most active class."

Every now and then, I read a letter filled with insight and understanding. Ria, for example, offered: "My opinion about middle school is that middle school is a place where you prepare yourself for high school. If there were no such thing as middle school and children left from elementary to high school, I believe there would be lots of lost souls."

Tasha's letter also expressed wisdom unusual in most of the letters:

School is harder, more homework that you have to keep up on if you want to pass. Trust me, you will want to still stay in elementary. You'll miss your younger friends 'cause they look up to you. That's a big responsibility that they respect. Maybe there's a teacher or principal that you like—you will miss them. The best part of the middle school is that it means you're growing up.

Taking the Students Seriously

As I mentioned in the beginning of this chapter, the majority of the students took writing to me very seriously. I have treated their opinions with that same seriousness. I give my thanks to all the students who wrote to me, just as many of them thanked me for reading their letters. "Nice talking to you!" wrote Adrianne. Tatiana wrote, "I would like to thank you for reading what I had to say, because adults rarely ask children their opinions." "Thank you for your interest in what us middle school kids feel and think," wrote Dana. "It feels good to know that someone really cares about our opinion or view on an issue like school."

Joe wrote, "Thank you, Dr. Gallagher, for being interested in people our age. Most people aren't very nice to us because they think we're all mischievous (Well, maybe some of us)." "I really appreciate your interest for our opinions," Brandi wrote. "It's not every day people ask our opinions."

Reflections

I was looking for remarks specific to the experience of middle school. For that reason, I didn't spend too much time on the various other standard common complaints about school—the cafeteria food, the need for more field trips, the desire to start school later in the day because getting up early is so difficult. Those kinds of remarks are the same ones that my generation made.

I attempted to reveal the opinions of the students in their own words. If there were two sides to an issue, I tried to present both. Because readers will form their own opinions as they read through the text of this paper, I will not invest many words rehashing what the students have said. I could not represent each student who wrote to me. As the person who read all 675 letters, however, I believe I have a clear understanding of the importance of some of the issues. The statements made about middle schoolers' perceptions about their world represent the middle school students I studied. Although limited to middle school students in two schools in northeastern Ohio, I believe that these students are typical of seventh and eighth grade students elsewhere.

When I began this inquiry, I thought there would be a major difference between the opinions of suburban students and small-town students. The only difference I noticed was the emphasis that students from suburban Lakeview placed on sports. Males and females alike mentioned the importance of sports in their lives. Often they told me what athletics they were involved in, and they shared their dreams of playing on professional sports teams. Sports were seldom mentioned by the students from Glenridge. Among the many possible factors contributing to that difference is the close proximity of Lakeview to a city that is home to professional football, baseball, hockey, and soccer teams. With the exception of the importance of sports, I found more similarities between the two schools than differences.

Friends are important to middle school students, and time in school to meet with friends is vital. Middle school students at Glenridge and Lakeview expressed a kind of stress caused by being kept in the building all day. They longed for the days when they had time to run and play with their friends. It would be an advantage if the schedule of the school day could be altered to include an opportunity to be outside in the fresh air.

Middle school students view teaming as an organizing structure for education. They seem willing to accept the teaming concept, and they like the idea that they can get all their make-up assignments by calling just one person. What they want most of all is caring teachers who make learning enjoyable. They want field trips and active learning. They want teachers to take a personal interest in them and to give them personal attention. All of these requests seem logical to me.

Teaming in the middle school is a step in the right direction because it breaks down the walls of isolation that so often separate teachers and departments in junior high and high school. Perhaps by integrating classes and curricula, middle schools can find time for field trips, fresh air, and personal relationships with their students.

Discussion Questions

1. This chapter presented an insider's view of the middle school. How do the views of these students support or counter the views of the authors of other chapters?

2. A 13-year-old girl, Kristin, began this chapter by saying that she doesn't understand why God created the middle school. Write a letter to Kristin, explaining why you believe the middle school is an effective organizational structure for adolescents.

Index

Winner, E., 159
Within-class grouping, 152–153
Wokott, L., 196
Word processing, 196–198
Wright, G. S., 81
Writing
  art and, 178–180
  Creative Hook method for encouraging,
    172–178
  encouragement of teachers, impact of, 170–
    171
  food coloring trails example, 173–174
  great pretzel, 177–178
  paper clip, 174–176
  red foil hearts, 176

student-generated topics, 171–172
Writing the Natural Way (Rico), 171

X

XYZ grouping, 151–152

Y

You Just Don't Understand (Tannen), 45

Z

Zern, D. S., 51